The American Model of
State and School

Books by Charles L. Glenn

The Myth of the Common School, 1988, 2002. Italian translation 2004; Spanish translation 2006

Choice of Schools in Six Nations, 1989

Educational Freedom in Eastern Europe, 1995

Educating Immigrant Children: Schools and Language Minorities in 12 Nations (with Ester J. de Jong), 1996

The Ambiguous Embrace: Government and Faith-based Schools and Social Agencies, 2000

Finding the Right Balance: Freedom, Autonomy and Accountability in Education, I & II (with Jan De Groof), 2002

Un difficile equilibrio: Europa continentale e mediterranea (with Jan De Groof), 2003

Balancing Freedom, Autonomy, and Accountability in Education, I–III (with Jan De Groof), 2005

Contrasting Models of State and School: A Comparative Historical Study of Parental Choice and State Control, 2011

African American/Afro-Canadian Schooling: From the Colonial Period to the Present, 2011

American Indian/First Nations Schooling: From the Colonial Period to the Present, 2011

The American Model of State and School

An Historical Inquiry

Charles L. Glenn

continuum

Continuum International Publishing Group
80 Maiden Lane, New York, NY 10038
The Tower Building, 11 York Road, London SE1 7NX

www.continuumbooks.com

ISBN: 978-1-4411-8842-7 (hardcover)
       978-1-4411-3530-8 (paperback)

Library of Congress Cataloging-in-Publication Data
Glenn, Charles Leslie, 1938-
The American model of state and school: an historical inquiry / Charles L. Glenn.
  p. cm.
Includes bibliographical references and index.
ISBN-13: 978-1-4411-8842-7 (hardcover : alk. paper)
ISBN-10: 1-4411-8842-8 (hardcover : alk. paper)
ISBN-13: 978-1-4411-3530-8 (pbk. : alk. paper)
ISBN-10: 1-4411-3530-8 (pbk. : alk. paper) 1. Education and state–United States–History.
2. Education–United States–History. I. Title.

LC89.G538 2012
379.73–dc23

                                                              2011039967

Typeset by Newgen Imaging Systems Pvt Ltd, Chennai, India
Printed in the United States of America

To my grandchildren Sam and Max, Lila,
Margaret, and Emmett, and those yet to come

Contents

Preface

In 1988, I published my first book, a study of the development of the idea of the "common" public school as a political program in France, the Netherlands, and the United States in the early nineteenth century, and the subsequent fate of that idea in the three countries. *The Myth of the Common School* showed how this idea became, in France, the justification for an attempt at State monopoly of the schooling of the common people in order to impose a unifying ideology of secular nationalism. In the Netherlands, by contrast, political mobilization of the Protestant and Catholic "little people" led to the present system of extreme diversity of schooling, with more than two-thirds of pupils attending publicly funded schools operated by religious or other civil-society associations.

The developments in the United States over the nineteenth and into the twentieth century did not follow either of these patterns. I focused much of my account on the ever-renewed tensions between American public schools and groups seeking to make available faith-based schools or challenging what they considered the hostility of public education to their own convictions. My book, I now realize, did not adequately capture what is distinctive about the American model of organization of schooling.

After more than 20 years of further reflection and study, and publication of analyses of how more than 40 other countries organize their educational systems, I believe that it is time for me to seek to provide a more adequate account of the development of this American model. The context for so doing is the publication of my *Contrasting Models of State and School*, which provides a more ample discussion of the developments in the Netherlands than does *The Myth of the Common School*, together with the parallel case of Belgium and the contrasting cases of Germany and Austria. The former, I show, rely heavily upon civil-society sponsors to provide schooling, while in the latter the State has taken a predominant role.

The present account argues that the American model represents a third way of organizing the provision of schooling, and that this accounts for some of its strengths as well as some of its weaknesses. While not abandoning the emphasis of *Myth* on the influence of certain ideas about the role of the public school in American life, this new study seeks to do justice to two other factors in the development of the present situation: the tradition of democratic localism in the management of schooling, and the powerful effect of an emerging education "profession" that has in some respects the characteristics of a religious movement.

"Interpretive history," Paul Mattingly has written, "should become particularly conscious of its joint responsibility to both past and present ... this sense of historicity cannot be unmindful of the hereditary lines between past problems and current dilemmas. If it achieves new dimensions of understanding, it will be because it has made different disciplines serve each other."[1] My goal has been to put history at the service of policy analysis, and to use the insights offered by current policy debates to illuminate history, without distorting either. My approach has been what David Labaree describes as "genealogical," focusing

> attention on the analytical task of examining the roots of the movement rather than on the more speculative project of divining its ultimate purpose. [This] frees us from the confining assumption that the movement is a result of a process of rational planning, deliberately invented as a rational mechanism for accomplishing a particular educational goal. Instead, genealogy opens up the possibility of finding a heterogeneous mixture of elements embedded within the movement, elements that may be rationally incompatible with the stated purposes of the movement.[2]

This strategy recommends itself to me, I suppose, because two decades in government convinced me it is impossible to overestimate the role of sheer muddle in courses of action which, to the academic observer, may seem evidence of deep-laid plans or sinister conspiracies.

The debates that have shaped my perspective on the developments recounted in this book are primarily those among policy-makers, both then and now, not those among professional historians. The Introduction offers a sketch of three issues that trouble American education today and their historical roots. This by no means exhausts the areas that cry out for reform and for which an historical perspective is important.

Two important topics left out of this account are the formal schooling of native peoples and that of African Americans. Some of the earliest measures taken by governments in the North American colonies to promote schooling were devoted—ineffectively—to that of native peoples, and government and tribal efforts have remained intertwined ever since. In particular, this has been the most significant sphere of direct federal government intervention in schooling. Federal and state governments did not become concerned with the education of African Americans until the 1860s, but (like) the education of native peoples that remains a major policy and equity challenge today.

Since such schooling was almost invariably separate (and continues, though unofficially, to be largely separate today), it seemed best to devote to it separate accounts that could do justice to the distinctive forms that it took, and I have done so in two recent books. Some of the major themes of American popular schooling were first worked out in relation to these two groups, and then applied to the schooling of the white majority, including especially the role of the federal government in defining ways and in providing means.

Another challenging issue continues to be the appropriate education of immigrant children, and their children, a focus of my professional career for many years; I dealt with this in a comparative study of twelve countries, published in 1996. The present account is concerned, by contrast, with how the reaction to (often, reaction against) the presence of immigrants shaped policy debates about education. The history of the schooling of immigrant children deserves a separate account, and perhaps one day . . .

The account which follows concerns popular schooling in the nineteenth century, the schooling of those not going on to careers for which academic preparation was necessary; thus it does not discuss secondary and higher education, which did not become generally available until well into the twentieth century. It was on what we now call "elementary education" that efforts to use schools to shape American society were focused. The development of "normal schools" to train teachers for those schools is a necessary part of this story, as are the ideas about education and educators that were fostered by these institutions and their successors.

My primary purpose, in offering this account of the development of the distinctive American model of schooling, is to illustrate the deep roots of ways of thinking about schools that have made it difficult for policy-makers and the public to do what needs to be done to enable schools to function as they should, to be academically effective and also responsive to the concerns of parents in our pluralistic society.

As I was finishing this book, I was asked to provide expert testimony in a case in Colorado, and my preparation for that task added some concrete instances to the account that follows. My gratitude to Martin Nussbaum, Esq. and University of Colorado Denver graduate student Craig Leavitt for some of the material that I have made use of.

Introduction

Weaknesses and Strengths of the American Model of Schooling

Public schooling in the United States has both distinctive weaknesses and distinctive strengths. Each of the areas of weakness can be seen as the flip side of an area of strength. The futility of many efforts to correct the weaknesses of American education arises from failure to take into account how they are anchored in its characteristic strengths. Our focus will be on three of these sources of mingled weakness and strength: the exalted meanings attached to the public school, the tradition of local control, and the substitution of consecration for professionalism among educators. We will see how these came to play an important role, keeping in mind that an "institution like public education gains coherence not only from organizational forms but also from the social meanings that people attribute to it."[1]

PUBLIC EDUCATION AS AN OBJECT OF FAITH

The first half of the nineteenth century was, on both sides of the Atlantic, a period of greatly increased interest in providing basic schooling to every child. For the first time, millions of children came to be in school, and societies were transformed as the horizons of those children were expanded.

The traditional explanation of this rapid spread of popular schooling gives primary credit to elite reformers who made effective use of government and new administrative structures that were developing during this period to standardize public schooling.[2] The reformers have been portrayed as battling against religious obscurantism and stubborn local resistance.

While this version of how education developed is at least partially accurate with respect to Germany, France, and—later in the century—Spain and Italy, it is a fundamental misrepresentation of the developments in North America. Popular schooling spread across the United States and Canada largely through a combination of local initiatives and religiously motivated associations and networks of influence. The rhetoric of education reformers like Horace Mann in Massachusetts, Henry Barnard in Connecticut, Calvin Stowe in Ohio, and Egerton Ryerson in Ontario was indeed profoundly influential, but it gained much of its influence from its consistency with themes and visions for the future that were already very much in the air in religious circles. Often, indeed, they borrowed familiar religious vocabulary to promote the public school cause.

To a remarkable extent the reformers were themselves clergymen: Ryerson was a leading Methodist minister, Stowe a Congregationalist professor of divinity, and Mann's successor in Massachusetts, Barnas Sears, was also a clergyman, as were Mann's Massachusetts allies in creating the first state teacher training institutions, Samuel May, Charles Brooks, Cyrus Peirce. Many others, including Thomas Gallaudet, the pioneer in the education of the deaf, saw no tension between their roles as ministers and as educational reformers. "The ease with which such men passed back and forth between the ministry and education . . . confirms how profoundly moral and spiritually regenerative education was thought to be."[3]

The "sacred" meaning which we will find attached to public schooling in its formative stages has continued to characterize how we think about it today, and to limit our ability to think freshly about how schools should respond to societal pluralism and the concerns of parents. After all, how we experience reality and seek to interact with it is shaped by the mental pictures that we use to make sense of it; these come, over time, to have an authority that resists evidence calling some aspect of them into question. The power of these mental pictures is all the greater because they are shared and thus receive constant social reinforcement. Thomas Kuhn's celebrated theory argued that prevailing models shape how scientists deal with phenomena and make it difficult for them to entertain alternative views of reality, until the dominant paradigm shifts as a result of unanswerable new evidence and what was almost literally inconceivable becomes the new shared understanding.[4] So it has been with education: the persistent resistance to according a role in the provision of public education to schools with a distinctive religious character is based not only upon fear of conflict and a belief that the common public school is the unique institution that knits the nation together, but also upon what it would not be inaccurate to describe as a competing belief-system.

Thinking about public schools has long been surrounded by emotion and largely impervious to criticism, even when the schools themselves are manifestly not. When, in an earlier book, I referred to the "myth" of the common public school, I was not using the word to denote something untrue, but rather something possessing a truth beyond empirical verification and of fundamental significance in policy debates and decisions. "It becomes very difficult to think outside the paradigm that the myth establishes and reflects because myth and reality become mutually reinforcing. Society is structured to conform to the apparent truths that the myth reveals, and what is taken as real increasingly takes on the color of the myth."[5] Thus the ubiquity of the public school and its central role in the life of most communities seems a confirmation of the special and irreplaceable function attributed to it by the myth. Ivan Illich went so far, in *Deschooling Society* (1971), as to compare it to an established church.

One of the most prevalent and unquestioned ideas in American culture, I argued, is that only the public school, in some uniquely powerful sense, creates citizens. Political scientist Terry Moe, analyzing a nationwide survey of current public attitudes toward parental choice of schools, found that

> What they have, in effect, is a normative attachment to the public schools—and an affective inclination to see the public schools in a sympathetic light, whatever the latter's actual performance might be. . . . two-thirds of Americans say the public schools deserve support even when they are performing poorly . . . many private school parents share this same attachment to the public school system. . . . Forty-three percent of public [school] parents say they wouldn't feel right putting their kids in private schools—a profoundly important fact, given that so many of these same parents think that private schools are actually *better* than public schools.[6]

In her influential book *Democratic Education*, political scientist Amy Gutmann reveals just how strong is the conviction, even (or perhaps especially?) among intellectuals, that schools operated by government are fundamentally different and uniquely capable of meeting the needs of society. After conceding that evidence "suggests that private schools may on average do better than public schools in bringing all their students up to a relatively high level of learning, in teaching American history and civics in an intellectually challenging manner, and even in racially integrating classrooms," Gutmann goes on to assert that "public, not private, schooling is an essential welfare good for children as well as the primary means by which citizens can morally educate future citizens."[7]

and to argue that private schools with a religious character should be expected to conform their mission to that of their public counterparts.

The prevailing "myth" of the unique role played by the common public school has made it far more difficult for such educational reforms as public charter schools and other forms of school-level distinctiveness to be implemented, even apart from religious factors. While the spread of charter schools nationwide has been impressive, they continue to serve less than 3.5 percent of the public school pupils in the United States, and there are constant efforts in state legislatures, promoted by the teacher unions, to force charter schools to become more closely conformed to the static models provided by regular public schools.

When it comes to the proposals for vouchers to allow families with limited resources to send their children to the private schools of their choice, and despite the green light provided by the Supreme Court, the barriers are infinitely higher. Campaigns in California, Michigan, and other states to create voucher programs through direct popular vote have been in every case defeated in the face of massively funded and well-organized opposition by the teacher unions. The argument against extension of the freedom of ordinary parents to make decisions about what is in the best interest of their children claims that vouchers are a direct assault on public education and thus on fundamental American values. It has become evident that the general public, influenced by the "myth," is overwhelmingly responsive to this argument.

Why does this matter? Not because the traditional public school should be abandoned or has failed to benefit millions of American families—including my own—but because the cloud of sentiment that surrounds it and the unrealistic meanings assigned to public schools make it extremely difficult to engage in straight talk about what needs to be fixed and what different organizational forms "public education" can legitimately take. As David Tyack and Elisabeth Hansot observed 30 years ago,

> [w]ith few exceptions, public educators have believed in the basic soundness of the American social order and the belief systems supporting it, including the value of controlled competition in such domains as politics, religion, and the economy. Within public education, however, they have sought to prevent organized opposition by stressing consensus, by claiming schools should be "above politics" or by absorbing, co-opting, or deflecting outside forces.[8]

Evidence from a variety of sectors of public services shows that monopoly can be as damaging to quality and efficiency as it commonly is in the private economy. The monopoly that prevails in American public education stifles the ability of schools to respond effectively to the changing demands that are placed upon them. Even the public school's ability to provide real education for citizenship and responsible adulthood—the central claim of the proponents of a public school monopoly of public support—is undermined by the lowest-common-denominator curriculum, the blandly neutral "values," the "defensive teaching" resulting from mandatory attendance at an assigned school in a pluralistic society.

There is abundant evidence that, at least among educational reformers, the myth has lost its power to convince. Charter schools, on-line "virtual schools,"[9] tax credits or vouchers for private school tuition are all on the agenda of reformers in a way that would have been unthinkable 40 years ago. Keeping up with state and local initiatives across the country could be a full-time job! While the conversation among reformers and the options that they are willing to consider have changed, the opponents of fundamental reform continue to be able to rely upon the persistent power of the myth of the common public school over the minds of voters.

LOCAL AND PARENTAL CONTROL

Among the weaknesses of American education compared with that in most Western democracies is an extreme variability in the quality of schools and the expectations that they have for their pupils, a variability that exists not only among the states but also within individual states. This variability grows out of the long tradition of local control of schools, despite the formal authority of state governments over the education provided. "As late as 1890 the median size of state departments of education was two, including the superintendent. . . . State officers complained that they had little power to compel local districts to do anything . . ."[10]

During the post-colonial period in the United States, popular schooling remained intensely local, though there were those who advanced ambitious proposals for what it could and should accomplish in transforming society if given a form and direction unlikely to occur to parents and local leaders. Thomas Jefferson and Benjamin Rush argued that schools could be made instruments of tremendous power . . . but neither their proposals nor their occasional gestures toward implementation made popular education a matter of effective governmental concern.

The extraordinary spread of schooling across the northern part of the country during the nineteenth century, with schools built and staffed almost as soon as farms were carved out of forest or prairie, owed almost nothing to government above the level of local face-to-face democracy. There was no

Loi Guizot or *Oberschulkollegium* to impel this process; it was local initiatives that created more than a hundred thousand public school districts by the end of the century, each a little democracy deciding who would teach and to a large extent what they would teach (by the selection of commercially produced and unregulated textbooks), and how much to tax themselves to maintain the school.

The positive effects were indisputable. Millions of Americans—including newly arrived immigrants—became accustomed to the process of democratic decision-making on issues of immediate concern; schooling, soon including secondary schools and even colleges, spread across most of the country far more rapidly than the governments of the time, with their limited revenues and administrative resources, could have achieved.

This unguided, almost spontaneous process of local effort was both a strength and a weakness. Soon after his arrival in the United States, in 1831, Alexis de Tocqueville wrote to his father that "this country, as to administration, seems to me to have gone to precisely the opposite extreme as France. With us the government is involved in everything. [Here] there is no, or at least there doesn't appear to be any government at all." A few months later, after his visit to New England, Tocqueville came to have a more positive view of the American model.

> Liberty does not carry out each of its undertakings with the same perfection as an intelligent despotism, but in the long run it produces more than the latter. It does not always and in all circumstances give the peoples a more skillful and faultless government, but it infuses throughout the body social an activity, a force, and an energy which never exist without it, and which brings forth wonders.[11]

The high degree of literacy that Tocqueville observed in New England and in the vast stretch of territory settled primarily from New England in northern New York State, Ohio, and on to the West was achieved by local efforts before Horace Mann and others began to promote the state role in schooling. Tocqueville admired what he described as the American system (though it was in fact confined to Northern states) of government stimulation of local initiative; "it is the provisions for public education," he wrote, "which, from the very first, throw into clearest relief the originality of American civilization."[12] He noted that government did not attempt to prescribe how local citizens would meet their obligation to provide schooling, in implicit contrast with the uniform schemes that had been adopted (though never effectively implemented) in France over the previous 40 years. In New England, "the establishment of a school is obligatory, but the township builds it, pays for it, and controls it."[13]

Why was this so important? Here Tocqueville comes to the heart of his analysis of the strength of American democracy. "Without local institutions, a nation may give itself a free government, but it has not got the spirit of liberty." Local institutions are not the same thing as branch offices of a bureaucracy, as when the government of Louis-Philippe, about the time Tocqueville was writing, sought to govern France more effectively by placing a gendarme and a schoolmaster in every village.[14] No, Tocqueville declared himself "persuaded that . . . the collective force of the citizens will always be better able to achieve social prosperity than the authority of the government."[15]

Though most of his contemporaries among French social theorists were strongly in favor of centralization and a strong state, Tocqueville insisted that

> administrative centralization only serves to enervate the peoples that submit to it, because it constantly tends to diminish their civic spirit. . . . It is true that centralization can easily succeed in imposing an external uniformity on men's behavior . . . [this can] maintain the status quo of society. . . . When it is a question of deeply stirring society or of setting it a rapid pace, its strength deserts it. Once its measures require any aid from individuals, this vast machine turns out to be astonishingly feeble; suddenly it is reduced to impotence.

Thus, "[w]hat I most admire in America is not the *administrative* but the *political* effects of decentralization." By "political effects," he meant the way that local responsibility taught the habits of responsible participation, which he considered essential to a healthy republican form of government, and to a healthy society. "How can liberty be preserved in great matters among a multitude that has never learned to use it in small ones?"[16] he asked. A threat is posed by the extension of the reach of government, not least in the education of children. In one of his typical paradoxes, Tocqueville notes that

> [e]very central power which follows its natural instincts loves equality and favors it. For equality singularly facilitates, extends, and secures its influence. One can also assert that every central government worships uniformity . . . all these various rights which have been successively wrested in our time from classes, corporations, and individuals have not been used to create new secondary powers on a more democratic basis, but have invariably been concentrated in the hands of the government. . . . In Europe in the old days almost all charitable establishments were managed by individuals or corporations.
>
> They are now all more or less under government control. . . . In most countries now education as well as charity has become a national concern. The state receives, and often takes, the child from its mother's arms to hand it over to its functionaries; it

takes the responsibility for forming the feelings and shaping the ideas of each generation. Uniformity prevails in schoolwork as in everything else; diversity, as well as freedom, is daily vanishing.[17]

Tocqueville was critical of political thinkers who assumed that formal structures alone, without the support of "habits of the heart" and social institutions, could suffice to protect the liberties won in recent decades. "They think," he wrote, "they have done enough to guarantee personal freedom when it is to the government of the state that they have handed it over. That is not good enough for me."[18] Thus the American (really New England) model of democratic localism was a constant training in political activism.

Although schools were by no means the only sphere of local decision-making—and thus of the political education of citizens—through the nineteenth century, they were a constant concern at the community level. Schooling was not thought of as an alien and irrelevant imposition, as was often the case in France and other countries where it was imposed from the center. By comparison, in France 20 years after the national government mandated a system of village schools (and Tocqueville visited New England), in one rural community that has been studied closely attendance was very uneven because parents saw no utility to sending their children to school. There were in this community in 1851–52 120 children from ages 7 to 13 who should have attended school; most did not do so.

> In 1851, there were 20 pupils January 1st, all boys; two of them remained in school one month, two others three months . . . three attended for five months. Ten new pupils entered in February. Two attended for one month, seven for two months, three attended for five months. . . . Thus almost all pupils attended school for only a couple of months [each year], mostly in winter.[19]

Only when the changing French economy—specifically, the possibility of employment on the growing railroad system—made the skills taught in school economically useful did parents begin to send their children to school consistently; the national government's political agenda of "forming citizens" found no resonance at the local level.

In addition to the positive effects of localism noted by Tocqueville and other observers, there have been negative effects, as well. One is that a school controlled by a local majority may be less open to the views and concerns of a local minority than is a school answerable to a much broader constituency. The framers of the American constitutional order understood this well.

Just over 220 years ago, James Madison pointed out, in *Federalist 10*, that local democracy can be dangerous to freedom, which is safeguarded by a broader republican order.

> The smaller the society, the fewer probably will be the distinct parties and interests composing it; the fewer the distinct parties and interests, the more frequently will a majority be found of the same parry; and the smaller the number of individuals composing a majority, and the smaller the compass within which they are placed, the more easily will they concert and execute their plans of oppression. Extend the sphere, and you take in a greater variety of parties and interests; you make it less probable that a majority of the whole will have a common motive to invade the rights of other citizens; or if such a common motive exists, it will be more difficult for all who feel it to discover their own strength, and to act in unison with each other.[20]

Schools have been a source of much conflict in American communities when local majorities have been unresponsive to the interests of individual parents or groups of parents whose concerns differed from those of the majority. In some highly significant cases it has been the state or national government, or more frequently the courts, that have intervened to overturn the tyranny of a local majority. Perhaps the most notable case was the decision of the Supreme Court to uphold the right of Jehovah's Witness children not to join in a patriotic ceremony in school, during the World War II.

> National unity as an end which officials may foster by persuasion is not in question. The problem is whether under our Constitution compulsion as here employed is a permissible means for its achievement.... Probably no deeper division of our people could proceed from any provocation than from finding it necessary to choose what doctrines and whose program public educational officials shall compel youth to unite in embracing.... freedom to differ is not limited to things that do not matter much. That would be a mere shadow of freedom. The test of its substance is the right to differ as to things that touch the heart of the existing order. If there is any fixed star in our constitutional constellation, it is that no official, high or petty, can prescribe what shall be orthodox in politics, nationalism, religion, or other matters of opinion.[21]

It is true that, in some cases, local solidarity has protected enclaves of difference in approach to education from the pressure of wider social forces. Sometimes the consolidation of small local school districts for the sake of economy or to offer a more extensive educational program has been experienced as oppressive by religious or language minority groups that had previously had their "own" local public school. Thus, for example, the establishment of private schools by Amish and Mennonite communities is a recent phenomenon, in response to the closing of the small local public schools that had previously reflected their conservative Protestant values without being explicitly religious. In such cases, local control of public schools had served freedom of conscience, through providing families with a way to have a direct influence on the schools that their children attend. In other cases, however, it has demonstrably had an oppressive effect, as Madison warned.

Decision-making about schools at the community level has changed in its meaning since before World War II, when there were 119,000 local school districts in the United States and the enrolment of the average school was 90 pupils. By 1990, the number of local districts had fallen through consolidation to 15,358, while the average school was five times as large as it had been a half-century before. Whereas the average district had enrolled only 187 pupils—of course, there were urban districts enrolling hundreds of thousands—by 1990 the average had risen to 2,460. Managing schools and school districts with budgets in the millions was no longer something for amateurs, and there was a well-established profession of school administration quite distinct from that of teaching.

It is evident that the nature of the engagement of parents and other local citizens in a school district enrolling 187 or fewer pupils, all of them very likely from families known to one another, and that in a school district of 2,460 (or 10,000, or 50,000) pupils will be very different. Political scientist Terry Moe, in his new book on the role of the teacher unions, clearly has in mind urban districts, where

> the equation of school boards with government by the people is one of the enduring myths of public education. . . . During the early years of the twentieth century, school boards were often under the thumb of party machines. Later, as Progressive reforms weakened the parties, local government of the schools shifted to newly powerful groups—business, middle-class activists, education administrators—with their own special interests to pursue. Then came the 1960s and 1970s, when the unionization of teachers led to yet another shift in the balance of power, and school boards found themselves under strong, special interest pressure from their own employees. The history of American school boards has never been a history of grassroots democracy. It has always been a history of special interests.[22]

Moe's conclusion seems too absolute, given the strong community mobilization that can still occur in smaller school districts over a controversial issue like sex education or a school closing, and the exquisite hierarchy of status that can be found among school systems in neighboring suburban communities. The ecology of schooling in the suburbs where most Americans now live "is remarkably flexible, adapting quickly to local market conditions and changes in consumer demand, and it is also remarkably differentiated, as particular institutions and individual school systems come to occupy specialized niches in the highly competitive educational arena."[23] But we don't need a sociologist to tell us that; ask any suburban realtor!

In general Moe is correct, however, that public school governance is no longer the education for citizenship that Tocqueville celebrated. As more and more activities of teachers and functions of the school are defined by union contract provisions on the one hand and state laws and regulations on the other, not to mention court decisions and the strings tied to federal and state funding programs, the scope for debate about curriculum and teaching has shrunk to marginal issues raised by small groups of parents and ignored by their neighbors. Elected school boards bargain over pension and health care provisions, not over the goals of education and how to accomplish them. School board elections are contested, in most cases, on issues of personality and group interests rather than of principle, with the local teachers union mobilized to "elect their employer."

Among the lingering negative effects of the American tradition of educational localism is the tremendous variation in expectations for academic rigor and pupil achievement among local districts as well as among states, evident as more and more data from standardized tests has become available.[24] The differences in outcomes reflect to some extent, of course, background factors of early stimulation and family support that pupils in different communities bring with them to school, but the fact that the schools of communities with similar demographics also produce very different results clearly reflects local culture and differing expectations about what pupils can be expected to achieve.

While organizational structures were imitated from local district to local district and from state to state, there was much less commonality of academic expectations, and this continued to be true throughout the twentieth century and into the twenty-first. Variation in performance—and in expectations for performance—was and remains dramatic in comparison, for example, with that in most countries in Western Europe.

In effect, the positive side of local decision-making about schools, its role in fostering grassroots democracy and the habits of citizenship, has largely faded away, while the negative side, the lack of common standards for education, has persisted and grown more problematic as the world economy and American society have made increased demands on education.

There are grounds for some optimism that the negative effects of the American tradition of educational localism on academic standards may be reduced as states adopt curriculum standards specifying measurable outcomes (and such standards begin to take shape at the national level), and as new strategies are adopted for accountability, including consequences for inadequate results. So far, those consequences primarily fall upon school administrators, and a major debate rages over to what extent teachers should be rewarded or sanctioned based on the measured achievement of their pupils. There are also well-founded grounds for concern that the role of states and local communities as laboratories for positive innovation may suffer from the push toward common standards; here, as so often, the challenge is finding the right balance between autonomy and accountability.[25]

Whether consequences for academic effort and performance will be extended to children and youth in ways that make them more engaged with academic learning remains to be seen. One of the other effects of educational localism is the apparent inability of many schools to persuade their pupils— particularly at adolescence—to take the content of instruction seriously as worth learning for its own sake rather than simply as a means to some extrinsic end. A nationwide study a few years ago found that "whether surrounded by suburban affluence or urban poverty, students' commitment to school is at an all-time low. . . . an extremely large proportion of students—somewhere around 40 percent—are just going through the motions. . . . According to their own reports, between one-third and 40 percent of students say that when they are in class, they are neither trying very hard nor paying attention."[26] It seems likely that to a considerable extent this attitude reflects the lack (except in inner-city areas) of a clear boundary between school and community. When the high school is the center of community social life and of youth activities (in contrast with Europe where youth sports and clubs are usually based in community institutions rather than in schools), it is not surprising that its academic mission would come to seem of secondary importance compared with social dimensions of the school experience.

PSEUDO-PROFESSION OR SECULAR CLERGY?

In my earlier account of the development of the role of government in popular schooling, I placed primary emphasis on the efforts of Horace Mann and his counterparts in France and the Netherlands to expand the reach of the State as an instrument of what François Guizot called "a certain governance of minds."[27] I see now that I missed an important element without which the present situation of popular schooling in the United States cannot be understood:

development of a set of ideologies, interests, and self-understandings among influential educators, attitudes that worked against the development of an effective state role. I missed, also, the significance of the meanings that came to be projected onto ordinary teachers.

It is easy to miss the scope of these beliefs about the vocation of educators because the story of the development of the modern educational system in the United States is dominated by the work of the so-called administrative progressives who created the structures and the justification for the bureaucratic organization of schooling that persist today. During the late decades of the nineteenth century, the earlier leadership role of the amateur reformers, ministers like Egerton Ryerson in Ontario and Calvin Stowe in Ohio, or lawyers like Mann and Henry Barnard in New England, was superseded by a new and self-conscious profession of educational administrators, closely networked like their predecessors and no less committed to a vision of social transformation through schooling.[28] Priding themselves as efficient managers,[29] rubbing elbows with local businessmen at the Rotary Club, practicing a new academic discipline called "Administrative Science," these high school headmasters and school system superintendents placed a mark on American schooling that still persists in routinized procedures and standardization, since reinforced—but not invented—by union contracts.

Meanwhile, teachers—primarily female and working at the lower grades that then enrolled the great majority of schoolchildren—were largely voiceless, poorly paid, young, and without career goals in education. Typically, they had received no professional training and stayed in the classroom an average of 3 years before marrying or finding other employment.[30] While the situation, both of women and of schools, had improved somewhat half a century later, teaching in common elementary schools was far from being considered a profession, or even a skilled trade. High school and academy teachers, mostly men, were in a very different position but in far smaller numbers and not nearly so influential in the evolving complex of ideas about the sacred mission of the educator.

Precisely because they were women and poorly compensated, teachers of children came to be seen as ministering angels, or at least as devoted religious missionaries, fulfilling a mission for which women were considered uniquely fitted. The aura surrounding them has endured, bringing into prominence the non-instructional side of their role. This has conveniently fortified the criticism, by the teachers unions, of the use of standardized testing to measure academic achievement as representing a distraction from "the real purposes" of the teacher's work. Without a way of measuring what pupils have learned, of course, it is difficult to hold teachers accountable for the quality of their performance.

In addition to this effect of justifying a focus on the work of teachers on unmeasurable qualities of caring and inspiration (not that these are unimportant, of course), the way that Americans came to think about teachers created a halo effect that makes it very hard to criticize how public schools perform or to propose reforms that could threaten what teachers see as in their interests. Even those most critical of the role of the teachers unions in blocking reform of American education commonly insist that they are not including ordinary teachers in this criticism.

It is in substantial part because of this understanding of the higher wisdom possessed by educators about what is in the best interest of children and youth that the prevailing argument used to counter all proposals to open up the system to new ways of thinking is not about efficiency or about test scores; it is about the alleged moral function of the traditional public school, a moral function that it is uniquely qualified to provide. Horace Mann and his allies who promoted the revival-like teachers' institutes were in accord with the position taken by Amy Gutmann 14 decades later that future citizens should be shaped through public schools alone.

SUMMARY

Three persistent themes, then, that we will be tracing in their historical development: the unique role of the common public school in the formation of citizens, the tradition of localism even after it has ceased to be a source of engagement by parents and other citizens in making decisions about their schools, and the special calling of educators that is used to insulate them from accountability to parents or to society at large.

In presenting the history of educational policy in France or most other countries, it is possible to concentrate in the first instance upon legislation and the policy debates that surround it. While, as in the case of the French Revolution, it is evident that the implementation and effect of laws was often very far from what was intended by those proposing them, it is nevertheless possible to trace the stages of thinking about education in developments at the governmental level.

This is much less fruitful when considering the history of education in the United States, where most of the decisions that have shaped schools have been made at the local level, until the states, relatively recently, began to play a larger role, and where professional associations have often filled the role played by government in other societies. Thus "coeducational public schools did not result from centralized state policy. Instead, they grew gradually from decisions made in tens of thousands of local school districts, usually with few records of debate on the question."[31] It would thus not be especially productive to trace the succession of federal laws—few and far between until the 1960s—affecting schools, nor even those in a sample state or two. It is necessary to treat the history of educational policy in the United States in large part in terms of *implicit policies* observed from actual practices, as a matter of social and intellectual more than of political history.

This is not to say that tens of thousands of local school districts invented their own ways of providing schooling, but rather that it was through what today we might call a viral process of connections and influences, exerted by professional associations, journals, and individuals with a knack for catching the ear of the public or at least of educators, rather than by government regulation, that the distinctively American forms of schooling have emerged and evolved. The impulse behind these patterns of influence and emulation was a shared conviction that popular schooling (what I have elsewhere called the "Myth of the Common School") was essential to societies lacking strong central authority or social hierarchies.

Chapter One

Colonial Background

Two issues—religion and language—that have caused conflict over educational policy over the past century and a half were seldom at issue during the colonial period. Population was largely dispersed into homogeneous communities that provided such schooling as was available according to local preferences. It was the late-nineteenth century institution of compulsory school attendance, in a social context of mobility and inter-group contact, that made the religious content conveyed by schooling and the language in which it was conveyed a matter of often intense conflict, co-existing uneasily with government efforts to form citizens through a unitary system of public schooling.

It is natural to assume that the reasons for going to school have always been pretty much what they are today: to prepare individuals to participate successfully, as adults, in a society and economy that require skills usually developed by schooling. That was not the case for most of those growing up in the American colonies of the seventeenth century; rather, "from the very beginnings, the expressed purpose of colonial education had been to preserve society against barbarism"[1] and to provide the basis for a religious life that required reading and understanding scripture and devotional texts. Literacy was not especially useful for the work that most men and women did. Indeed, there is evidence that many who learned to read as children lost the skill subsequently, unless it was maintained for religious reasons. Inventories of the estates of men and women who died during the eighteenth century have found a "continuing massive preponderance of religious books. . . . The flood of 'how-to' books expected to accompany an increase in the need for literacy simply does not materialize, and the focus of literacy remains essentially religious."[2]

NEW ENGLAND

Colonists in Massachusetts and Connecticut settled initially near the coast and along the Connecticut River in organized and compact communities; a law of 1635 in Massachusetts required that settlers live within a half mile of a town church.[3] It has been suggested that "the pattern of settlement of New England—in compact villages rather than scattered farms [as in other regions]—was a deliberate decision taken in order to create close-knit communities of educated Christians. The concern or lack of concern with education was as much a cause as it was an effect of the varying patterns of settlement in colonial America."[4] The New England colonists placed a high value on raising children who would achieve knowledge of God's plan of salvation through independent study of the Bible as well as through faithful attendance at preaching. For many, indeed, this was a primary motivation for leaving England. "Why came you into this land?" asked one Puritan preacher in 1671. "Was it not mainly with respect to the rising generation? . . . Was it to leave them a rich and wealthy people? Was it to leave them Houses, Lands, Livings? Oh, No; but to leave God in the midst of them."[5]

It is not that the formal schooling of Puritan children was focused primarily on religious instruction; that was the responsibility of the home and the church. Parents and community leaders were generally concerned to reproduce the conditions of English town life, including the availability of primary schools and, for the more able and ambitious older boys, grammar schools where Latin was taught and classical authors read. Girls were not generally encouraged to carry their education so far in a literary direction; John Winthrop wrote in 1645 about the talented wife of the governor of the Hartford colony who had lost her mind "by occasion of her giving herself wholly to reading and writing. . . . if she had attended her household affairs," Winthrop commented sadly, "and not gone out of her way and calling to meddle in such things as are proper for men, whose minds are stronger &c. she had kept her wits."[6]

We should not underestimate the difficulty of creating adequate provision of schooling, under the conditions that the settlers of New England faced; indeed, old England would not do so until late in the nineteenth century. Even the fundamental goal of nearly universal literacy was not achieved for several generations, but

> [t]he evidence is that between the middle of the seventeenth century and the end of the eighteenth New England evolved from a society little more than half-literate to a society of nearly universal male literacy. This was part of a trend toward higher

literacy throughout the western world, but literacy rose faster and to a high level in New England than in most areas.[7]

The Massachusetts colonial legislature, in 1642, required town officials "to take account from time to time of all parents and masters, and of their children, concerning their calling and employment of their children, especially of their ability to read and understand the principles of religion and the capitall lawes [sic] of this country." As we can learn from court records, parents and masters who neglected this duty to see to the education of children under their care were fined. The law of 1642 also provided that local authorities could "divide the towne amongst them, appointing to every of the said townesmen a certaine number of families to have special oversight of";[8] thus, the following year, Cambridge appointed various citizens to be responsible for ensuring that all children in their carefully defined sections of the town were adequately educated.[9] This was not a requirement of school attendance; parents and masters could choose other means of ensuring that their children and apprentices were prepared for life in church and society, but they would be sanctioned if they did not do so. In 1648, a further school law was passed, complaining that "many parents and masters are too indulgent and lenient of their duty" and requiring local officials to keep "a vigilant eye over their brethren and neighbours, to see, first that none of them shall suffer so much barbarism in any of their families as not to indeavour to teach by themselves or others their children and apprentices so much learning as may inable them perfectly to read the english tongue, and knowledge of the Capital laws; upon penaltie of twentie shillings for each neglect therein."[10]

Massachusetts legislation throughout the seventeenth and eighteenth centuries made it the responsibility of local elected officials to determine the qualifications of the teachers they employed and also of private schoolmasters, except in the case of grammar-school teachers, whose competence to teach Latin and Greek was to be determined through examination by several local ministers. "The selectmen were directed to pay particular attention to the character and religious qualifications of schoolmasters before granting them permission to teach in the commonwealth."[11]

Despite the best efforts of legislators, the New England population in these early decades earliest was not sufficiently concentrated in residence for the school laws to have their intended effect. As population became more concentrated, schooling became more widely available. The growth of a market economy and trade with other colonies, including the West Indies, and with England, made the need for literacy more evident. The increasing significance of its foreign and inter-colony trade, for example, may help to account for the unusually high level of literacy in Essex County, Massachusetts, which had been in sixth place in that respect in 1710 but was tied for first place among the counties in 1760.[12]

The expansion of literacy should not be attributed entirely to the greater provision of schooling; in some respects schooling became less available while literacy rose during the eighteenth century, as the population spread out from town centers and more and more families lived on their farms. Cultural factors made literacy highly valued in New England, and it increased steadily in New Hampshire, for example, where school laws were weak. Lockridge suggests that literacy in New England was unusual for the time because it was not strongly linked with occupation and with wealth, but was spread generally throughout the population, both men and women. In the whole Atlantic world, "the only areas to show a rapid rise in literacy to levels approaching universality were small societies whose intense Protestantism led them widely to offer or to compel in some way the education of their people. In Calvinist Scotland, a system of compulsory elementary education appears to have raised adult male literacy from 33% around 1675 to nearly 90% by 1800. . . . As a result Scotland reached the threshold of universal male literacy simultaneously with New England."[13]

In 1647, perhaps concluding that more institutional support was needed, the Massachusetts legislature required communities of appropriate sizes to maintain schools, with tuition paid either by parents "or by the inhabitants in generall." The preamble to this law has become celebrated, and is worth quoting:

> It being one chief project of that ould deluder, Satan, to keepe men from the knowl-edge of the Scriptures, as in former times by keeping them in an unknowne tongue, so in these latter times by perswading from the use of tongues, that so at last the true sence and meaning of the originall might be clouded by false glosses of saint-seeming deceivers, that learning may not be buried in the grave of our fathers in the church and commonwealth, the Lord assisting our endeavors—It is therefore ordered, that every township in this jurisdiction, after the Lord have increased them to the number of 50 housholders, shall then forthwith appoint one within their towne to teach all such children as shall resort to him to write and reade, whose wages shall be paid either by the parents or masters of such children, or by the inhabitants in general [sic].[14]

Towns with one hundred families or householders were required to maintain a grammar school as well, "the master thereof being able to instruct youth so farr as they may be fited for the university;" towns neglecting this obligation were required to pay £5 to the nearest grammar school (presumably as tuition for pupils resident in the delinquent town) until they came into compliance.[15] Nine communities were already operating grammar schools. The school regulations adopted, in 1645, by Dorchester (then an independent town and one of the largest in New England) required that the schoolmaster "equally and impartially receive and instruct such as shall be sent and committed to him for that end, whether their parents be poor or rich, not refusing any who have right and interest in the school."[16] This law of 1647 needed little enforcement with respect to the obligation to provide primary schools, though the grammar school obligation was increasingly evaded: "while there are numerous instances where the compulsion of the courts was necessary for the maintenance of the Latin grammar schools, there are few where disobedience to the law concerning the elementary school called for any exercise of power from the outside."[17]

Similar requirements were enacted, almost verbatim, in the sister-colonies of Connecticut (1650), New Haven (1656), and New Hampshire (1693), while Plymouth was incorporated into Massachusetts in 1692 and thus became subject to the school law of 1647. In 1690, the Connecticut legislature noted that "notwithstanding the former orders made for the education of children and servants, there are many persons unable to read the English tongue, and therefore incapable to read the holy word of God, or the good laws of the colony," and ordered that "all parents and masters shall cause their respective children and servants, as they are capable, to be taught to read distinctly the English tongue." In addition, the legislators ordered that two "free schools"— grammar schools—be established in Hartford and New Haven, to teach Latin and Greek. The costs of these were to be shared by the colony, individuals, and the two towns.[18]

While many schools in England had been endowed by the crown with confiscated church properties, or by wealthy benefactors, or by town guilds, this was not possible in colonial New England, where there was little accumulated wealth and where land was too plentiful for rents to produce a reliable income for a school. New England schools, then, were supported by general taxes in addition to the fees paid by those parents who could afford it. "If their lack of endowment denied them a measure of security and independence, their dependence upon taxes made them intellectually responsive to the society for which they acted."[19] Here we see the origins of the localism that has always been a defining characteristic of American schooling.

Monroe observes that "there was no presupposition or theory in favor of free schools. They grew out of the experience of the town." In England, free schools—"charity schools"—had been for paupers, and self-respecting parents were reluctant to send their own children; in the North American colonies in general, tuition continued to be paid by those parents who could afford it throughout the colonial period and beyond. The New England requirement that every town have a school, however, created pressure to use general taxation to support that school, since otherwise compliance with the law was dependent upon whether parents chose to send their children. Gradually, the operating costs of schools and teacher salaries were paid out of general town revenues, and tuition became less and less important as a source of support, until in many communities it was abandoned altogether by the middle of the eighteenth century, "quite a century earlier than a genuine free school system was built up in any state west of New England."[20] Thus the common claim that there were no "public schools" before the 1830s is inaccurate with respect to New England.

The reasoning behind the assumption of school costs by general taxpayers was that free schools, unlike schools supported by tuition and fees, existed "for the benefit of the Poor and the Rich; that the children of all, partaking of equal Advantages and being placed upon an equal Footing, no Distinction might be made among them in the schools on account of the different Circumstances of their Parents, but that the Capacity & natural Genius of each might be cultivated & improved for the future Benefit of the whole Community."[21]

It is often assumed that colonial New England was a sort of educational paradise, with every community centered around its white church and its little red schoolhouse. There were indeed famous schoolmasters like Elijah Corlett, who taught in Cambridge for at least 50 years and was described as one of the ornaments of the colony, and Ezekiel Cheever, who died in 1708 after teaching in New Haven for 12, in Ipswich for 11, in Charlestown for 9, and at the Boston Latin grammar school for 38 years,[22] and there were many others whose schools enjoyed strong support from parents and local ministers.

This was not universally the case, however, nor could it have been as families kept moving away from settled communities to find more farmland. The institutions of church and school, and effective local government, were slow to follow in New Hampshire,[23] Maine, and rural areas of central and western Massachusetts. On the other hand, schools were in general established as soon as there was a sufficient concentration of families to support a teacher with their tuition fees or in-kind contributions, or local government became prosperous enough to contribute to a teacher's salary. In the settled towns, there were well-established schools and these in general enjoyed strong support.

In New England, . . . owing to the uncertainties of support by endowment and tuition rates, schooling had early become a function of the towns, with funds generally deriving from taxation supported by tuition and control increasingly exercised by the town meeting and the selectmen. But the development had been far from

uniform, with constables, justices, [church] elders, deacons, ministers, and overseers of the poor assuming various roles at different times in the different localities.
Meanwhile, the selectmen of a number of towns began to appoint special committees or subcommittees to give continuing attention to the care and oversight of
schools and especially to the employment of teachers, the erection of schoolhouses,
and the management of school funds—the town of Dorchester provided for a committee to oversee such matters as early as 1645. And as towns dispersed precincts
were created, which were either assigned or arrogated unto themselves the responsibility for managing education. . . . The result, by the time of the Revolution, was
the popular control of schooling as a civil responsibility by elected laymen at the
provincial, town, and precinct (later district) levels.[24]

Although historians are fond of citing the Massachusetts legislation requiring
that youth be educated, Mattingly points out that the "striking feature of this
legislation was its repeated endorsement of the provisions for basic instruction. Progressive historians have interpreted this repetitiousness as evidence of
America's early and firm commitment to notions of public education. As likely,
the necessity of passing virtually the same laws over and over indicated the
practical frustration of those notions."[25] The adequacy of schooling depended
considerably upon local conditions and initiatives, as population scattered out
from the originally compact agricultural communities and as religious fervor
faded or took more emotional forms that placed less emphasis upon biblical study. "Those negligent communities were not indifferent to education,
but the desolation caused by Indian warfare and the scarcity of teachers often
hindered" complying with the legislation.[26] The provision of schooling in the
eighteenth century in the smaller rural communities could often be far from
adequate, since

> even in normal circumstances, the learning experience of colonial children was
> disadvantaged, for the environment of New England schooling consisted of smoky
> rooms, unevenly heated and poorly ventilated, backless seats, full of unsuspected
> splinters and agonizing projections, inadequate lighting, and ceilings that were
> oppressively low, even for small children. It is a tribute to the tenacity and stern stuff
> of New England's children that they crowded such schools in increasing numbers
> before the Revolution, and indeed that they learned as much as contemporaries and
> visitors boasted they did.[27]

While there was a general provision of elementary schooling, though of
uneven quality, the requirement that larger communities maintain grammar
schools teaching Latin and Greek was increasingly resisted, as "townspeople

bickered over the necessity of a classical education and attempted to evade requirements set by the magistrates. . . . That devotion to the ideal of the classical grammar school, so apparent during the first decades of settlement, by the eighteenth century seems to have been gradually disappearing." Already in 1677 the New Haven Town Meeting had expressed a desire that a teacher be appointed for the town school who would "teach English allsoe [sic] and to write, at present being few Latin scholars [students]."[28] In response to this changing demand, there developed a network of private schools teaching the writing and other skills required for employment in business and commerce. In these schools writing and arithmetic were taught by masters skilled in penmanship and accounts. Now, provided with professional instructors, writing and arithmetic were no longer neglected. Future bookkeepers were taught to cast accounts and future scriveners were instructed in the various ornate hands popular in the seventeenth and eighteenth centuries. The flourishing trade of Boston demanded an educated commercial class with a mastery of figures and a legible hand, and with the establishment of writing schools this demand was satisfied. The numerous private schools of eighteenth-century Massachusetts offered instruction in other vocational subjects. In 1709, Owen Harris placed an advertisement in the *Boston News-Letter* for his school offering instruction in "Writing, Arithmetick in all its parts; And also Geometry, Trigonometry, Plain and Sphaerical, Surveying, Dialling, Gauging, Navigation, Astronomy; The Projection of the Sphaere, and the use of Mathematical Instruments." Other private school masters of eighteenth-century Boston taught fortification, gunnery, "Bookkeeping after the Italian Method of Double Entry," "Foreign Exchanges, either in French or in English," "divers sorts of Writing, viz., English and German Texts; the Court Roman, Secretary and Italian Hands."[29]

These private establishments not infrequently received town subsidies as well as tuition from parents. Thus, in addition to the town and district schools required by law (but also, of course, by local demand), there were many private-venture schools in New England. With the decline in interest in classical study as the first generations of what has been called a "meritorious aristocracy" passed away and was replaced by an elite of merchants, "the best education to be obtained in New England by the middle of the eighteenth century was usually that of the entirely private schools in the largest towns, which offered their pupils training in a wide variety of commercially useful disciplines."[30] Advertisements for these schools appeared frequently; typical is one from Boston in 1720:

At the house formerly Sir Charles Hobby's are taught Grammar, Writing after a free and easy manner, in all the hands usually practiced, Arithmetick Vulgar and

Decimal in a concise and practical Method, Merchants Accompts, Geometry, Algebra, Mensuration, Geography, Trigonometry, Astronomy, Navigation and other parts of the Mathematicks, with the use of the Globes and other Mathematical Instruments, by Samuel Grainger.

They whose Business won't permit 'em to attend the usual School Hours, shall be carefully attended and instructed in the Evenings.[31]

The Latin grammar school in Roxbury served for a number of decades as the town school, though it continued to be governed by self-perpetuating trustees and eventually evolved into the private school that it continues to be today. There were also "dame schools," as in England, which provided the basic instruction required before admission to a town school, which "often provided 'that no children shall be admitted into such schools who have not perfectly learned the letters of the alphabet.'" Dame schools also admitted girls, who were not always welcome in the town schools. "Scattered population and smaller group settlements demanded more and cheaper schools. How common these private ventures were in some towns is indicated by the Concord report of 1680, 'in every quarter of the town men and women that teach to write English when parents can spare their children and others go to them.'"[32]

SOUTHERN COLONIES

The picture was very different in the South, where the dispersal of population was much greater and where immigrants did not come as covenanted church members with a strongly Calvinistic emphasis upon the reading of the Bible and thus the need for literacy. After all, even in the eighteenth century the "Atlantic world lacked those powerful forces that today revolutionize the breadth, structure, and very meaning of literacy in developing nations. Protestantism was perhaps the sole force that could rapidly increase literacy to high levels."[33] The forms of Protestantism in Virginia and the other southern colonies did not create a strong popular demand for reading. In addition, many of those who came to the southern colonies were indentured servants who were required to work for a number of years to pay for their passage, and of course many others were brought as slaves from Africa.

Equally important were factors of occupation and residence. Southern settlers planted tobacco and—the more fortunate among them—sought to live the lives of country gentlemen, in dispersed settlements; New England settlers planted subsistence crops, lived in towns and villages, and cultivated a strong community life. Governor Berkeley of Virginia, when asked, in 1671, what the colony was doing about education, replied "the same that is taken in England [by families living] out of towns: every man according to his own ability instructing his children." After some negative remarks about the Anglican clergy in the colony, he adds, "but, I thank God, there are no free schools, nor printing, and I hope we shall not have these three hundred years, for learning has brought disobedience, and heresy, and sects into the world, and printing has divulged them, and libels against the best government. God keep us from both!"[34] Monroe notes, however, that "the partial quotation is not only misleading but is probably inaccurate, for there are documents that seem to indicate that there were 'free schools' in operation at that time. . . . the governor himself had but a short time before made a generous contribution to a free school."[35]

Virginia enacted a law in 1631 or 1632 that required all parents and masters of apprentices to ensure that their children were taught, by sending them to church for catechism instruction, and a decade later another law required that those responsible for orphans "educate and instruct them according to their best endeavours in Christian religion and in rudiments of learning."[36] Such requirements were not followed up as in Massachusetts, however, with a mandate that local communities maintain schools.

As prosperity grew, the wealthier planters and merchants employed domestic tutors. The diaries and letters of a young man from the North who served as tutor on a plantation in 1773–1774 give a vivid picture of how demanding this instruction could be. He taught the children and a nephew of the owner, reporting that "the oldest son is turned of seventeen, and is reading [Latin author] Sallust and the greek grammar; the other [boys] are about fourteen, and in english grammar, and Arithmetic. He has besides five daughters which I am to teach english, the eldest is turned of fifteen, and is reading the spectator; she is employed two days in every week in learning to play the Forte-Piano, and Harpsicord—the others are smaller, and learning to read and spell."[37]

It was at such a plantation school, at Tuckahoe on the James River, that, with his sisters and cousins, young Thomas Jefferson received his early schooling.

Nothing like adequate coverage of schooling developed in the South, apart from some of the larger towns like Charleston. In 1724, the Archbishop of Canterbury (head, under the king, of the Church of England) asked the parishes in Virginia to report on a number of aspects of their situation; twenty-nine replied, more than half of the administrative units in the colony. Four of them reported the existence of a "public" (i.e., a free—usually endowed) school, of which two offered only reading, writing, and arithmetic; thirteen other parishes reported only private or "little" schools, and another thirteen had no schools at all to report.[38]

MID-ATLANTIC COLONIES

In the mid-Atlantic colonies, schooling was provided largely by individual churches, which led to great diversity given the pattern of settlement, and by individual schoolmasters for whom it was often a temporary occupation; in both cases, fees were charged, except in the charity schools maintained expressly for poor children. "Competing schoolmasters offered to teach anything from the ABC's to astronomy, at all times of the day, to students of widely varying ages. Schoolteaching was more a trade than a profession." In New York, "a 'school' in most cases was simply a person who taught, and when he stopped, the 'school' stopped. The only collective efforts in schooling in this period were the three denominational charity schools and King's College," the ancestor of Columbia.[39]

Colonists came not only from England (as, generally, in the colonies to the north and south), but from Scotland and Ireland and Wales, Sweden, Finland, Norway and Denmark, France, Germany, and the Netherlands. Paul Monroe's description of the settlers who came to New Netherland in the early seventeenth century applies to many others in the region: they came "with no purpose of reform, were moved by no spirit of protest. As traders, merchants, and the craftsmen and workers subordinate to these, they would naturally reproduce the life and institutions with which they were familiar at home."[40] This was true of the schooling that they provided or neglected to provide to their own children, and it was also characteristic of their general lack of interest in government policies to impose schooling on the children of others. The "others," indeed, were remarkably heterogeneous for that time and in contrast with the prevailing homogeneity in New England and (among whites) in the southern colonies. In New Amsterdam, for example, one could find not only the Dutch but also Protestant refugees from Catholic Europe: Huguenots from France, Waldensians from Italy, Moravians from Germany, as well as Baptists and Quakers from England and New England, and Jews whose ancestors had been expelled from Spain and Portugal. "It has been estimated that before the end of the Dutch period [in 1674] fifteen languages could be heard in New Amsterdam."[41] This diversity reflected the tolerance of the Dutch.

As in The Netherlands in the seventeenth century, schooling was provided in New Amsterdam by cooperation between the established Reformed Church in the Netherlands, which examined and certified the teacher, and the municipality, which provided the schoolhouse and sometimes also supplemented the income that the teacher received from tuition. In 1637, Adam Roelantsen was examined and licensed to go to New Amsterdam as schoolmaster and also reader and song-leader for the church. As in the Netherlands, he and subsequent teachers worked under the joint supervision of church and town authorities, and were partially funded by both, as well as by parents. There were ten other chartered towns in the Dutch colony, including Beverwyck (Albany), Breukelen, and New Haerlem, all but one of which had a school by the 1660s. "On the whole it appears a just generalization to say that the Dutch village in New Netherland reproduced as nearly as could be the parish school of the mother country."[42]

These arrangements were by no means automatic, since the colony was run on a commercial basis; it had been necessary for residents to petition that "there should be a public school, provided with at least two good masters, so that first of all in so wild a country, where there are many loose people, the youth be well taught and brought up, not only in reading and writing, but in the knowledge and fear of the Lord. As it is now, the school is kept very irregularly, one and another keeping it according to his pleasure and as long as he thinks proper."[43] In addition to the town schools there were private schools, whose teachers also required licensing by church authorities.

With the growth of the colony, the authorities in the Netherlands were persuaded, in 1659, to appoint a schoolmaster for a Latin school and provide a salary for him as well. The town provided the schoolhouse, and parents paid tuition as well.[44]

When the colony came under British rule (temporarily in 1664 and permanently in 1674), the Dutch schools generally continued in existence, and local communities often helped to support them. For several generations, "these schools of the Dutch churches were concerned chiefly with the preservation of the Dutch tongue. . . . In some English began to be taught with Dutch early in the eighteenth century. In others Dutch was used exclusively until near the Revolutionary War. At all times the English governor claimed the right of licensing such teachers and on occasion exercised this right to the chagrin, often as they thought to the danger, of the Dutch community."[45]

There was a marked contrast between this practice of supporting schools in the Dutch communities, even under British rule, and the hands-off policy (apart from licensing teachers) in the English communities that grew up in the colony. "In all of these Dutch settlements a community school existed as one essential part of the structure of society and of the local system of government. . . . while the school was immediately under the church, it was essentially a town school." Children of the English-speaking population, by contrast, were schooled primarily by private-venture teachers and by schools maintained by the Church of England's Society for the Propagation of the Gospel in Foreign Parts (SPG), founded in 1701, which "developed the largest, most systematized, and best-financed program of education in provincial America, establishing and subsidizing churches, schools, and libraries by the score."[46] Over the course of the eighteenth century the SPG sent 309 preachers to the American colonies, nearly half of them to New York, Pennsylvania, and New Jersey, but the teachers employed by the Society were almost all recruited in the colonies.[47] "For the most part the schools of the society were 'charity schools'; that is, the master was subsidized by the society on condition that he be an adherent of the Church of England and teach so many children free.... Schools were also maintained for the negroes [sic] by an affiliated society, and missionaries and teachers were sent out among the Indians."[48] Often Anglican, Dutch, and Jewish congregations would hire teachers to give basic religious and literacy instruction to the children of the poor of their congregations. "A 'common education,' as it was then conceived, could be acquired in about three years, after which charity school boys were to be apprenticed and girls usually put out to service."[49]

The colony of New Jersey, created in 1665 by separation from New York, was under "concessions and agreements" that guaranteed liberty of conscience, with the result that—like New York and Pennsylvania—it became a preferred destination for settlers of various religious groups that were experiencing difficulties or persecution in Europe. "To most of these groups of religious devotees, the school was as essential to the maintenance of their denominational entity as was the church." It was highly satisfactory to these groups that the colonial government left the sponsorship and control of schools up to local churches.[50]

Similarly, in Pennsylvania, the deliberate policy of William Penn to establish religious freedom in the colony attracted a wide variety of immigrants. The role of government was limited to requiring that children be educated, not that schools be established and maintained. Under a Pennsylvania law of 1683,

> to the end that poor as well as rich may be instructed in good and commendable learning, which is to be preferred before wealth, Be it enacted, etc., That all persons in this Province and Territories thereof, having children ... shall cause such to be instructed in reading and writing, so that they may be able to read the Scriptures and to write by the time they attain to twelve years of age; and that then they may be taught some useful trade or skill, that the poor may work to live, and the rich if they become poor may not want ... and in case such parents, guardians, or overseers shall be found deficient in this respect, [they] shall pay for every such child, five pounds, except there should appear an incapacity in body or understanding to hinder it.[51]

No measures were taken, however, to create a system of schooling in Pennsylvania. Religious groups established their own schools and sometimes subsidized them—or appealed to their "mother churches" in Europe for help— for parents who could not afford the tuition. The various groups of German immigrants, in particular, established and sustained schools, sometimes with help from the great center of Pietist missionary effort in Halle (Prussia).[52] Similarly, schooling for the children of English-speaking settlers was often, as in New York, provided through the efforts of the SPG.

A few scattered voices called for schools to be organized by public authorities (Thomas Budd, in 1685, even called in vain for a law requiring parents to put their children in school for at least 7 years), but it was not for more than 100 years that government action became even minimally effective in this respect. Some colonial leaders, it is true, were concerned about the deliberate isolation of immigrant groups. Benjamin Franklin wrote, in 1753, that "measures of great Temper are necessary with the Germans. . . . Those who come hither are generally of the most ignorant Stupid Sort of their own Nation . . . and as few of the English understand the German language, and so cannot address them from either the Press or Pulpit, 'tis almost impossible to remove any prejudices they once entertain. . . . Few of their children in the Country learn English. . . . Yet I am not for refusing entirely to admit them into our Colonies; all that seems to be necessary is, to distribute them more equally, mix them with the English, establish English Schools where they are now too thickly settled . . ."[53] In general, however, the diversity of religion and language among settlers, given their dispersal in communities with limited outside contact, seems to have caused little concern or policy debate during the colonial period, and there were few if any suggestions that compulsory schooling be used to reshape their children.

On the other hand, "religious benevolence supported the education of paupers far more generously in Pennsylvania than in New York,"[54] and this would continue well into the nineteenth century. For example, the Anglican organization Dr Bray's Associates established a school for free blacks in Philadelphia in 1758, and the Quaker Monthly Meeting, in 1770, started a class for the slaves of Quakers who were being prepared for manumission and for free blacks.[55]

The male literacy rate in Pennsylvania had reached two-thirds by the early eighteenth century, a level it would not exceed for the rest of the colonial period. Lockridge suggests that "in all respects this is a literacy environment very like that of eighteenth-century England. It is the environment of pre-industrial English and American society in the absence of intense Protestantism" of the sort found in New England.[56] It would perhaps be more accurate to say that the heterogeneous character of the Pennsylvania population, and its greater dispersal in a much richer farming environment than New England offered led to an uneven development, with communities of intense religious and educational commitment interspersed with others that were more indifferent to both.

One should not confuse the provision of schooling with the attainment of literacy and other skills, which was quite general in the Middle Atlantic colonies. "Many children could learn the three R's at home, accounting could be learned in the counting house, and navigation at sea. Each man decided how much, when, and what kind of schooling he needed or could afford for his children." As a result, "schooling was haphazard, and arrangements were often temporary. Students came and went, enrolled in schools and changed their minds. They went to different schoolmasters for different subjects and quit school often to change masters, to work, or to travel."[57]

Kaestle attributes the lack of urgency about the provision of schooling during the eighteenth century to the relatively homogeneous population, divided among Protestant groups that had no fundamental antagonism and yet none of which could impose its own version of education. "In late colonial New York there was neither a cultural threat nor a cultural hegemony. The group that later became the dominant city leaders, native Protestants, were divided in the eighteenth century" between the Dutch and several English denominations. Thus "Huguenot, Dutch, Anglican, Presbyterian, Deist—each arranged his child's moral and doctrinal education to his liking, not only at home and at church as in later periods but also in school."[58] Those who valued formal schooling for their children took pains to provide it, but education was not perceived as a public responsibility as in New England.

The line between primary and secondary schooling was not clearly drawn. Rather than a sequence of grades that led from one to the other, as we understand the distinction, there were two types of schools that served different clienteles and led to different destinations in life. Indeed, they developed in different ways from different demands.

What we think of as primary or elementary schools, teaching the fundamentals of literacy and numeracy to all the children of a community, began to develop only in the seventeenth century as a function of local government, and were still limited and altogether absent in many places well into the nineteenth century . . . indeed, into the twentieth, in parts of the South. The great theme of the history of education in the nineteenth century (starting in the 1830s) was the extension of such primary schooling, usually through initiatives at the local level but, where these were lacking, by government at the state though not yet at the national level, spurred on by an inter-communicating group of reformers and publicists who have been called "the school promoters."

Benjamin Franklin, born in Boston in 1706, received only 2 years of formal schooling, after learning to read at home.

> My elder Brothers were all put Apprentices to different Trades [he writes in his *Autobiography*] I was put to the [Boston Latin] Grammar School at Eight Years of Age, my Father intending to devote me as the Tithe of his Sons to the Service of the Church. My early Readiness in learning to read (which must have been very early, as I do not remember when I could not read) and the Opinion of all his Friends that I should certainly make a good Scholar, encourag'd him in this Purpose of his. . . . I continued at the Grammar School not quite one Year . . . but my Father in the mean time, from a View of the Expence [*sic*] of a College Education which, having so large a Family, he could not well afford, and the mean Living many so educated were afterwards able to obtain . . . took me from the Grammar School and sent me to a School for Writing and Arithmetic. . . . At Ten Years old, I was taken home to assist my Father in his Business . . .[59]

What would later be called "common schools" were thus instruments of social cohesion and moral governance, but were not seen as part of an inevitable continuity with secondary schooling. As in Europe until after World War I, there were in colonial North America in effect two parallel types of schools, the schools that most children attended at most until their early teens, receiving general instruction through English, and the elite grammar schools that a Franklin might enter at eight or even younger for instruction largely focused on mastery of the classical languages and intended to prepare for what were considered the learned careers of the ministry and law.

The limited schooling received by Benjamin Franklin, who came to be revered in both France and the young American Republic as one of the foremost philosopher/scientists of his day, reminds us that formal schooling during the colonial era did not play the role that it has today, of gate-keeper to almost all career and other opportunities. In a classic essay, historian Bernard Bailyn described how much of *education* occurred outside of schools in colonial America.

> What the family left undone by way of informal education the local community most often completed. It did so in entirely natural ways, for so elaborate was the architecture of family organization and so deeply founded was it in the soil of a stable, slowly changing village and town communities in which intermarriage among the same groups had taken place generation after generation that it was at times difficult for the child to know where the family left off and the greater society began. The external community, comprising with the family a continuous world,

naturally extended instruction and discipline in work and in the conduct of life. And it introduced the youth in a most significant way to a further discipline, that of government and the state.[60]

Noah Webster, the influence of whose spellers and readers on schooling in the United States in the first decades of the nineteenth century can scarcely be over-stated, paid tribute to this education outside of school in recalling his own youth before the Revolution:

> More explicit in its educational function than either family or community was the church. . . . It furthered the introduction of the child to society by instructing him in the system of thought and imagery which underlay the culture's values and aims. It provided the highest sanctions for the accepted forms of behavior, and brought the child into close relationship with the intangible loyalties, the ethos and higher principles, of the society in which he lived.[61]

Webster is one of the figures who bridged the transition from the traditional to the Enlightenment understanding of the purposes of schooling. It was during his lifetime that publicly managed schools without an explicitly religious character began to provide an *education* that was concerned with the formation of values and worldview.

In 1803, the Reverend Samuel Miller published *A Brief Retrospect of the Eighteenth Century*, with "high praise for the educational revolution that was obviously under way. The means of learning had been brought to almost every door, the curriculum had been rendered 'more conducive to the useful purposes of life,' servility and 'monkish habits' had been abandoned, opportunity had been opened to women, and the advantages of education had been 'more extensively diffused through the different grades of society than in any former age.'"[62]

It was in the 1830s and 1840s, in the United States and Canada as in much of contemporary Europe, that universal and uniform primary schooling, under the direction of the State, became a policy agenda of political leaders and the shapers of opinion. Immigration and the mixing of populations through the westward movement led to conflicts over religion and language that had seldom occurred during the colonial period, especially with respect to schooling, precisely because of the drive to make schooling uniform. Formal schooling and the credentials that it offered began—though there was a long way to go—to exercise the gate-keeper function that is so nearly absolute today. For all of these reasons, educational policy, and debates over the purposes and means of schooling, would come to have a significance far beyond their modest role during the colonial era.

It was the development of secondary and higher education in the late nineteenth and twentieth centuries—a story that we do not attempt to chronicle here—that made schooling the gate-keeper of economic opportunity. As we will see, the focus of popular schooling in the nineteenth century was on participation in the civic, moral, and religious community, primarily on a local level but increasingly at the national level as well.

Chapter Two

The Idea of
Forming Citizens

Although opportunities for schooling continued, in the early National period, to be highly dependent upon local initiatives and thus in turn upon settlement patterns as well as initiatives by church leaders, families, or teachers themselves, in elite circles there was a certain amount of discussion of the role that popular education could be expected to play in the formation of citizens. Some of this discussion reflected mistrust of what parents could be expected to demand for the schooling of their children, and of the education that they would provide for them at home.

As so often, Benjamin Franklin was ahead of his time. Writing to an English educator whom he attempted in vain to recruit to head the new Academy in Philadelphia, Franklin stressed that "nothing is of more importance for the public weal, than to form and train up youth in wisdom and virtue. Wise and good men are, in my opinion, the strength of a state." Although education might be effective with only a few, "yet the influence of those few and the service in their power, may be very great."[1]

It is easy to overlook how fragile the United States seemed to many during the first decades of its existence. As in Europe at the time, many political theorists called for the use of schooling to solidify the sense of nationhood and commitment to social order. Noah Webster wrote, in a series of articles that appeared in 1787–1788, that "our national character is not yet formed." "Education, in a great measure," he wrote, "forms the moral characters of men, and morals are the basis of government. Education should therefore be the first care of a legislature. . . . A good system of education should be the first article in the code of political regulations. . . . no legislature can be justified in neglecting proper establishments for this purpose."[2]

As it took the lead in the struggle for American independence, in January 1776, the Massachusetts legislature proclaimed, in words composed by John Adams, that "As a government so popular can be supported only by universal knowledge and virtue, it is the duty of all ranks to promote the means of education for the rising generation, as well as true religion, purity of manners, and integrity of life among all orders and degrees." The legislators ordered that this resolution be read at every court opening and every annual town meeting and urged the clergy of Massachusetts to read it to their congregations after the next Sunday service.[3] Four years later, with Adams again the drafter, the new Massachusetts *Constitution* proclaimed that

> Wisdom, and knowledge, as well as virtue, diffused generally among the body of the people, being necessary for the preservation of their rights and liberties; and as these depend on spreading the opportunities and advantages of education in the various parts of the country, and among the different orders of the people, it shall be the duty of legislatures and magistrates, in all future periods of this commonwealth, to cherish the interests of literature and the sciences, and all seminaries of them . . . to encourage private societies and public institutions . . . to countenance and inculcate the principles of humanity and general benevolence, public and private charity, industry and frugality, honesty and punctuality in their dealings, sincerity, good humor, and all social affections, and generous sentiments among the people.[4]

Such admonitions were characteristic of the laws bearing on education in the new republic. "With the exception of language in the declaration of rights, no other sections contained so much exhortation to virtue or justificatory prose. Sections on the legislative branch did not extol the virtues of representative government, nor those on the judiciary the glories of justice. . . . In contrast, the high-flown justifications of the common school declared public education to be a shared value, like those embedded in the declarations of rights, a common good above the squabbles of political party or sect."[5] This reliance upon rhetoric also reflected the lack of direct control by legislatures over local schooling.

It was considered necessary, in some cases, to use the schools to guard against disloyalty. The Pennsylvania legislature required, in 1777, that all teachers and trustees of public and private schools and colleges take an oath of loyalty to the Commonwealth of Pennsylvania, promising that "I will not at any time do or cause to be done any matter or thing that will be prejudicial or injurious to the freedom and independence thereof" and to report to the authorities "all treasons or traitorous conspiracies which I may know or hereafter shall know to be formed against this or any of the United States of America."[6]

A number of leaders among the founding generation were convinced that government could and should play a role in ensuring that children grow into virtuous citizens of the new nation.

"The instruction of the people," John Adams wrote in 1778, "in every kind of knowledge that can be of use to them in the practice of their moral duties, as men, as citizens, and Christians, and of their political and civil duties, as members of society and freemen, ought to be the care of the public. . . . It is not too much to say, that schools for the education of all should be placed at convenient distances, and maintained at the public expense." Seven years later he wrote, "the whole people must take upon themselves the education of the whole people, and must be willing to bear the expenses of it."[7]

This concern was widely shared. Samuel Adams wrote to his cousin John, in 1790,

> What then is to be done?—Let Divines [clergymen], and Philosophers, Statesmen and Patriots unite their endeavours to renovate the Age, by impressing the Minds of Men with the importance of educating their *little boys*, and *girls*—of inculcating in the Minds of youth the fear, and Love of the Deity, and universal Phylanthropy; and in subordination to these great principles, the Love of their Country—of instructing them in the Art of *self* government, without which they never can act a wise part in the Government of Society great, or small—in short of leading them to the study, and practice of the exalted Virtues of the Christian system, which will happily tend to subdue the turbulent passions of Men, and introduce that Golden Age beautifully described in figurative language.[8]

Six weeks later, he wrote to his cousin again:

> Should we not, my friend, bear a gratefull remembrance of our pious and benevolent Ancestors, who early laid plans of Education; be which means Wisdom, knowledge, and Virtue have been generally diffused among the body of the people, and they have been enabled to form and establish a civil constitution calculated for the preservation of their rights and liberties? . . . This Constitution was evidently founded in the expectation of the further progress, and "extraordinary degrees" of virtue.[9]

A crucial factor in development of a government role in education was the expansion of the concept of the citizen under a republican government. With increased discussion of alternative forms of political authority, there was a renewed appreciation of Aristotle's argument that citizens should be shaped by state-directed education to match the form of government under which they would live.[10] While this applied to all forms of government, according to French *philosophe* Montesquieu in *The Spirit of the Laws,* widely read by American leaders, it was especially the case in republics:

> It is in republican government that the full power of education is needed.... One can define this virtue as love of the laws and the homeland. This love, requiring a continual preference of the public interest over one's own, produces all the individual virtues; they are only that preference.... in a republic, everything depends on establishing this love, and education should attend to inspiring it.[11]

This theme was echoed constantly throughout the decades after the Revolution, though little was accomplished by government above the local level. George Washington, in his First Annual Message to Congress (1790), urged attention to the general diffusion of knowledge, arguing that it was essential for "teaching the people themselves to know and to value their own rights, to discern and provide against invasions of them; to distinguish between oppression and the necessary exercise of lawful authority; between burthens proceeding from a disregard to their convenience and those resulting from the inevitable exigencies of Society; to discriminate the spirit of Liberty from that of licentiousness."[12]

Similarly, in his *Farewell Address* (1796), Washington pointed out that

> of all the dispositions and habits which lead to political prosperity, Religion and morality are indispensable supports. In vain would that man claim the tribute of Patriotism, who should labour to subvert these great Pillars of human happiness, these firmest props of the duties of Men and citizens.... And let us with caution indulge the supposition, that morality can be maintained without religion.... 'Tis substantially true, that virtue or morality is a necessary spring of popular government.... Promote then as an object of primary importance, Institutions for the general diffusion of knowledge. In proportion as the structure of a government gives force to public opinion, it is essential that public opinion should be enlightened.[13]

And in his will, dated 1799, Washington expressed his concern that youth sent to foreign countries to complete their education would acquire "principles unfriendly to Republican Governmnt [*sic*], and to the true and genuine liberties of mankind.... For these reasons, it had been my ardent wish to see a plan devised on a liberal scale which would have a tendency to sprd [*sic*] systematic ideas through all the parts of this rising Empire, thereby to do away with local attachments and State prejudices." In support of this goal, he made a bequest for the endowment of a national university "to which the youth of fortune of talents from all parts" of the country "might be sent for the completion of their education in all the branches of polite literature" and "(as a matter of infinite importance in my judgment) by associating with each other, and forming friendships in Juvenile years, be enabled to free themselves ... from those local prejudices and habitual jealousies" which were "pregnant of mischievous consequences to this Country."[14] A proposal to give the national government the authority to create such an institution had, however, been voted down at the Constitutional Convention.[15]

While this and other proposals for a national role in schooling republican citizens had little practical effect or even apparent resonance, there was widespread concern at the state and local level, reminiscent of that many decades before when the first settlers in New England sought to establish their "city on a hill" on the basis of appropriate moral education. In 1805, the newly established Society for the Education of Poor Children in New York City pointed out that "the blessings of such a Government can be expected to be enjoyed no longer than while its citizens continue virtuous, and while the majority of the people, through the advantage of a proper early education, possess sufficient knowledge to enable them to understand and pursue their best interests."[16]

THOMAS JEFFERSON

Histories of American education commonly cite Jefferson's "Bill for the More General Diffusion of Knowledge" (1778) as a landmark, though they do not always mention that the bill failed to pass the Virginia legislature and that Virginia did not implement anything like a universal system of public education for white children—not to mention black children—for another 100 years. Ambitious proposals for educational reform bear no necessary relationship to actual provision of effective schooling!

Jefferson made two arguments about the need for a state-managed system of education, in the preamble to the bill. The first was that a general education, especially in history, would enable the citizens at large to detect the first signs of tyranny on the part of those in office over them. It was important to "illuminate, as far as practicable, the minds of the people at large." The second argument was that, by judicious selection and education, a worthy ruling class could be formed, "able to guard the sacred deposit of the rights and liberties of their fellow citizens." These natural leaders should be selected "without regard to wealth, birth or other accidental condition or circumstance." This, however, required public funding, since

> the indigence of the greater number disabling them from so educating, at their own expense, those of their children whom nature hath fitly formed and disposed to become useful instruments for the public, it is better that such should be sought for and educated at the common expense of all, than that the happiness of all should be confided to the weak or wicked.[17]

The bill called for a system of schools under the supervision of local community leaders, at which "all the free [white] children, male and female, . . . shall be entitled to receive tuition gratis for the term of three years, and as much longer, at their private expense, as their parents . . . shall think proper." The local leaders ("overseers") would select from among the boys in these schools "whose parents are too poor to give them farther education, some one of the best and most promising genius and disposition, to proceed to the [proposed] grammar school of his district." The fortunate boys thus selected would thus go to one of 20 regional schools with tuition and board paid by public funds. Each year a visitation would be made to these grammar schools for the purpose of weeding out any of the students who had not lived up to expectations: a third of the students who had completed one year were to be "discontinued." An even more stringent selection would follow for those who had continued longer, with a very few selected boys sent on to the College of William and Mary.[18]

In this manner, he proposed, the Commonwealth of Virginia would provide universal elementary schooling and selective secondary schooling for a very few poor children of "the best learning and most promising genius and disposition." Of course, the sons of more prosperous parents would not be subject to this strict selection, but could continue their schooling at their parents' expense.

In a 1786 letter, Jefferson wrote, "I think by far the most important bill in our whole code is that for the diffusion of knowledge among the people. . . . Preach, my dear sir, a crusade against ignorance; establish & improve the law for educating the common people."[19] The following year, in a letter from France which was no doubt influenced by the contemporary discussions of education in that country,[20] he wrote that it was "the most certain and the most legitimate engine of government."[21]

More extensively, in his *Notes on the State of Virginia* (intended to correct negative French stereotypes about American conditions), Jefferson described his proposal "to diffuse knowledge more generally through the mass of the people." One poor boy would be selected each year, as described above, from each of the primary schools to attend a grammar school, and one would in turn be selected from each grammar school "and continued six years, and the residue dismissed. By this means twenty of the best geniuses will be raked from the rubbish annually."

> The ultimate result of the whole scheme of education would be the teaching all the children of the state reading, writing, and common arithmetic; turning out ten annually of superior genius, well taught in Greek, Latin, geography, and the higher branches of arithmetic; turning out ten others annually, of still superior parts, who, to those branches of learning, shall have added such of the sciences as their genius shall have led them to; the furnishing to the wealthier part of the people convenient schools, at which their children may be educated, at their own expence [sic].[22]

These provisions reflect his belief, expressed in a letter to John Adams (1813), that "there is a natural aristocracy among men. The grounds of this are virtue and talents. . . . The natural aristocracy I consider as the most precious gift of nature for the instruction, the trusts, and the governance of society." In view of their importance, Jefferson still regretted the defeat of his proposal, under which "worth and genius would thus have been sought out from every condition of life, and compleatly [sic] prepared by education for defeating the competition of wealth and birth for public trusts." Although the bill, finally enacted in 1796 with a provision leaving it up to the counties whether to put it into effect, had never been implemented seriously, Jefferson expressed the hope that "some patriotic spirit will, at a favorable moment, call it up, and make it the key-stone of the arch of our government."[23] In fact, however, Norfolk was the only county where public schools were started under the provisions of the 1796 legislation; "other counties chose not to raise the necessary taxes, and Jefferson's idea foundered."[24]

Jefferson returned to this theme in a private letter in 1816, reacting to the new liberal (and short-lived) Spanish Constitution, urging

> Enlighten the people general and tyranny and oppressions of body and mind will vanish like evil spirits at the dawn of day. Although I do not, with some enthusiasts, believe that the human condition will ever advance to such a state of perfection as that there shall no longer be pain or vice in the world, yet I believe it susceptible of much improvement, and most of all in matters of government and religion; and that the diffusion of knowledge among the people is to be the instrument by which it is to be effected.[25]

In another letter the same year, he spelled out a process for putting the languishing state law into effect by stimulating the creation and maintenance of schools through local initiative in a manner that would not depend on state regulation or support; it would, indeed, have replicated

> many of the features of what had been the system in New England for nearly two centuries: explain the object of the law to the people of the [local militia] company, put to their vote whether they will have a school established, and the most central and convenient place for it; get them to meet and build a log school-house; have a roll taken of the children who would attend it, and of those of them able to pay. These would probably be sufficient to support a common teacher, instructing gratis the few unable to pay. If there should be a deficiency, it would require too trifling a contribution from the county to be complained of . . . Should the company, by its vote, decide that it would have no school, let them remain without one.[26]

In a proposal for schooling that he spelled out in 1817, Jefferson subordinated it entirely to the goal of forming citizens by stipulating that no one over the age of 15 would be considered a citizen of Virginia "until he or she can read readily in some tongue, native or acquired."[27] This was consistent with the concern he had expressed, 35 years earlier, in his *Notes on the State of Virginia*, that immigrants "will bring with them the principles of the governments they leave, imbibed in their early youth; or, if able to throw them off, it will be in exchange for an unbridled licentiousness. . . . In proportion to their numbers, they will share with us the legislation. They will infuse into it their spirit, warp and bias its direction, and render it a heterogeneous, incoherent, distracted mass."[28]

Although he is often cited as a prophet of American popular education, however, Jefferson's deeds belied his fair words. When public funding became available as a result of the national government repaying its debt to the states for costs incurred during the War of 1812, he opposed the efforts of Charles Fenton Mercer to use the Literary Fund for the schooling of poor and elementary school children (as Massachusetts would later use those federal funds to support local schools). "Jefferson wanted to start at the tip of the pyramid with his university; Mercer wanted to build elementary schools first as a building block, partly because he thought the American Revolution had cut off the flow of good teachers from Britain. . . . Jefferson needed the aristocracy's support to build his university, and relinquishing support for primary schools was the political cost he paid."[29] Jefferson encouraged his legislative allies to block bills supporting the development of common school provision statewide. As a result, until late in the nineteenth century most schools in Virginia were "essentially private, but partially reimbursed by city or county governments" for enrolling children from poor families.[30]

THE ALLIES OF JEFFERSON

The United States was, in the 1780s, almost alone among nations in possessing a republican form of government. The events in France in 1789 and 1790 seemed to provide a confirmation that republicanism was the way of the future, and were greeted with enormous enthusiasm by most Americans. It was claimed that more cannons were fired by Americans in 1791 to celebrate the fall of Amsterdam to the French revolutionary forces than the French had fired in taking it,[31] and "when the news arrived in the United States that the French had turned back the invaders at Valmy on September 20 [1792], and that France had declared itself a republic two days later . . ., all America went wild with joy. There were bells and illuminations in Philadelphia on December 14, the day the news came in, and huge civic celebrations were held in place after place throughout the succeeding six weeks."[32] Alexander Hamilton warned, in 1793, that "the popular tide in this country is strong in favor of the last revolution in France."[33] This enthusiasm for the French Revolution—at least until the Terror and French efforts to embroil the United States in another war with Britain turned most Americans against it—created an interest in radical French ideas about education and the State. Proponents of "republican" education were often admirers of the Jacobin program, though their admiration was shaken by its violent phase and its hostility to Christianity; John Adams wrote in 1790 that he did not know "what to make of a republic of thirty million atheists."[34] On the other hand, Benjamin Franklin Bache, an influential Republican journalist and grandson of his namesake, wrote in 1792 that no one could "seriously suppose that the present struggle of that nation is not the beginning of that universal reformation which is about to take place in the world for the general benefit of the human race." Bache frequently used his newspaper to argue for the establishment of a public school system as a means of "instilling republican virtues."[35]

> In the 1790s, during the period of intense emotional debate about the French Revolution, the intellectual representatives of the Revolutionary Enlightenment reached impressive heights of popularity in America. Rousseau, long familiar, was read as never before, and all his major works were republished in America.[36]

Even Noah Webster's early thinking about the political order of the new nation and the role of schooling in establishing that order was influenced by reading Rousseau's *Social Contract*, "from which he admitted be 'imbibed many visionary ideas' that he later rejected."[37] By 1794, however, Webster was asserting in his newspaper "that the French, far from being the true liberals they claim to be, are in reality the most implacable persecutors of opinion, and he went on to argue that the Revolution is necessarily fatal to morality, that by removing all religious restraints it has increased violence, which will in time 'decivilize' the people, and is indeed fast doing so."[38]

Robert Coram of Delaware, a leading anti-Federalist journalist, published an essay of political reflections in 1791, in which he argued that "the education of children should be provided for in the constitution of every state," as it was indeed already in those of Massachusetts and several other states. Coram would go farther, however, in the spirit of contemporary proposals in France. "By incorporating education with government," he promised, "*This is the rock on which you must build your political salvation!*"[39] In order to accomplish this salvation, it was necessary to convert "private schools into public ones," and to ban from them all religious instruction: "modes of faith."[40] As May points out, "most of this program and the attitudes underlying it had a big future in American educational reform. [But] It was much too sweeping to get far in practice in the America of the 1790s."[41]

The American Philosophical Society—in imitation of the practice of eighteenth-century learned academies in Europe—sponsored an essay contest in 1795 about the best "plan for instituting and conducting public schools in this country." The prize was shared in 1797 by Samuel Knox (a Scots-Irish clergyman sympathetic to the religious views of Jefferson) and Samuel Harrison Smith (editor of the official newspaper of the Jefferson administration). Smith did not mince his words: "it is the duty of a nation to superintend and even to coerce the education of children," he wrote. In light of this duty, "high considerations of expediency not only justify but dictate the establishment of a system which shall place under a control, independent of and superior to parental authority, the education of children."[42]

With respect to the content of such instruction, Smith argued that it must give primacy to development of that "virtue" essential to the civil order and that "wisdom" necessary to the exercise of virtue. It should limit itself to "those truths in which all men agree," and "the most solemn attention must be paid to avoid instilling into the young mind any ideas or sentiments whose truth is not unequivocally established by the undissenting suffrage of the enlightened and virtuous part of mankind."[43] What he intends, obviously, is the exclusion of beliefs based upon revelation or tradition and the teaching instead of those convictions that men of the Enlightenment liked to believe were based upon the pure exercise of reason.

This education, Smith argued, must be compulsory and not left up to the decision of parents, a tacit admission that there would not be universal acceptance of the program recommended. He discusses the need to commission schoolbooks "defining correctly political, moral, and religious duty in the place of those which are at present in use," and require their use to prevent teachers from conveying their own "immature ideas" to their pupils. It is clear that Smith's concern is not with improved methods of teaching reading or arithmetic, that is with *instruction*, but with the ideological content of schoolbooks, and thus with *education* . . . or, indeed, indoctrination.

Knox acknowledged recent efforts, in France, to establish a national system of education, but pointed out that he knew of no other "plan devised by individuals or attempted by any commonwealth in modern times that effectually tends to the establishment of any uniform, regular system of national education." Much had been spent on education for the children of the elite, "while the poor and such as most wanted literary instruction or the means of acquiring it have been almost totally neglected." Although something was being done in different parts of the new nation, there were serious problems for the development of a sense of national unity arising from the different approaches taken, differences causing "many other inconveniences and disagreeable consequences that commonly arise in the various departments of civil society or even the polished enjoyments of social intercourse." A national system of education, by contrast, would remove these regional and other differences, including those arising from a population "blending together almost all the various manners and customs of every country in Europe." In the face of this challenge, "nothing . . . might be supposed to have a better effect towards harmonizing the whole in these important views than a *uniform system of national education*."[44]

BENJAMIN RUSH

In some ways a more interesting example of Enlightenment ideas in an American form than Jefferson and his allies is found in proposals by Benjamin Rush, a physician and (like Adams and Jefferson) a signer of the *Declaration of Independence*, for a system of popular schooling in Pennsylvania. Rush urged, in 1786, that "Our schools of learning, by producing one general and uniform system of education, will render the mass of the people more homogeneous and thereby fit them more easily for uniform and peaceable government."[45] "I consider it as possible," he wrote, "to convert men into republican machines. This must be done if we expect them to perform their parts properly in the great machine of the government of the state. That republic is [vulnerable to] monarchy or aristocracy that does not revolve upon the wills of the people, and these must be fitted to each other by means of education before they can be made to produce regularity and unison in government."[46] Rush's proposal owed more to Franklin's concern about the acculturation of the Germans in Pennsylvania than it did to French prophecies of human progress through education.

After proposing that Pennsylvania support, with state funds, one university and four colleges, he went on to call for an academy in each county "for the purpose of instructing youth in the learned languages and thereby preparing them to enter college," and an elementary school in every township or other districts with at least 100 families. These "free schools" would be supported by a tax on every district for the support of its schoolmaster, who in addition would receive tuition payments from families "to prompt him to industry in increasing his school."[47]

In his enthusiasm for his proposed system, Rush anticipated the exaggerated claims that Horace Mann and his allies would make for the "common school." "I can form no idea of the golden age, so much celebrated by the poets," he wrote, "more delightful than the contemplation of that happiness which it is now in the power of the legislature of Pennsylvania to confer upon her citizens by establishing proper modes and places of education in every part of the state."[48]

Unlike Jefferson, Rush was not hostile to the teaching of revealed religion in the schools, believing that "the only foundation for a useful education in a republic is to be laid in Religion. Without this there can be no virtue, and without virtue there can be no liberty, and liberty is the object and life of all republican governments."[49]

Nor did he believe, as Horace Mann and the New York Public School Society would later contend, that it was possible to provide a non-denominational religious instruction; "it is necessary," he wrote, "to impose upon them the doctrines and discipline of a particular church." He was careful to deny any attempt to promote an established form of religion: "Far be it from me to recommend the doctrines or modes of worship of any one denomination of Christians. I only recommend to the persons entrusted with the education of youth to inculcate upon them a strict conformity to that mode of worship which is most agreeable to their consciences or the inclinations of their parents." The emphasis upon district schools would ensure "that children of the same religious sect and nation may be educated so much as possible together."[50]

Religious instruction was the basis for morality, and Rush did not consider leaving it to the responsibility of the home or the church. Indeed, he wrote, "I had rather see the opinions of Confucius or Mohammed inculcated upon our youth than see them grow up wholly devoid of a system of religious principles."[51] He urged, in fact, that public funds be provided to each denomination to make it possible for poor children to attend its schools. Rush tackled head-on the charge, still often heard today, that "it is improper to fill the heads of children with religious prejudices of any kind, and that they should be left to choose their own principles."

> Could we preserve the mind in childhood and youth a perfect blank this plan of education would have more to recommend it; but this we know to be impossible.... Do we leave our youth to acquire systems of geography, philosophy, or politics, till they have arrived at an age in which they are capable of judging for themselves? We do not.[52]

"I add further," Rush concludes, "that if our youth are disposed after they are of age to think for themselves, a knowledge of our system [of religion], will be the best means of conducting them in a free enquiry into other systems of religion."

In 1791, Rush published a letter calling for the use of the Bible as a text in elementary schools. "We profess to be republicans," he wrote, "and yet we neglect the only means of establishing and perpetuating our republican form of government, that is, the universal education of our youth to the principles of Christianity, by means of the Bible; for this Divine book, above all others, favours that equality among mankind, that respect for just laws, and all those sober and frugal virtues which constitute the soul of republicanism."[53]

While (like Benjamin Franklin several decades earlier) Rush was concerned about the assimilation of Pennsylvania's large German population, he suggested that they be given the option of having their children taught in German as well as in English. He was particularly concerned that poor parents be enabled to educate their children, and devoted one of his written pleas to the public to that cause. When a group of German Pennsylvanians asked his support for a college that would use their language, Rush published an essay seeking to answer objections to "sectarian education," arguing that it would be easier to provide the essential religious instruction in institutions where all the children were of the same denominations. Use of German for instruction would not prevent the integration of Germans into American life, since "once a thirst for learning has been created, they will turn naturally to English to further their education, especially when they realize that language leads to distinction in medicine, law, and politics. Would not such a college make a separate people more separate? 'It is *ignorance* and *prejudice* only that keeps men of different countries and religions apart. . . . A German college, by removing *these*, will prepare the way for the Germans to unite more intimately with their British and Irish fellow citizens and thus form with them one homogeneous mass of people."[54]

THE LIMITED EFFECT OF SUCH PROPOSALS

While some of Jefferson's allies remained under the influence of the radical ideas from France, and floated proposals for a national and uniform system of education capped by a national university, this approach found little practical resonance in American political life. "As the most ardent reformers were well aware, far the greatest steps toward free and equal education had been made in Federalist New England, under auspices far removed from those of the Revolutionary Enlightenment."[55]

Alexander Hamilton, like Edmund Burke in England, was quick to perceive the utopian and unbounded nature of the ideas promoted by influential intellectuals through adoption of the *Rights of Man and the Citizen* and other measures, even before the most radical phase of the Revolution. "I dread the reveries of your Philosophic politicians," he wrote to Lafayette.[56]

Similarly,

> celebrating the anniversary of American Independence in New Haven in 1798, Noah Webster declared: "Never . . . let us exchange our civil and religious institutions for the wild theories of crazy projectors; or the sober, industrious moral habits of our country, for *experiments* in atheism and lawless democracy. *Experience* is a safe pilot; but *experiment* is a dangerous ocean, full of rocks and shoals."[57]

John Adams, in turn, "ridiculed Condorcet's dogmas about the limitless perfectibility of man and unstoppable progress. But especially he disdained Condorcet's belief that intellectuals were humanity's 'eternal benefactors.'"[58]

The resistance to French-inspired proposals for society-transforming education was part of a broader aversion to the "French Philosophy and Illumination" associated with Jefferson,[59] who was widely suspected of being a deist and "immoralist." "By the end of the [eighteenth] century, even as Americans were electing their most enlightened president, this form of Enlightenment was already being rejected by an overwhelming majority."[60]

Though support had not yet developed for a strong state role in directing education, there was general agreement among political elites on the almost unlimited potential for schooling to create free citizens. "We do not, indeed, expect all men to be philosophers or statesmen," Senator Daniel Webster proclaimed in 1820, "but we confidently trust . . . that, by the diffusion of general knowledge and good and virtuous sentiments, the political fabric may be secure, as well against open violence and overthrow, as against the slow, but sure, undermining of licentiousness."[61] New York Governor De Witt Clinton urged his state legislature, in 1826, that

> the first duty of government, and the surest evidence of good government, is the encouragement of education. A general diffusion of knowledge is the precursor and protector of republican institutions . . . I consider the system of our common schools as the palladium of our freedom; for no reasonable apprehension can be entertained of its subversion, as long as the great body of the people are enlightened by education. To increase the funds, to extend the benefits, and to remedy the defects of this excellent system, is worthy of your most deliberate attention.[62]

A former mayor of New York City (and an early leader of the Public School Society of that city), Clinton was very much aware of how the institutions of government and the functioning of society were being challenged by the first effects of urbanization. Nor was this all: the arrival of refugees from revolutions and civil unrest in France, Ireland, and the West Indies "sent a new group of impoverished radicals" who—so some believed—threatened the political stability of the new nation.[63] Gradually the conviction grew that state government should not leave the provision of schooling entirely up to local initiatives.

At the beginning of the nineteenth century, the schooling available was in general quite adequate to the economic needs of the day. There is little evidence of grass-roots demand for fundamental reform of the schooling available through local initiatives; to the extent that parents were dissatisfied, they made their views known locally and, if these were not addressed adequately, they turned to the private academies that were so widely available. The "common school revival" that began in the late 1820s and received definitive form under the leadership of Horace Mann, Henry Barnard, and their allies to the west was a struggle over *education,* over the political role of schooling in shaping the character of the American people, not over *instruction*, the imparting of skills and objective knowledge. Ironically, in view of the alienation of many present-day evangelical Protestants from the attempts of public schools to promote values that they find objectionable, it was, as we will see in the next chapter, evangelicals who prepared the ground for the acceptance of this broader role in the nineteenth century.

UTOPIAN REFORMERS

Another strand of thinking and advocacy about popular education in the antebellum period came from abroad. The new American nation seemed, to

European visionaries, to offer endless possibilities for experiments in the fundamental reordering of human relations in society. Many of these experiments were communitarian, reacting against the social disruption of revolutions and industrialization through seeking to reproduce on a secular basis the cooperative spirit of religiously based communities of which there were many at the time in the United States. Ideas associated with Swiss educator Heinrich Pestalozzi played a key role in most of these schemes, offering the promise of remaking humanity.[64]

> The communitarian idea was peculiarly attractive because alternative methods of social reform appeared to have reached a dead end during this particular period. Individualism seemed incapable of answering the nineteenth-century need for collective action. Revolution had revealed itself as a dangerous two-edged sword in the quarter-century of French and European history between 1789 and 1815. And the problems created by industrialization appeared to have so far outdistanced the ability of gradual methods to solve them that society itself was retrograding. Drastic reform was the demand, but drastic reform without revolution. Such a program the secular communitarians offered, and during the half-century following 1815 they were listened to with attention.[65]

Among the Britons who tried, in various ways, to carry out such plans in the United States were William Maclure (1763–1840), Robert Owen (1771–1858), his son Robert Dale Owen (1801–1877), and Frances Wright (1795–1852). Bronson Alcott (1799–1888), an American educator, became for a time a favorite of British enthusiasts for his utopian program of a "New Moral World."

Maclure was a successful businessman who became an American citizen, retiring early to devote himself to the first extensive geological survey of the United States. Interested in social reform, he became convinced that only an appropriate schooling of young children could produce fundamental change: "I have so far lost the little confidence I had in adults or parents that I believe no good system of education can have a fair trial but with orphans."[66] Concluding that the education he had himself received was useless ("In reflecting upon the absurdity of my own classical education, launched into the world as ignorant as a pig of anything useful . . . I had long been in the habit of considering education one of the greatest abuses our species were [sic] guilty of"),[67] Maclure decided that the new methods of Pestalozzi, which he observed in Switzerland and in Paris, could produce more positive effects. He financed the move of several Pestalozzian educators to Philadelphia, where he had become president of the Academy of Natural Sciences. One of them, Joseph Neef, published in

1809 a *Sketch of a Plan and Method of Education*, the first book on pedagogical method published in America.[68]

Like Maclure, Robert Owen was a successful businessman who turned to social and educational reform. Owen managed for more than 20 years a cotton mill which his father-in-law had built in a sparsely populated area of Scotland, housing a labor force gathered from the Highlands and from urban orphanages. New Lanark was an early "company town," and Owen took advantage of his complete control to experiment in a variety of ways with improving the attitudes and habits of his workers. Widely admired by contemporary reformers was the significantly named Institution Established for the Formation of Character, in which children were enrolled as soon as they could walk since, Owen was convinced, "in ninety-nine cases out of a hundred, parents are altogether ignorant of the right method of treating children." Children under 10 were "trained collectively," while those older and employed in the factory had an evening school. Owen insisted that "the children were not to be annoyed with books, but were to be taught the uses and nature or qualities of the common things around them."[69] This schooling of children was the crowning element of the "total institution" which Owen had created, in which all the residents were directly dependent on him and through which he sought to direct their lives both on and off the job.

Intoxicated with the celebrity of New Lanark, Owen distributed widely his book *A New View of Society* (1816). "The fundamental principle," he wrote, "on which all these Essays proceed is, that 'Children collectively may be taught any sentiments and habits'; or, in other words, 'trained to acquire any character.'" Through state-controlled schooling, "the governing powers of any country may easily and economically give its subjects just sentiments, and the best habits." This would be the basis for a new social and economic order and for universal peace and progress; through the right sort of education, man would come to understand "that his individual happiness can be increased and extended only in proportion as he actively endeavours to increase and extend the happiness of all around him."[70] Villages of Unity and Mutual Cooperation would create a surplus of production that would make all prosperous.

Disappointed by the reluctance of British policymakers to restructure society according to his prescription, and convinced (in part by reading about Shaker and other flourishing religious communities) of the greater openness of America to such ideas, Owen purchased property in Indiana from one such community. In a series of lectures, including several to members of Congress and President John Quincy Adams, Owen announced that he was ready to institute his New System in Indiana, and predicted that its benefits would be so obvious that it would soon be emulated nationwide. "I am come to this country," he told the gathered settlers in his community of New Harmony in April 1825, "to introduce an entire new state of society, to change it from the ignorant, selfish system, to an enlightened social system, which shall gradually unite all interests into one, and remove all cause of contest between individuals."[71]

Owen persuaded Maclure to join him in the venture, transferring the scientific and educational work he had been sponsoring in Philadelphia. So was born, in 1825, the short-lived New Harmony community. Nothing, Owen told the colonists, had ever produced so much evil as individualism, and they would show by their example how the human race could be transformed. Almost immediately, however, they broke into squabbling factions, with a succession of short-lived arrangements for governance and economic affairs that collapsed entirely after 2 difficult years.

Despite the failure of New Harmony as a utopian community, the educational institutions sponsored by Maclure, including free schools for girls as well as boys, the first "infant school" in America, a school for teens that combined study with productive work, all strongly Pestalozzian in inspiration, and (after his death) the Working Man's Institute and Library, made New Harmony for decades a center of practical research and education on the frontier.

A visitor to New Harmony during its brief "Owenite" phase was Frances "Fanny" Wright, a Scottish heiress who shared Owen's enthusiasm for communities as a means of social reform. Wright founded, in 1825, the Nashoba Community in Tennessee, intended to allow slaves to purchase their freedom through cooperative work while living together with white and free black fellow-workers. This effort, despite an international board chaired by General Lafayette, soon collapsed like other communities without a religious basis of unity, in this case partly because of reports of inter-racial co-habitation.

Owen's oldest son, Robert Dale Owen, published in 1824 a highly Pestalozzian account of the education provided in New Lanark and in New Harmony, became one of the primary leaders in the frequent absence of his father. After the failure of plans for communal living, he and Frances Wright moved in 1829 to New York City, where they published the *Free Enquirer*. This newspaper promised to expose the tyranny of organized religion and called for what they called State Guardianship Education. They proposed that all children aged 2 and older should be enrolled in government boarding schools, wear the same clothes, eat the same food, receive the same education; this, they predicted, would eliminate the influence of family wealth and culture in giving some children advantages over others. In this manner the "children would be separated from the pernicious influences of existing society . . . raised in an atmosphere of perfect equality, trained in both manual and intellectual skills, and graduated at last as citizens capable of remaking the institutions of the old immoral world."[72] Under this proposed system, "parents interested in maintaining contact with their children would be allowed occasional visits, but were to have neither control nor supervision over their nurture."[73]

This idea was not original with them; it had been a cornerstone of the Jacobin program of education during the radical phase of the French Revolution, and Maclure had also argued for boarding schools since, he contended, pupils were confused by the contrast between harmony in school and the social contradictions experienced at home.[74]

It happened that the same year, influenced by a slightly earlier development in Philadelphia, an organization of discontented working men formed in New York; Robert Dale Owen was chosen as one of the secretaries of the new political party, while Wright became a fiery orator for the movement, which was able to elect two candidates to the state Assembly. "Republican education," Wright wrote in 1829, "alone, as it seems to me, can set the vessel of the republic fairly and safely afloat." A system of national boarding schools "would lift from parents the burden and responsibility of their children while educating the generations to come" as "new people" with progressive ideas about economics and male-female relations.[75]

Establishment of state-controlled systems of schooling was in fact one of the regular demands of these associations;[76] indeed, for a couple of years, it became "the nucleus of the Working Men's position everywhere. They called above all for free, tax-supported school systems of high quality to replace the stigmatized 'pauper schools.'"[77] In 1830, the workers' association in New York City declared schooling their first priority and a similar group in Boston urged that "the establishment of a liberal system of education, attainable by all, should be among the first efforts of every lawgiver who desires the continuance of our national independence."[78] This brief agitation led, in the early twentieth century, to claims that it was to organized labor that America owed the creation of popular schooling; as one labor newspaper put it in 1924, "Labor was the first to fight for the public schools in America."[79] In fact, however, the efforts of the short-lived Working Men's Party had no more lasting impact on the provision of schooling than did those of Thomas Jefferson or of Robert Owen.*

---

* One of the sources of this claim was Carlton (1910), who wrote "In those eventful years, 1829, 1830 and 1831, of the first organized agitation by American workingmen, an impetus was given to the movement for free and universal education which led directly to the general adoption of the free-school system. The American public-school system owes much to Robert Dale Owen, to his father, and to New Harmony" 190. Pawa (1971) points out, more accurately, that the "public schools in New York emerged not as a result of labor agitation but as the by-product of a religious clash" 291.

The party line was too radical to find wide acceptance: "religion was super-stition, traditional education irrational, capitalism unnatural, the subordina-tion of women artificial, and all of it inequitable. Through the proper sort of education, said Wright, 'a revolution would indeed be effected; the present order of things completely subverted.'"[80] Less radically, John Eldredge told his fellow workingmen, at a New England conference in 1832, that "'a democratic form of government . . . is incomplete and insufficient' without a state-run edu-cation system."[81]

The association with Fanny Wright—called by the mainstream press the "great Red Harlot of Infidelity" and by Lyman Beecher "the female apostle of atheistic liberty"—and with an educational proposal that laid "siege to the very foundation of society" proved fatal to the new party, and the majority of its members, opposed to state assumption of the family's role, abandoned it. One newspaper called the idea of government boarding schools "one of the wild-est fancies that ever entered into the brain of the most visionary fanatics"—a system designed "to sever those strong ties of affection that keep families together."[82] By the 1830 election the party had lost its drive and was decisively defeated. Kaestle notes that the activist workers themselves "were not in gen-eral committed to religious skepticism, to women's rights, or to attacks on marriage and the family. Owen and Wright and their sympathizers had tried to engraft a thoroughgoing critique of capitalist society onto a stripling labor organization whose members were largely motivated by specific work-related grievances. The effort proved futile."[83]

While Robert Owen and Frances Wright had no significant role in later developments in the United States, and William Maclure retired to Mexico for his health, Robert Dale Owen was later elected to Congress from Indiana, had a major role in creation of the Smithsonian Institution (to which he attempted to assign a teacher-training role),[84] and served as the American envoy in Naples. As a framer of the Indiana Constitution of 1850, he incorporated language for a uniform system of common schools with state and local tax support, and after the Civil War had a role in drafting the Fourteenth Amendment to the US Constitution. Like his father and other militant nineteenth-century secu-larists, he became a convert to Spiritualism, publishing several books on com-munication with the spirits of the dead.

Amos Bronson Alcott established, in 1834, the Temple School in Boston, which enjoyed a brief vogue among the Unitarian elite. Alcott (the "Papa" of *Little Women*) sought to elicit the "spiritual existence" of his pupils by having them maintain journals to record their most intimate thoughts, convinced that education was not so much a matter of pouring knowledge into the children as of drawing out the divine wisdom which each possessed. Children were innately good. "I said Christianity, art, beauty, all are in the soul of the child, and the art of the teacher consists in drawing it out . . ."[85] An account (1835) by his assistant Elizabeth Peabody (one of whose sisters married Horace Mann, the other Nathaniel Hawthorne) of the instructional method used made Alcott internationally known, though English visitor Harriet Martineau predicted that "a few weeks are enough to convince sensible parents of the destructiveness of such a system."[86] Sure enough, Alcott's own *Conversations with Children on the Gospels* (1836) caused such a scandal that the school closed, and Alcott went to England, where some saw him as "the American Pestalozzi."

Returning to Massachusetts in 1842 with two English admirers, Alcott started a communitarian experiment called "Fruitlands," intended as a model of education and society; this attracted many visitors but fell apart after 7 months because of internal disagreements and the failure of their farming efforts to produce enough to eat. "Charles Lane, Alcott's associate at Fruitlands, identified what he considered the basic social question of the day—'whether the existence of the marital family is compatible with that of the universal family, which the term "Community" signifies.'"[87] It is safe to say that most Americans were not prepared to embrace a universal family in place of the ones, however limiting, that they already possessed. The Fruitlands property subsequently became, appropriately, a refuge for former reformers.

Although the efforts of the Owens, Wright, and Alcott to implement new models of community all ended quickly in failure, their widely publicized optimism about the transformative power of education on individuals and, through them, on society as a whole, helped to create the climate of ideas that fostered the rapid spread of the Common School movement. "Few social reformers have accorded education such a central place in their philosophy as the Owenites. They spoke in lyrical terms of what could be achieved by it and attributed vast power to its influence."[88] The success of the Common School reformers, in contrast with the failures of the Utopian predecessors and contemporaries with whom they shared many assumptions and hopes, can be attributed in part to the respect of the former for the role of families, a respect, it is true, forced upon them by the fact that they were operating in the real world of popular democracy and the local control of schools.

A longer-term effect of the Utopian reformers was the popularization, among educators, of the educational theories of Pestalozzi (and, ultimately, of Rousseau), which introduced to an American audience the idea that education should focus on the child's interests rather than on the skills and knowledge to be taught, a theme recurring more persistently in educationist circles here than in other countries, as we will see in Chapter Eight.

The largely peaceful development of the American educational system, at least until the controversies over religion in the 1870s, may in large part be attributed to the fact that proposals to create a national educational system were resisted and decisions about the content of schooling were left to local officials with basically conservative and non-theoretical concerns. "Among American republicans the French revolutionary mania for centralization was almost entirely lacking."[89] Making decisions about schooling in the United States remained primarily a local matter until the last few years, though with sporadic prodding from the states—some more than others—and, recently, from the national government.

Chapter Three

Religion as Source of Cooperation

Early in the nineteenth century, it was primarily religious motivations that led to the establishment and maintenance of schools. While in some areas this led to separate denominational schools, in others cooperation among Protestants who differed on various points of doctrine and practice led to schools with a religious character that all could support. Even Horace Mann, though criticized by some evangelicals for attempting to promote his own Unitarian beliefs through the public schools,[1] enjoyed strong support among the Protestant clergy of New England and beyond.

This situation changed with the arrival of tens of thousands and eventually millions of Catholic immigrants, most from countries where schools—including those funded by government—were organized on a denominational basis. Anxiety over the assimilation of these newcomers (discussed in Chapters Five and Seven), as well as a trans-Atlantic climate of distrust between Catholics and those committed to republican governments meant that the cooperation among Protestant groups was not extended to Catholics.

American intellectual and social life throughout the nineteenth century was profoundly influenced by the evangelical form of Protestantism, a sometimes-uneasy blend of orthodox Calvinism and the Pietist and Methodist movements of the eighteenth century. This received a great impulse from the Second Great Awakening early in the century and shaped how Americans thought about themselves and about the millions of non-evangelical immigrants who arrived in great numbers beginning in the 1840s. Evangelicals believed that the nation faced a choice between "superstition and evangelical light," and that the appointed role of Protestant churches and associations was to shape the culture, its institutions, and its future citizens.

The leaders of these associations were by no means opposed to government action to further their various causes; most were Whigs—"as far as is known no Democratic politician was ever a national officer of the voluntary societies"[2]—and just as comfortable promoting public funding as encouraging private benevolence. In many respects, indeed, the evangelical initiatives of the early nineteenth century prepared the way for the government efforts which, by mid-century, were increasingly supplementing them.

The profound influence of Protestant believers and institutions was exercised despite a lack of official connections between government and churches; indeed, it seems likely that it was precisely the lack of an established church that made religion such a vital force in American life.[3]

Legal "disestablishment," the termination of the arrangements in most colonies by which public funding was provided to churches, occurred not as a result of the First Amendment to the Federal Constitution but through a series of decisions at the state level: North Carolina in 1776, New York State in 1777, Virginia between 1776 and 1779, Maryland in 1785, South Carolina in 1790, Georgia in 1798, Vermont in 1807, Connecticut in 1818, New Hampshire in 1819, Maine in 1820, and Massachusetts in 1832–1833. Nor was it as a result of Thomas Jefferson's efforts that even his Virginia ended its support for the Episcopal Church; "Robert Baird, whose *Religion in America* appeared in various editions between 1842 and 1856, pointed out that 'it was not Jefferson that induced the State of Virginia to pass the act of separation. That must be ascribed to the petitions and other efforts of the Presbyterians and Baptists.'"[4]

The leaders of the new nation had no intention of excluding Christianity in an interdenominational form from public life. Alexander Hamilton called in 1802 for a "Christian Constitutional Society" to aid immigrants and win their loyalty, and many voluntary associations—such as the Massachusetts Society for Promoting Christian Knowledge (1807), the Boston Society for Religious and Moral Instruction of the Poor (1816), and the Society in Lynn for the Promotion of Industry, Frugality, and Temperance (1826)—included this among their objectives.[5]

It was a matter of course that most leaders in civic and benevolent enterprises would be clergymen, based on their education, their social position, and the networks of communication and influence that they often possessed. "Clergymen inspired the dominant social movement of the period, the crusade for humanitarian reform, at every stage. They were the principal arbiters of manners and morals and the most venerated citizens of every community."[6]

Later historians, concerned to demonstrate that public education had been emancipated from religious influences, chose not to report how close the relationship between (nonestablished) church and school remained. "In listing ten representative leaders of the [common-school] movement, Cubberley neglects to mention that five of them were ministers. About one-third of the contributors to Barnard's *American Journal of Education* were ministers."[7]

The Reverend Thomas Gallaudet, for example, played an active role in a variety of good works, including the evangelical Tract Society; he is best known as the pioneer of the education of deaf mutes in the United States. The Reverend Horace Bushnell, whose *Discourses on Christian Nurture* (1847) caused a stir among his fellow Congregationalists by downgrading the significance of conversion and urging that children could be educated into Christian faith,[8] became a major critic of Catholic schooling as a threat to American society. The Reverend Lyman Beecher, born in 1775, was "the outstanding revivalist produced by New England Calvinism during the Second Great Awakening … [and] a leading figure in the moral reform movement and missionary activities of the day"[9] as early as 1813, when he co-founded the Connecticut Society for the Promotion of Good Morals, and did much to create concern about schooling on the western frontier.

Among Beecher's 13 children, daughter Catharine was a pioneer in the education of women and helped to create an influential set of assumptions about the special gifts and character possessed by women, and their role in society. Another daughter married a leading education reformer in Ohio and, as Harriet Beecher Stowe, wrote the novel that roused antislavery sentiment across the North and in Britain. It is possible to trace among the members of this family the shift from orthodox Calvinism, with its emphasis upon man's depravity and the sovereignty of God, to a moralizing emphasis upon free will and good works. This shift was already evident in the school for girls that Catharine founded in the 1820s, where strongly religious instruction nevertheless reflected "the transposition of the drama of salvation from theological to social grounds, the creation of a moral code designed to check behavior even without the existence of an angry God, and the assertion of a new class of moral guardians empowered to enforce this code."[10] That does not mean, it should be noted, that she had transmuted religious teaching into a general moralism suitable for a secularized society. As she wrote several decades later, the growing religious diversity of American communities if anything increased the responsibility of the teacher to serve as a sort of pastor and religious teacher to his or her pupils:

> It is at the head of a school from diverse families, whose children have experienced diverse modes of training, that a teacher is enabled to retrieve parental neglect or

mistakes, and add new power to parental influence. This is especially the case in reference to the employment of the motives of the spiritual world. A large portion of every school comes from families whose spiritual religious training is entirely neglected, or where it is administered with great mistakes and deficiencies. For this reason, the teacher needs to begin with explaining to his flock that the great end of school education is *to train them to a loving and prompt obedience to the laws of God*. . . . The Bible should be appealed to as the book in which this loving Parent [that is, God] has given all needful rules for right feeling and action in order to attain the best and highest happiness.[11]

The salience of this theme of religious nurture helps to explain why, in the national movement to support the "common school," the emphasis (as Horace Mann wrote) was upon finding "teachers of pure tastes, of good manners, of exemplary morals";[12] these characteristics, invariably associated with religious convictions, and not intellectual qualities or extensive knowledge, were considered essential. It did not, therefore, seem out of place when the editor of the *Wisconsin Journal of Education*, himself a clergyman, reported of a teachers' institute that "[a] religious revival, in which many of the teachers found a hope in the Saviour, added greatly to the interest and benefits of the occasion,"[13] or that when, in the same state, it was proposed in 1858 to remove the Bible from public school classrooms, the state superintendent replied that "Christianity is everywhere incorporated in the law of the land," and to remove the Bible from the schools would endanger "all we now hold dear and sacred: our homes, our country, Christianity . . ."[14]

A decade later, National Education Association delegates voted unanimously that the Bible should be both read and taught in public schools, and this continued to be a regular theme at NEA conventions into the early twentieth century: "Its use was regarded as indispensable for the development of character, morals, citizenship, and patriotism."[15]

The success of this version of evangelicalism, emphasizing its moral implications and the less divisive aspects of traditional Protestantism, was such that

by 1830 [the evangelicals] had succeeded so well that deism was virtually extinct in America and rational Christianity (as Unitarianism described itself), which Jefferson fondly expected to be the religion of the new republic, was thoroughly on the defensive where it remained for the rest of the century. Given the choice between deistic rationalism and common sense piety, the Americans chose the latter.[16]

In the antebellum period, however, Unitarians and more orthodox Protestants were often in alliance to support popular education. Lawrence Cremin points out that "the liberal Christian paideia we associate with Channing's Unitarianism was more than a matter of particular churches or a particular philosophy. It manifested itself rather in the broader cultural efflorescence that made the Boston-Cambridge region the moral and cultural hub of the Republic for at least a generation ... they penetrated to the farthest reaches of American society, imparting a view of man and the world that had an enduring effect on education."[17] It was transplanted by New Englanders who established schools and organized systems of schooling in Baltimore, New Orleans, California, and elsewhere around the country.

Governor Edward Everett of Massachusetts, under whose leadership the first state board of education was established in 1837, with Horace Mann as its executive Secretary, gave a speech that year about "the one living fountain, which must water every part of the social garden, or its beauty withers and fades away. Of course I mean, sir, moral and religious, as well as mental education."[18] A quarter-century later, the superintendent of public instruction in Illinois insisted that "the chief end is to make GOOD CITIZENS. Not to make precocious scholars ... not to impart the secret of acquiring wealth ... nor to qualify directly for professional success ... but simply to make good citizens."[19]

Mann's staunch ally, the Rev. Charles Brooks, gave an address in 1837 to the citizens of Quincy, Massachusetts in which he expressed the "wish that every school committee could feel that they have a divine command to bring up every child in the nurture and admonition of the Lord. Words cannot tell the loss our community has sustained in expelling the spiritual nature from our school houses. It is my firm conviction that the omission of christian instruction in our schools accounts for half the crimes and more than half the unhappiness of society."[20] Thirty years later, Brooks continued to make the same argument in *An Appeal to the Legislatures of the United States in Relation to Public Schools*: "Education, especially moral education, underlies all the sources of human power, action, and hope. Religion, enthroned in the lives of its citizens, is the cheapest police that any country or government can maintain."[21]

This was a period when, as Mann wrote in the Massachusetts Board of Education's *Eleventh Annual Report* (1848),

> The subject of education has been very much "agitated," particularly in the northern portion of our country, within the last dozen years. There can be no hazard in affirming, that far more has been spoken and printed, heard and read, on this theme, within the last twelve years, than ever before, were it all put together, since the settlement of the colonies. The consequence certainly has been a very marked development of the merits of the subject, and a corresponding opening or expansion

of the public mind, for their recognition. To many sensible men, it has come like a revelation, inspiring hopes for the amelioration of mankind, and for the perpetuity of our institutions, which they had never dreamed of before. There are thousands of persons amongst us, whose once darkened minds have been so quickened with life, and illuminated with wisdom, on this subject, as to beget an intolerable impatience under old imperfections . . .[22]

The climate of ideas that placed such confidence in the redeeming capacity of public schools had been created, over the previous decade, by James Carter, Mann, and others, who had asked (adapting evangelical vocabulary to their purposes),

> How shall the rising generation be brought under purer moral influences [so that] when they become men, they will surpass their predecessors, both in the soundness of their speculations and in the rectitude of their practice? . . . The same nature by which the parents sank into error and sin, preadapts the children to follow in the course of ancestral degeneracy. Still, are there not moral means for the renovation of mankind, which have never yet been applied?[23]

The question had already been answered in Mann's previous annual report. "How many are there of those, who swarm in our cities, and who are scattered throughout our hundreds of towns," he had asked rhetorically, "who, save in the public schools, receive no religious instruction? They hear it not from the lips of an ignorant and a vicious parent. They receive it not at the sabbath school, or from the pulpit. And, if in the Common School, the impulses of their souls are not awakened and directed by judicious religious instruction, they will grow up, active in error, and fertile in crime."[24]

Some orthodox Protestants saw Mann's emphasis upon religious instruction as a ruse to divert attention from his efforts to expel from the schools any reference to central Christian doctrines. They opposed the lowest-common-denominator religion that he insisted alone could be taught in common schools. Despite occasional attacks upon this watered-down version of Christian beliefs for school purposes,[25] the religiously orthodox critics of the common school program did not prevail. It was a time of transition to a more moderate form of Calvinism, as expressed in Lyman Beecher's influential sermon "The Faith Once Delivered to the Saints" (1823) and in Bushnell's book on how children could be nurtured, rather than converted, into faith.[26] Evangelicals sought to express their beliefs in a form that could gain the broadest possible acceptance. Inevitably, hard points of doctrine—even some core Christian beliefs—were not emphasized. In addition, evangelicals were devoting enormous energies to evangelization of the cities, the western frontier, and the world beyond the United States, and had little interest in controversies with those who shared their concern for social reform.

In fact, orthodox Protestants did not gain an easy victory. In the first decades of the nineteenth century, in Massachusetts,

> to be an evangelical leader or devout layman . . . was often to feel oneself under siege. . . . Far from being disheartened, however, American evangelicals reacted with an aggressive counter thrust. Revivalism was one expression of this response. Another was a lush flowering of voluntary moral and religious societies led by evangelicals, financed by evangelicals, and dedicated to furthering evangelical purposes. Transcending denominational bounds and closely patterned on British precedents, these associations promoted a wide variety of causes: training foreign missionaries; printing Bibles, tracts, and uplifting books; founding domestic missions and Sunday schools; marshaling public opinion against a broad range of moral evils.[27]

To give some sense of the scale of such activities, "from its beginnings to 1828, the United States government spent nearly $3.6 million on internal improvements (roads, canals, communications). In that same span of years the thirteen leading benevolent societies, overwhelmingly evangelical in constituency and purpose, spent over $2.8 million to further their goals."[28] It was, arguably, the absence of an established church that explained the dynamism of religion and religious institutions in the United States and "the shift of religious authority away from the state and toward the 'voluntary' institutional bodies. Out of this shift came an extraordinary expansion of religiously-informed institutions, new means to reach great numbers of individuals and groups, and a new confidence to shape society and its values."[29]

The flourishing of voluntary associations which so struck Alexis de Tocqueville during his visit in the early 1830s has sometimes been characterized as the "Evangelical United Front." German political refugee Carl Schurz was wrong when he observed that, "Here in America you can see every day how slightly a people needs to be governed. In fact, the thing that is not named in Europe without a shudder, anarchy, exists here in full bloom."[30] The growing and effective role of civil society institutions in the United States was by no means random or anarchical; there was constant coordination through interlocking leadership and regular communication among leading evangelical clergy and laymen.

English Protestants had made frequent use of voluntary societies to carry out public purposes since the organization, in the late seventeenth century, of the Society for the Propagation of the Gospel, which provided so much of the schooling available during the colonial period. In the United States, one researcher has identified 24 societies established between 1801 and 1812, and another 32 between 1812 and 1816. "No other organized promoter of values, no other generator of print, no other source of popular music or compelling public imagery, no other comforter (and agitator) of internal life—none came anywhere near close to the organized strength of the evangelical churches in the three-quarters of a century after the dawn of the republic."[31] In no sphere of American life was this more evident than in the promotion of education, at a period when government was only fitfully committed to supporting schools.

The American Bible Society, founded in 1816 by the amalgamation of state and local societies, sought to distribute Bibles on the Western frontier and to ensure that families were able to read them; the Sunday and Adult School Union (founded in 1817; renamed the American Sunday School Union in 1824) was also concerned with literacy. In communities which had not yet developed weekday schools, Sunday schools were often the means of providing basic education, as had been the case in eighteenth-century England. Benjamin Rush helped to start a First Day Society in Philadelphia in 1790, and by 1816 there were about 50 Sunday schools with more than 6,000 pupils in New York City.[32] In 1850, the American Sunday School Union began to employ young men who were studying for the ministry during their summer vacation, and in 1853, 214 of them organized 695 Sunday schools and recruited more than 4,000 teachers. "They were very active in city slums, where they served as unofficial truant officers, rounding up many children for the public schools." In New York City, at that time, "the average weekly attendance [in Sunday schools] of 30,000 equaled three-fourths of that in 'public, ward and corporate' schools," and there were similar proportions in Cleveland, Philadelphia, and Boston.[33] Many Sunday school pupils attended public schools during the week, but for many others, even in the 1850s, it was the only instruction they received, and Sunday schools commonly taught reading and other skills.

In David Tyack's words, "missionaries attempted to provide a Protestant paideia for settlers on the frontier: a total education through the common school, sectarian academies and colleges, Sunday Schools, the pulpit, religious reading, and a number of formal and informal associations."[34] Quite naturally, it has been pointed out, "the same local evangelical group that originally organized a Sunday school was often in due course the prime mover in the establishment of a common school, in the process overseeing the selection of teachers, the organization of curricula, and the choice of textbooks."[35]

These efforts were not all local and spontaneous, as though the only alternatives were central government action or that of local communities. The role of what sociologist Peter Berger calls "mediating structures" of the civil society[36]—in this case, predominantly of religious inspiration and including Catholic and Jewish as well as Protestant organizations—was essential in mobilizing local efforts through denominational and other religious publications (of which there were hundreds), conferences, missionaries, the transfer of Methodist and other clergymen, and in countless other ways.

> The young Congregationalist ministers sent out by the American Home Missionary Society after 1827 ... professed amazement at the ignorance they found in southern Illinois when they first encountered frontiersmen from Kentucky and Tennessee who had known no Puritan tradition in education. The smoothly operating Roman Catholic schools in St. Louis and Vincennes seemed to them an alarming contrast to the educational neglect of children which they observed in Methodist, Baptist, and Presbyterian families. The missionaries immediately reacted by shifting their emphasis from a primarily pastoral and evangelistic ministry to an educational one. At Vandalia, Illinois, for example, Theron Baldwin enrolled 105 pupils in his Sunday school in the spring of 1830 but found that only thirty-seven were able to read. Of the fifty-two families he visited at a nearby settlement, composed chiefly of people from Tennessee, not half contained even one literate person, child or adult. Baldwin organized a Sunday school there "to gather in if possible young and old, and learn them to read." But Sunday school was obviously not enough. In May he wrote Absalom Peters in New York the first of many letters urging the American Home Missionary Society to send schoolteachers to the West.[37]

On the Mississippi Valley frontier, the Sunday School Union reported, most children did not have schools available, and it urged that "Sunday-schools be established as widely as possible, and they will remedy some measure of the evil"[38] by teaching children to read. This remedy was needed just as urgently, evangelicals believed, in the growing cities of the East. "From the time the earliest American Sunday schools were established in New York, Philadelphia, Boston, Baltimore, and other coastal cities around 1815, the surging pace of urban growth was a matter of profound and continuing concern. 'Vice is pouring into the city like a torrent, the population is wonderfully increasing,' said the New York *Christian Observer* in 1827, 'and the best shield against immorality is the sabbath school institution.'"[39]

In one of the earliest American industrial communities, Pawtucket, Rhode Island, the industrialist Samuel Slater paid the expenses of Sunday schools as part of an effort to bring civilizing influences to a population of worker families drawn in many cases from remote rural areas, "from places where the general poverty had precluded schools and public worship." These families, "brought up illiterate and without religious instruction, and disorderly and vicious in consequence of their lack of regular employment, have been transplanted to those new creations of skill and enterprise, and by the ameliorating effects of study, industry, and instruction, have been reclaimed, civilized, Christianised."[40]

The influence of these evangelical reform groups was evident at the Sunday School Union's meeting in Washington, in 1831, to discuss its efforts in the Mississippi Valley, where local churches that otherwise were in fierce rivalry for members worked together to provide "union" Sunday schools teaching literacy and a generic Protestantism. President Jackson sent his apologies, and speeches were given by leading senators, putting aside for the occasion their bitter political rivalries. Daniel Webster "spoke of the legal provision made for the mind even by heathen legislators, but of 'the far superior value and efficacy of a system of instruction founded on the Bible, that grand textbook for universal commentary.'"[41]

> In Delaware the state legislature granted a per pupil subsidy to Sunday Schools throughout the state. By 1827 a newspaper in Springfield, Massachusetts estimated that 200,000 children attended Sunday schools in America. . . . the highly organized Union Sunday School movement was one means by which a standardized, nondenominational Protestantism was exported to the countryside.[42]

In more settled circumstances, "the Sunday school was taking on the role of parallel institution to the common school. It would [also] teach morality, but morality buttressed by evangelical religion, while at the same time preparing children for salvation through the conversion experience." After all, the evangelicals believed, "people had to be educated, not just for heaven, but for the immediate moral crusades and for the prosperity which would accompany the kingdom."[43] Many children attended both public schools and Sunday schools, which "were seen as essential for all Protestant children because public schools were becoming more nonsectarian" or, indeed, secular.[44]

In Rochester, New York, the effect of religious revivals was to inspire evangelical churches to provide education beyond their own congregations; "the congregations at First Presbyterian, St. Luke's Episcopal, and Free Presbyterian Churches organized schools to teach reading, writing, and proper thoughts to poor children, and to keep them away from 'the highways and resorts of dissipation.'"[45]

Whether in the Deep South, in New Orleans, or on the Pacific coast, New England ministers and teachers (often they were the same) created schools as soon as they arrived:

> School accompanied Church in the New England program of settlement [in California]. Many ministers taught during the week, and New England laymen

accounted in the main for the establishment of California's common school-system. . . . ministers managed to found schools, libraries, and philanthropic agen-cies. They put into public discourse great questions which might otherwise have gone unasked, questions of history and moral choice, social responsibility, and cultural growth.[46]

For local Protestant as well as Catholic churches, providing schooling seemed a natural part of their ministry, and it was as Protestants formed a united front against what they perceived as the threat of Catholic immi-gration they rallied behind the common public school and abandoned, to a great extent, any efforts to provide general education on a denominational basis.[47] The exceptions, Protestant denominations that made major efforts to create their own schools in the later nineteenth century, were themselves largely made up of immigrants, such as the Missouri Synod Lutherans and the Dutch Reformed. Just as native Protestant leaders "saw Christianity and republicanism as mutually supportive and dependent upon one another, so did they see the common school, teaching a truth properly grounded in evangelical doctrine, as an instrument of their movement and a bulwark of the Republic."[48]

So thoroughly did the evangelical spirit permeate social reform in the ante-bellum period that its vocabulary was used heavily by promoters of public schooling, including Horace Mann, who made no secret, privately, of his hos-tility toward the orthodox Calvinism in which he had been brought up, and who relied heavily on fellow-Unitarians like Governor Everett and the Rev. Charles Brooks as allies. His friend Theodore Parker, also a Unitarian, wrote of Mann that "I know no politician who so hated Calvinism; none who used its language so much, or who, to the public, appeared so much the friend" of evangelicalism.[49]

> The leading Unitarian preacher of the period, William Ellery Channing, wrote in 1833 that it is important, that [teachers] should be able to cooperate with parents in awakening the religious principle in the young. We would not of course admit into schools the peculiarities of the denominations which divide the Christian world. But religion in its broadest sense should be taught. It should indirectly mix with all teaching. The young mind should be guided through nature and human history to the Creator and Disposer of the Universe; and still more, the practical principles and spirit of Christianity should be matters of direct inculcation.[50]

The essay that Mann (a member of Channing's Boston congregation) included with the Massachusetts Board of Education's *Eighth Annual Report*, stressed "the importance of cultivating, as well the moral and religious, as the intellectual faculties of our children by the frequent and careful perusal of the Sacred Scriptures, in our schools," and reported that, of 308 cities and towns, the schools of 258 were using the Bible as a reading book. In the Board's own teacher-training normal schools, he reported, the Bible was "used" every day.[51]

Mann took care to demonstrate the close relationship between religion and popular schooling in many articles carried by his *Common School Journal*, distributed widely across Massachusetts and with readers in Europe and South America as well. In the issue of June 15, 1841, for example, he reprinted an article from another publication which argued that "the only foundation in which a child's character can be laid, so that he may perform his part well in the drama of life, are firm religious principles imbedded deep in the youthful heart." But, the author warned, the fact that very many children did not receive from their parents instruction in "the necessity of their religious duties" explained "much of the crime and dissipation which darken the fair prospect of our country." This made it necessary that religious instruction be given in school so that "children of such parents will there receive what ought to have been impressed upon their minds at home."[52]

A subsequent issue of Mann's journal printed a lecture given by Amherst College President Heman Humphrey before the leading educational institution of the day, the American Institute of Instruction, in which the gathered education reformers were told that "the most successful teachers have found the half hour devoted to moral and religious instruction more profitable to the scholar [that is, pupil] than any other half hour in the day." Because of the importance of this instruction, no teacher

> ought ever to be employed, who is not both able and willing to teach morality and religion in the manner which I have just alluded to. Were this faithfully done in all the primary schools of the nation, our civil and religious liberties, and all our blessed institutions, would be incomparably safer than they are now. The parent who says, I do not send my child to school to learn religion, but to be taught reading, and writing, and grammar, knows not "what manner of spirit he is of." It is very certain that such a father will teach his children anything but religion at home, and is it right that they should be left to grow up as heathen in a Christian land? . . . if the parent means to say, I do not send my child to school to have you teach him to fear God, and to keep his commandments, to be temperate, honest and true, to be a good son and a good man, then the child is to be pitied for having such a father; and with good reason might we tremble for all that we hold most dear, if such remonstrances were to be multiplied and to prevail.[53]

Humphrey was by no means presenting a minority view; the controversies of the time were not over whether schools should provide religious instruction, indeed permeate their instruction with religious perspectives, but over whether that could be done in a single "common school" teaching a neutral form of Protestantism or whether different religious groups should define the form that this instruction would take in the schools attended by their children. Mann was an emphatic supporter of the former alternative and, during the 1840s and 1850s most Protestant churches (apart from those based in immigrant communities), faced by what they perceived as the threat of Catholic separatism, abandoned their own schools for the common school and for a form of religious instruction focused on what Mann called "the pure religion of heaven," stripped of any elements with which Unitarians could not agree.[54]

The American Institute of Instruction, though all of its founders were from Massachusetts, from the start had national ambitions, as its name suggests. More than half of its original 250 members were teachers in academies; the second largest group were clergymen. Nearly all the prominent ministers of the leading Protestant denominations belonged to the Institute.

> Those from Boston and surrounding towns were mainly Unitarian—the denomination known as the "Boston religion." Although these religious liberals frowned on immoderate responses to the revivalism of the Second Great Awakening, they were as convinced as other churchmen that the republic could not survive without a Christian people. As heirs not only of rationalism but of the warm and sentimental piety of eighteenth-century Arminianism, they were caught up in their own version of evangelicalism and contributed to the revival of religion in the early nineteenth century. They were active in their own missionary societies, in temperance and other moral reform causes and in the improvement of education in Boston and at Harvard College. The Unitarian clergy were prestigious men with important social, cultural and political connections throughout the state. But most of the clergy in the Institute, like most of the church-going population of Massachusetts, were orthodox evangelical Congregationalists. The majority had reputations extending beyond parochial circles; few were poor or obscure parsons. They held executive posts in rapidly growing evangelical societies like the American Sunday School Union or the American Tract Society, trained future clergy at the Andover Theological Seminary, edited or contributed to religious journals and participated in a variety of moral reform causes. They formed part of the "interlocking directorate" of Protestant crusaders and were a formidable force in Massachusetts.[55]

In his own annual report for 1847, Mann stated that the "policy of the State promotes not only secular but religious instruction,"[56] the following year he claimed that "[i]t is not known that there is, or ever has been, a member of the Board of Education, who would not be disposed to recommend the daily reading of the Bible, devotional exercises, and the constant inculcation of the precepts of Christian morality, in all the Public Schools,"[57] and the year after that, in his final report, he made the religious character of the common school his central theme.

After a panegyric to the importance of moral education as the central mission of the common school, Mann pointed out that

> it will be said that this grand result, in Practical Morals, is a consummation of blessedness that can never be attained without Religion; and that no community will ever be religious, without a Religious Education. Both these propositions, I regard as eternal and immutable truths. Devoid of religious principles and religious affections, the race can never fall so low but that it may sink still lower; animated and sanctified by them, it can never rise so high but that it may ascend still higher.... The man ... who believes that the human race, or any nation, or any individual in it, can attain to happiness, or avoid misery, without religious principle and religious affections, must be ignorant of the capacities of the human soul, and of the highest attributes in the nature of man.[58]

As a result, "I could not avoid regarding the man, who should oppose the religious education of the young, as an insane man," and, in his role as Secretary of the Board of Education, he had "believed then, as now, that religious instruction in our schools, to the extent which the constitution and laws of the state allowed and prescribed, was indispensable to their highest welfare, and essential to the vitality of moral education."[59]

Mann's successor as Secretary of the Massachusetts Board of Education, the Rev. Barnas Sears, reinforced this emphasis, writing in the Board's *Fifteenth Annual Report* that

> The most perfect development of the mind, no less than the order of the school and the stability of society, demands a religious education. Massachusetts may be regarded as having settled, at least for herself, this great question of the connection of religion with the Public Schools. She holds that religion is the highest and noblest possession of the mind, and is conducive to all the true interests of man and of society, and therefore she cannot do otherwise than seek to place her schools under its beneficent influence. The constitution and laws of the Commonwealth enjoin it upon teachers to inculcate piety and Christian morals, love to God and love to man.... The formation of a virtuous character is the natural result of a right religious training.[60]

But this praise of religious instruction was limited to that instruction as provided in the common public school; Mann and the other common school promoters were in general strongly opposed to non-public schools, and especially those with a religious character.

Not only did Mann and other leaders in the common school movement employ the language of evangelical and humanitarian reform, they also urged the clergy to play a key role in overseeing and promoting these schools, just had been the case in colonial times. The report, in Mann's *Common School Journal* of February 15, 1839, on the convention of the Middlesex County Association for the Improvement of Common Schools summarized speech after speech, almost all of them by clergymen of various Protestant denominations, each of them expressing strong support for the role of the common school in educating in the fullest sense, not just instructing. Just a year later, an article in the *Common School Journal* (February 15, 1840), quoting from its Connecticut counterpart, praised the clergy as devoting more of their time to supporting schools than all other members of the community put together. Continuing this theme, the issue of August 15, 1846 of the same journal carried a long lead article on the "Duty of Clergymen to Our Schools," urging that visitation of their local common schools was among their pastoral duties.

It is worth noting that in Prussia at the same period the oversight of the clergy was one of the primary grievances of schoolteachers.[61] The difference is that in Prussia popular schooling depended ultimately on the central government and teachers wanted to see themselves as government employees, while in Massachusetts schools continued to a great extent to depend upon local support, for which the clergy were key, and the protection or patronage of state government meant little or nothing to schoolteachers.

In New York State, "the legislature left decisions about the religious character of school instruction to the democratic determinations of individual districts—except in New York City, where, as a result of the 1842 resolution of the controversy between the Public School Society and Bishop Hughes, publicly funded schools were placed under the control of the elected officials of local wards within the city, remaining so for the rest of the century."[62] Naturally, the religious flavor of these ostensibly neutral schools was Protestant or Catholic depending upon the population of each district. In 1869, the growing political clout of Catholics at the state level led to a provision that 20 percent of the excise tax funds in New York City would go to "schools, educating children gratuitously in said city who are not provided for in the common schools thereof." According to *Harper's Weekly* in 1871, over $700,000 in public funds was provided to parochial schools.[63] This direct support ended in 1872, when the Republican-dominated state legislature abolished public funding of private charitable institutions, but with victory by the Democrats (the party for which almost all immigrant Catholics voted), the provision for state aid to "church-affiliated charities, including orphan asylums," but not day schools, was restored and expanded in 1875, and a decade later their number had doubled.[64]

As we will see in Chapter Seven, the Protestant majority became agitated after the Civil War about demands that public schools be purged of religious exercises and curriculum content to make them acceptable for Catholic pupils, on the one hand, and, on the other, that thoroughly religious Catholic schools share in the available funds for public education. Many feared that the common public school was under attack and would be profoundly damaged. This was rather different than the antebellum concern, expressed by Horace Bushnell and others, that immigrant children would not benefit from the Americanizing effects of public schooling.

Some worried that giving in to Catholic demands would lead to different demands from other groups, and thus the public schools would come to lack any character at all. Influential editor Horace Greeley "urged no concessions to the Catholic position. . . . He charged that the Roman Catholic church would continue to oppose public schools under any and all conditions short of winning state support for their own religious schools. Indeed, Greeley reasoned, removing the Bible would only weaken the public schools by alienating 'many of its oldest and firmest supporters.'"[65]

As Greeley suggested, Catholic leaders used the religious practices in public schools as a wedge issue to argue for the establishment and support of parochial schools. The Second Plenary Council of Baltimore (1866) ordered clergy to "diligently guard that the books and practices of [non-Catholic character] not be introduced into public schools to endanger [Catholic children's] faith and piety." Bishop McQuaid of Rochester was an especially prominent spokesman for this position, accusing "public schools of teaching Protestant religion when they conducted religious exercises and of teaching atheism when they did not." Catholic leaders avoided stating clearly "whether religious exercises could be truly nonsectarian for all faiths, or whether the common practice of reading the Douay (Catholic) version of the Bible in all-Catholic public schools was acceptable. Concessions along those lines would hurt the Church's arguments in favor of church-controlled, publicly funded schools."[66]

A study of complaints to the New York official responsible for schools concludes that, in fact, most communities found it possible to reach compromise on the issue of Bible reading and other religious exercises, such as singing hymns. "Surveys from the late 1880s and 1890s suggest that roughly half of all district schools conducted some form of opening religious exercises, usually Bible reading without discussion. Yet religious exercises excited little controversy in appeals." The state Superintendent of Public Instruction ruled, in 1866, that "a teacher has no right to consume any portion of the regular school hours in conducting religious exercises, especially when objection is raised. The principle is this: Common schools are supported and established for the purpose of imparting instruction in the common English branches; religious instruction forms no part of the course." On the other hand, the predecessor organization to the National Education Association voted, in 1869, that "The Bible should not only be studied, venerated, and honored as a classic for all ages ... but devotionally read, and its precepts inculcated in all the common schools of the land."[67]

The most common practice was for the teacher to conduct a devotional exercise before the school day officially started. By the last decades of the century, in New York State, "Bible use had climbed to roughly half of all school districts, and if we consider New York City's massive population, probably close to three quarters of the total state school enrollment."[68] In parts of the country with fewer Catholics, the rate was probably considerably higher, though it was reported that in California, by 1880, use of the Bible in public schools was "all but extinct" as a result of Catholic protests.[69]

If the religiously heterogeneous population of the United States did not lead to consistent demands from the majority Protestant population for denominational public schools—as in Germany, the Netherlands, or England—it was in part because of the strength of democratic localism. As a local school superintendent in New York State wrote in 1874, "Probably no two cities or localities in the State conduct their schools on the same plan. Each locality determines its own methods, selects its own teachers, and textbooks, in fact makes its own schools. More than this, teachers even in the same system of schools differ widely as to what shall be taught."[70]

In rural areas, where often each school served only a dozen or so families, with a single teacher chosen locally, it was not difficult to reflect the religious convictions of this limited clientele; people who shared common views often chose to live nearby each other, or the accidents of propinquity led to common views. In such cases, a common public school could be quite distinctive in terms of religious content in the curriculum as well as in the use of Bible readings and Christian hymns as opening ceremonies each day.

In some cases, the distinctiveness went even farther. In one community in New York State made up of members of the Shaker religious sect, for example, the public school was staffed by a member of the group and—consistent with its communitarian structure—the state funds were paid into the community's treasury.[71]

Since the settlement pattern in most cities created ethnically identifiable neighborhoods, public authorities sometimes found it expedient to enter into various arrangements with a local Catholic pastor to take over a parochial school and operate it as part of the public system, under an agreement that the pastor would approve the teacher employed by the school district and the books used in the school, but that explicitly religious instruction would be provided only outside of regular school hours. Such an arrangement was adopted in Lowell, Massachusetts in the 1830s, and in Elmira and Poughkeepsie, New York, decades later. In addition to helping to solve problems of facilities, the adoption of a Catholic school into the public system removed a source of competition.

In Lowell, where Catholic immigrants were replacing the factory workers drawn from the New England countryside, the public School Committee agreed to take over support and management of two parochial schools. The Committee would examine and employ the teachers, and prescribe the same books as for its other schools, but the teachers would be Catholic and the books would be examined to ensure that they contained no content reflecting negatively upon Catholicism. The arrangement continued from 1836 to 1852, and was praised by Horace Mann and others.[72]

Corning, New York rented St. Mary's School between 1868 and 1898, paying the teaching sisters to provide "public education," while they provided religious instruction outside of school hours. In Elmira,

> the board of education welcomed an offer in 1867 from the pastor of Saint Peter and Paul's School to place it within the city's system of public schools. As a result, the city found more space for children without the cost of a new building, reduced competition with a parochial school, and catered to the interests of a large number of Catholic parents. The parochial school, in return, got rent and public school salaries for its teachers [who were members of a teaching order].

In order to satisfy the demands of Catholic parents, the authorities allowed children from other attendance districts to attend the school. The pastor recommended, each year, what teachers should be employed by the school district. This arrangement continued until 1876, when it was ended by the church.[73]

In Poughkeepsie, in 1873, the board of education, facing severe overcrowding, agreed to rent two parochial school buildings for a token fee and operate them as public schools. The board

> would select, pay, and have power to dismiss the teachers, though, as in Elmira, it tacitly agreed to hire the church's selections. The board would also pay for expenses

and repairs. Reverend McSweeny agreed to forbid all religious teaching during public school hours and to open the school to children of all denominations. The two schools were to remain single sex, and children from other [attendance] districts could attend them, but in other respect they functioned as regular public schools.

The daily schedule included secular instruction from 9 to 12 and from 1:30 to 4, with religious exercises at 8:45 and at 4 and religious instruction from 1 to 1:30; thus while the secular instruction was distinct, it was framed within Catholic religious elements.

Of particular significance is the fact that, while the "Poughkeepsie Plan" was criticized by outside commentators (including some Catholics concerned that it watered down religious instruction) there were apparently no local complaints at all; in 1887, it was estimated that four-fifths of the Catholic children in the city were attending the two schools, and the arrangement continued until 1898. In fact, a review of the records of the state education office found that "not a single resident of Elmira, Poughkeepsie, Utica, Corning, or any other city challenged Poughkeepsie-like plans."[74]

In short, the prevailing localism in the management of schools made it possible to reach accommodations in the great majority of communities, with the religious character of schools reflecting that of families, and compromises reached as necessary. As we will see in Chapter Seven, it was developments at the national and state levels, stimulated in part by those in Europe, which made the religious character of schooling a major political issue in the 1870s and led in turn to its removal from the sphere of democratic decision-making. The result has been that since the late nineteenth century the United States, unlike other Western democracies, has never engaged in serious deliberation about how the religious convictions of parents and teachers should be accommodated in public education.

Chapter Four

Schooling and Local Democracy

Bernard Bailyn, in a celebrated essay, concludes that after the Revolution "a process whose origins lay in the half-instinctive workings of a homogeneous, integrated society was transformed in the jarring multiplicity, the raw economy, and the barren environment of America. No longer instinctive, no longer safe and reliable, the transfer of culture, the whole enterprise of education, had become controversial, conscious, constructed: a matter of decision, will, and effort."[1] Until the 1830s, however, those decisions and efforts were widely dispersed, local, and uneven, and this continued to be the case, though to a decreasing extent, in subsequent decades.

During the first third of the nineteenth century, the amount and quality of schooling available in the settled areas of North America was dependent on local conditions, and developed very unevenly. The nature of the local economy made a difference—more formal schooling was useful in commercial communities including seaports than in farming areas—as did the prevailing religious makeup of a local population, or the traditional attitude toward schooling of the immigrant group predominant in the area.

As a result, "the spread of common schools across a vast nation in the mid-nineteenth century resembled the building of Protestant churches, where local leaders mobilized their fellow citizens by persuading them to invest their money, time, and commitment to realize their common purpose."[2] These local efforts—which varied enormously in different parts of the country and were based on dynamics of ethnic tradition and of leadership in each community, as well as settlement patterns—were not altogether spontaneous; however; they were effectively encouraged by what historians refer to as the "Evangelical

United Front," by the Catholic hierarchy and religious orders, and by Jewish organizations in some communities.

One notable result of the extreme localism of schools was a close relationship between families and schools, and a consonance between the worldview of most parents and that presented by teachers. This does not necessarily imply much explicit religious instruction; it was simply the taken-for-granted world of the school and the local community. Perhaps the best way to get a sense of what that may have been like is a recent book about Old Order Amish and Mennonite schools in the late twentieth century. Many of these are recent creations that took over one-room public schoolhouses as school districts were consolidated in ways that the parents of these religiously and culturally conservative groups believed would threaten their ability to convey their convictions and way of life to their children. The researcher found, contrary to her expectations, that many of these schools did not provide religious instruction, leaving that to church and family, and also that they produced good academic results. Most important, these schools maintain a close linkage with and support by families.[3]

In the American context, it was taken for granted, at least across the North, that as new communities developed along the ever-expanding frontier, the settlers would come together to establish a school and to employ someone to teach the community's children. As a Pennsylvania educational leader wrote in 1886,

> [t]hus were planted thousands of schools along the valleys and among the hills of Pennsylvania. There were no laws to regulate, no officers to guide, no system to conform to—all that was done was accomplished by the voluntary efforts of the people, directed solely by their own notions of what was best under the circumstances... it taught the great lesson of self-dependence, and prepared the people for that efficient local management which has done so much already for the Public School System of the State, and which in the end is to be its crown of glory.[4]

Even in antebellum New England, of course, the quality of what was provided to schoolchildren depended on the vigilance and the resources of the local community, as we know not least from the complaints of Horace Mann and the annual reports through which he sought to shame laggard school districts in Massachusetts into "keeping school" more days and providing more adequate schoolhouses.

It was because popular schooling in North America developed in such intensely localized forms that it was in most cases based upon local consensus, mostly on the basis of a common Protestant worldview, but in some (mostly urban) cases on that of a Catholic perspective. Teachers taught as parents and local communities wanted them to teach, and there is scant evidence that it occurred to many to teach otherwise. What would subsequently become the tension between "local" and "cosmopolitan" perspectives much noted by sociologists of education was not generally a problem in the first half of the nineteenth century and before compulsory schooling and the monopoly, by public schools, of tax-supported free schooling.

Local efforts to provide schooling were encouraged by government land grants—over 77 million acres—and other subsidies that helped to support what we would now consider private as well as public schools and academies, but they were supported primarily by local taxpayers and by the tuition and fees paid by parents.

REALITIES OF LOCAL SCHOOLING

The typical pupil who was fortunate enough to be in school, in the early years of the Republic, studied "reading, writing, spelling, arithmetic, English grammar, and morality; that is a good summary of a common education, the relation of such schooling to further literary education and to occupational training is difficult to define because there was no system, one did not "graduate" from common school, and no particular pattern prevailed except that many boys were apprenticed at age fourteen." [5]

The decades of political turmoil, inflation, and war that led up to and followed the establishment of the new nation saw a weakening of actual provisions for education; "the Revolutionary War and the formation of the new nation did not bring in a great educational revival. Rather was the reverse true. The emphasis on individualism was too strong, the interest in new political and economic developments appealed too powerfully to the efforts of a newly liberated people." Provision of schooling was very uneven and, even at its most extensive, far from adequate in quality; there is reason to believe, indeed, that many schools in New England villages had been better in the early colonial days, because supported with a greater sense of religious zeal and urgency to transplant the acquisitions of civilization into the "wilderness," and by the clustering of population in town and village centers where children could reach school easily. Even in this region, "during the early National period the standards of length of term and character of studies were greatly lowered or wiped out altogether."[6]

A major factor in the decline of the quality of schooling during this period was the dispersal of population away from town centers to outlying farms, and to the frontier of northern and western New England and then beyond to the west. Bailyn points out that "the broad stream of enforcing legislation that flows through the statute books of the seventeenth century thinned out in the eighteenth century as isolated rural communities, out of contact, save for some of their Harvard- and Yale-trained ministers, with the high moral and intellectual concerns of the settling generation, allowed the level to sink to local requirement,"[7] which was often quite low.

Evidence of this general neglect of schooling is available from the account by an English traveler in 1795. He found no public school system at all outside New England, and even there noted a tendency for the grammar schools to degenerate into providing little more than basic skills. In New York, he mentions Columbia College and the semi-public academies, and adds, "besides these, there are schools established and maintained by the voluntary contribution of parents." Noah Webster, in 1806, reported much the same haphazard provision of schooling outside and even within New England.[8] In Rhode Island "there was no provision for the public support of schools prior to 1800. In that year, responding to the agitation of the Providence Association of Mechanics and Manufacturers, the General Assembly passed an Act to Establish Free Schools," requiring towns to support schools, but most ignored the law and it was only in commercial communities like Providence, where a demand for schooling existed, that there was adequate provision. The unpopular law was then repealed in 1803. A survey in 1832 found that there were more private than public schools in Rhode Island, and that provision of schooling was very unequal across the state.[9]

Uneven provision of schools did not mean—at least in New England and the frontier areas of northern New York, Ohio, and beyond that were settled largely from New England—that the population was illiterate. The rate of literacy was high in the northern states as a result of intense community life and the value assigned to the reading of the Bible. John Adams claimed, in 1765, that "all candid foreigners who have passed through this country, and conversed freely with all sorts of people here, will allow that they have never seen so much knowledge and civility among the common people in any part of the world."[10] Researchers have concluded that "about 90 percent of men and 60 percent of New England women were literate by 1790. . . . only 1.1 percent of the white population aged twenty and above in Massachusetts in 1840 were illiterate."[11]

Adams wrote to a Virginian correspondent that the New England character was formed in "town meetings, militia musters, town schools, and churches,"[12] and it was this active community life, in large part, that stimulated the acquisition of literacy. Bailyn points out that

> more explicit in its educational function than either family or community was the church. . . . It furthered the introduction of the child to society by instructing him

in the system of thought and imagery which underlay the culture's values and aims. It provided the highest sanctions for the accepted forms of behavior, and brought the child into close relationship with the intangible loyalties, the ethos and highest principles, of the society in which he lived.[13]

The ability to read was often acquired in literate homes;

the young Horace Mann followed his sister Rebecca about the house, holding a Noah Webster grammar in his hand, as she listened to his lesson while attending to her chores. . . . when a biographer suggested that Mann's achievements were largely self-attained, [his other sister] curtly reminded her brother that "every day of your life when with your parents and sister, at least, you were *at school* and learning that which has been the foundation of your present learning."[14]

Mann's Franklin, Massachusetts, like many other New England villages in the early nineteenth century,

did not create a single building near the center of the town as had been tried earlier in other communities, but instead organized six school districts, each with its own crude one-room edifice. In addition to contributing firewood and labor, the Manns and their neighbors squeezed about $100 a year out of their meager cash earnings to pay a teacher who "kept the winter school" six or seven weeks for the older children whose labor was needed less on the farm during this season. Hopefully, they also had a small residue with which to hire a woman in summer to keep the younger children out from underfoot during the harvest time.[15]

These district schools responded to the reality that population had long since dispersed from the village centers of the early colonial period as families moved onto their farms, and made schools accountable to those living near enough to send their children each day.

Each district had its own school committee, and the system had become so intensive that in rural Berkshire County, for example, 30 towns divided into 225 districts. The term "system" was really a misnomer as the schools varied from district to district; the only common feature was that none of the schools opened for the full school year required by law. The more affluent towns supported winter and summer schools open for a few months each season. Poorer districts—and they were in the majority—provided only summer schools where children learned the rudiments from female teachers who "came cheap." Some towns hired college-educated males—usually students on their long college vacation—for the winter season;

these were the grammar schools. Others made do with local residents looking for extra money in the slow season for farmers, fishermen, and tradesmen. School committees exercised little authority beyond decisions on budgets, hiring of teachers and maintenance of the schools. District schooling was a practical solution to the problems of growth and dispersal of population, equitable division of tax monies and the needs of a predominantly agricultural population. The schools were cheap and open in the seasons when help was less urgent for the farms and fishing fleets. Children were close to schools in the severe New England winters, and teachers were local residents, or outsiders who boarded with families in the still largely homogeneous communities. The schools were ungraded so children could attend them intermittently for years, and they taught the basic skills needed to get along in life. Parents who wanted more for their children could send them, for a price, to local private schools or academies.[16]

The district—as contrasted with town—organization of school governance was the result of practical realities as population spread out. The new state legislature of Massachusetts required, in 1789, every community to provide a schoolmaster "to teach children to read and write, and to instruct them in the English language, as well as in arithmetic, orthography, and decent behaviour," with the number of annual days of instruction required by law varying according to the size of the community. The local selectmen were confirmed in their responsibility for determining whether a teacher was qualified, and for inspecting schools.

The 1789 law provided that, when the size of a town made it impossible for all the children to be gathered in one place, districts could be created within the town, each with its own school, and another law of 1800 gave the inhabitants of the school districts the authority to tax themselves to build and maintain schoolhouses where they thought most convenient. In 1817 the districts were given full legal existence with responsibility and authority distinct from that of the town, and an 1827 law required that districts be created in all towns. "The town determined the amount of tax and the qualifications of the teacher, but the district had full control in employing and supervising the teacher, and expending such school funds as were raised."[17] This district system was

the nearest approach to a voluntary system according to which a group of private persons maintain a school for their own children. A little settlement of families, homogeneous in their needs and standards, could be formed into a district and have a school, however poor it might be, without waiting for neighboring settlements, composing with it the next larger civil district, to come to the same desire of having their children instructed in the three R's.[18]

This accommodation to local priorities was later deplored by Mann as "the most pernicious law ever passed in this Commonwealth, on the subject of schools," when he became the first state education official in Massachusetts. He estimated that by the 1840s there were some 2,500 school districts in the state, with "disastrous and blighting effects."[19] Under the conditions in many areas, the district schools did not offer much beyond what was already provided at home; on the positive side, the system left responsibility and management of schools with parents and neighbors in what Governor Marcus Morton called "little pure democracies."[20]

English visitor Harrier Martineau, in the 1830s, reported that:

All young people in these villages are more or less instructed. Schooling is considered a necessary of life. I happened to be looking over an old almanack one day, when I found among the directions relating to the preparation for winter on a farm, the following: "Secure your cellars from frost. Fasten loose clap-boards and shingles. Secure a good school-master."[21]

While it brought decision-making about schooling even closer to parents and other citizens than did town governance, the district system made its quality very much dependent upon local factors. From the perspective of education reformers, "this system produced the most general indifference to education on the part of all concerned; it prevented the establishment of any general standards; it fostered a pernicious and mean spirit; and it proved the greatest obstacle to technical educational advance."[22]

The population of the United States at this time was still overwhelmingly rural; 95 percent lived in communities with fewer than 2,500 inhabitants, and this was still true of 91 percent of Americans in 1830, and of 80 percent in 1860. As virtually all children walked to school, most schools were very small; even in 1850, "the census counted 80,978 public schools but only 91,966 teachers."[23]

It will not do to romanticize the provision of schooling in the early republic. Governor George Clinton "warned the New York legislature in 1782 that the war had created a 'chasm in education.'"[24] and Robert Coram, an English immigrant to Delaware, wrote in 1791 that "the country schools through most of the United States, whether we consider the buildings, the teachers, or the regulations, are in very respect completely despicable, wretched, and contemptible."[25]

A few years before the Revolution, in Connecticut, young Noah Webster's

teachers were untrained transients whose names went unrecorded in town annals. Sometimes they were college students in need of funds to continue their own education, but more often they were unskilled, out-of-work passersby with little intellect or love for children. Webster recalled the teachers of his youth as the "dregs" of humanity. . . . "The instruction in schools was very imperfect," Webster explained. "No geography was studied . . . no history was read . . . no book for reading was used."[26]

Even a half-century later, Catharine Beecher would arouse

her audiences' sympathy for the sufferings of masses of American children under cruel teachers and in degenerate environments. She quoted from several reports to state legislatures that described "the comfortless and dilapidated buildings, the unslung doors, broken sashes, absent panes, stilted benches, gaping walls, yawning roofs, and muddy moldering floors," of contemporary schools and "the self-styled teachers, who lash and dogmatize in these miserable tenements of humanity." Many teachers were "low, vulgar, obscene, intemperate," according to one report to the New York State legislature, "and utterly incompetent to teach anything good."[27]

The actual development of schooling in the American colonies and the early Republic depended largely upon the growth of demand. No one understood this better, or took better advantage of it, than Noah Webster, whose influence on the actual development of American education was much greater than that of Thomas Jefferson, Benjamin Rush, and other advocates of state intervention. One of the most successful self-promoters in American history, Webster insisted that "as an independent nation, our honor requires us to have a system of our own, in language as well as government." England could no longer be the model for the language used in the United States, "for the taste of her writers is already corrupted, and her language is on the decline."[28] An authentically American language could be taught and learned with the series of "spellers" and "readers" compiled by Webster, the first of which was published in 1783 and which, together, sold as many as 100 million copies by the end of the nineteenth century.[29] Publication of textbooks was one of the earliest nationwide enterprises; in Hartford alone, there were more than 30 firms producing textbooks for the national market during the 1820s.[30]

Webster was also a powerful and tireless advocate for popular schooling. As he wrote in 1787, when the state and federal constitutions were in the works, "the only practicable method to reform mankind is to begin with children. . . . Education, in a great measure, forms the moral characters of men, and morals are the basis of government. Education should therefore be the first . . . article in the code of political regulations."[31]

In the early Republic, as during the colonial period, most children acquired basic literacy at home or in a "dame school" in the home of a woman who was also teaching her own children to read and count; gradually towns began to pay these women to take on the teaching of children from families too poor to pay their fees. Eventually, "the dame school or woman's school became incorporated as the primary branch of a complex system of public education, as when Boston tardily adopted primary schools . . . into its structure of schools in 1818."[32]

Over time, and with the development of the economy shifting agricultural production from subsistence farming to cash crops and creating more positions in commerce, the nature of the demand for schooling beyond the preliminary stages was transformed. "The world of cash was a world of literacy and numeracy."[33] Parents and local government began to look for training in the skills useful for commerce and navigation, rather than in those, useful to only a few, preparatory to entering Harvard or Yale and then the ministry or the law.

Despite the influence of the Prussian example on American educational reformers,[34] the New England model "was not for *Das Volk*, but of and by the people. It was not an institution designed to fit the common people for the role in which the ruling classes cast them, but one controlled by themselves and in their own interests. . . . Poor and inefficient as it was for many years after its origin, it was theirs, and theirs it has always remained."[35]

Secondary education was even less of a state concern since it was considered to benefit only a small proportion of teenagers from more prosperous families, and until late in the nineteenth century it was provided largely by private academies. Larger communities in Massachusetts, with two hundred or more families, were legally required to provide grammar schools to teach Latin and Greek as well as other subjects; admission to these would be restricted to youth who had already learned to read. This law, Kaestle suggests, was limited in its effects. "Because most towns already provided partially free elementary schools, because the grammar-school provisions were widely unheeded and unenforced, because the law provided no state financial aid, and because the permissive clause authorizing the organization of school districts merely recognized an already common practice, the law probably had a very modest effect on popular schooling in Massachusetts."[36]

In some communities, however, it had happier effects; in Boston the new law "revived interest in education, which had waned during the Revolution,"[37] and led to the adoption of a system of public education with three geographically distributed "writing schools" and "reading schools," capped by the single Latin School—already by then in existence for more than 150 years. Boston began licensing "dame schools" in 1789. Five years before, a committee appointed by the Town Meeting had expressed its "Veneration of our Ancestors for their Wisdom, Piety and early Care in providing for the Instruction of Children" and called upon the elected selectmen "to take Care that no Person may be Allowed to Open a Private School without their Approbation." In addition, the committee, in an anticipation of vouchers, recommended "that the Overseers of the Poor be Authorized, to give Certificates to such Parents or Guardians as may apply, or who, they may be convinsed [sic], are not able to bear the expence [sic] of having their Children instructed in the early Stage of School Instruction . . . & that they allow such Schoolmasters & Schoolmistresses as they shall direct, the usual Sum given per Week for the Instruction of each of such Children."[38]

There were six schoolmasters in 1786, assisted by four "ushers," who taught the 564 youngsters attending Boston's three "writing and arithmetic" schools and three grammar schools that operated under public auspices. When a rumor spread that the committee of the Town Meeting charged with review-ing expenses was considering a reduction in their salaries, a citizen using the pen name Crito published a letter expressing what would be a characteristic Boston attitude toward the community's public schools for the next century and more:

> Our Publick Schools the people are convinced ought to be well endowed—this will encourage men of abilities to undertake the education of our children . . . we cer-tainly wish for such, and if we pay well we have a claim to be well served . . . if those now in service are faithful, let us "strengthen their hands and encourage their hearts" . . . . Mark those who speak flightily of publick tuition—you will find their children, if they have any, at private academies—if not, they are men of narrow, con-tracted, arbitrary principles—or sly, artful and ambitious, whose object is power, and whose Deity is mammon. Of Such beware . . .[39]

A subcommittee of the Boston School Committee carried out a ward-by-ward census in 1817, coordinated by architect Charles Bulfinch, which found that public school enrollment had increased to 2,365 students, though over 4,000 students attended free or tuition-charging private schools. Since children could not enroll in town grammar schools until they could read and write, this prevented children from poor families from pursuing an education. Bulfinch suggested that the hundreds of students not attending any school could be accommodated within the existing structures, with the Overseers of the Poor continuing to pay tuition for those children whose parents could not afford to send them to private schools. He found important moral advantages to

expecting those parents who were able to do so to take responsibility by paying tuition and thus devoting attention to the education of their children.[40]
The report concluded that "the establishment at the public expense of primary
schools for children under the age of seven years, is not in their opinion expedient, and that an increase of the number of the reading and writing schools is
not required by any evident public necessity."[41]

Other citizens did not agree, insisting that the city should take responsibility
for the education of all children in common schools in order to bring together
in mutual harmony children of all the nationalities and social and economic
classes in Boston. It was this view that ultimately prevailed in the establishment of a few free primary schools under public control for children aged four
to six. These schools were managed by a Primary School Board made up of
"the godly and well-to-do," appointed by the School Committee. The private
charity schools and those that educated students from moderate-income families were quickly driven out of business, whereas private schools for the more
affluent continued to serve their clientele.

In the writing schools, both boys and girls (though at different times) were
to be taught writing and arithmetic, while pupils in the reading schools would
practice on the Bible and several of Noah Webster's ubiquitous schoolbooks.
It appears that pupils in the Latin School might also attend a writing school
for those aspects of instruction that were not offered in a curriculum heavily
oriented toward Greek and Latin. Pupils could be admitted to the reading and
writing schools at age seven, provided that they had already learned to read
in a dame school, and to the Latin School at age ten, provided that they were
"well instructed in English grammar."[42] Thus, in 1818 Boston established public primary schools to provide basic literacy and prepare children to enter the
more advanced schools.[43] Over the next decades, and quite independent of and
in advance of state efforts to promote schooling, Boston developed a bureaucratically integrated model of education that was widely emulated across the
country.

[M]ore than 85 percent of all children who attended school in Boston in 1855 and
1860 went to public schools. This fact was widely known, not only in Boston but
throughout the American educational community. Beginning early in the nineteenth century, Boston educators had devoted major efforts to unifying the city's
many independent schools, centralizing their management and standardizing their
methods of classifying and instructing students, and by mid-century they had
achieved their goal of creating what would be called a school system, which became
a prototype for other cities around the country. . . .; the steady growth of public
school enrollment during the 1830s and 1840s combined with the stagnation of

private enrollment to reduce the share of the private schools from more than one-third of school children in 1829 to little more than one-tenth 30 years later. Boston's educators were proud of this history. As for example in 1846 an examining committee for the public schools declared that "the common-school system of New England is its pride and strength; and the public schools of Boston, are the richest jewel in its crown."[44]

It was no accident, for example, that the first superintendent of the Chicago Public Schools, appointed in 1854, had been a school principal in Boston.

FUNDING AND LOCAL CONTROL

The history of popular schooling in France or Germany since the late eighteenth century cannot be told apart from the ebb and flow of national legislation and administrative intervention in regions where local efforts lagged; in the United States, by contrast, central direction of schooling, still only partial, is largely a phenomenon of the twentieth century. Until then,

> there was no clearly defined prerogative of the state authorities to demand educational improvements of the local communities, while on the contrary there was a substantial tradition of local autonomy in the details of school administration .... A law calling for educational improvement was secure only when the voting public had been convinced of its desirability. . . . legislation in most cases has had as its source the improved practice of local communities acting on their own initiative

which was then generalized by legislators to more backward communities.[45]

Apart from charity schools, there was very little free education in the early Republic. As provided by the Massachusetts school law of 1789, towns collected tuition—so-called "rate bills"—from householders with children attending school. While this system was abolished in Massachusetts in 1827, it persisted in New York, Connecticut, Rhode Island, Pennsylvania, New Jersey, and Michigan until after the Civil War. Historian Carl Kaestle has shown that most elementary schooling was provided by "common pay schools" established by individual teachers in order to make a living. In New York State, by 1812, central state authority for schooling was enacted and a system of schools was to be supported by taxes and by rate bills on parents, but the office of Superintendent of Common Schools was abolished in 1821 and its duties assigned to the Secretary of State. A separate position responsible for education was not reestablished until 1854. Schooling was not made free for all children in the state until 1867, while, in Pennsylvania, despite a series of laws calling for free schooling, it was not universal until 1886.[46]

In the Midwest, also, enrollment in local schools increased well before the effective establishment of state leadership in education. State legislatures typically allowed but did not require towns to tax property to provide partial subsidies to schools, and provided little state oversight of local efforts. Ohio passed a school bill in 1821 that authorized local communities to tax property for common schools. Reformers managed to replace this in 1825 with a bill that required towns to provide schools, to tax property for part of the cost, and to set up a mechanism for teacher certification. This requirement was unpopular and unenforceable, and schools were supported by tuition and held short sessions in inadequate schoolhouses.

The efforts especially of New Englanders who settled the northern part of the state and of Calvin Stowe and others in Cincinnati led, in 1837, to establishing the office of State Superintendent of Common Schools, with two chief duties: (a) collecting information on schools; and (b) seeing that the school laws were being properly observed. Dr Samuel Lewis, originally of Falmouth, Massachusetts, was appointed the first state superintendent for a period of one year and, as a result of his efforts, the Assembly in 1838 passed the school law that established a state system of education. "Many people, however, were opposed to the new "centralization" and Superintendent Lewis—weary of facing constant indifference and even criticism—resigned in 1840. The legislature promptly abolished the office, and the paper work envisaged by the law of 1838 was transferred to the Secretary of State's office." It was another 15 years before Ohio enacted a comprehensive law requiring free schooling paid for by local taxes, clarifying the authority of town and district committees, prescribing county examinations of teacher competence, and providing for segregated schools for black pupils.[47]

On the western frontier, in Illinois, there was mixed public-private provision of schooling.

The census of 1850 reported the existence of seventy-two public schools in Macoupin County taught by seventy-three teachers and enrolling 1,958 pupils. Moreover, the same census reported 3,365 youngsters in school attendance. . . . the larger figure doubtless included youngsters attending private schools, Sunday schools, and quasi schools of every sort and variety. What is important . . . is that some 90 percent of a total population of 3,695 between the ages of five and fourteen was spending some time in some kind of school, and this fully five years before the Illinois legislature established a state-wide, tax-supported, public school system.[48]

The Illinois legislature had enacted a law in 1825 calling for free, tax-supported schools, but public reaction had been so negative that the following session abandoned the requirement. Local voters could decide whether to provide the whole cost of the school, or only half of it, leaving the balance up to parents, while a fatal provision was inserted that "No person shall hereafter be taxed for the support of any free school in this state unless by his own free will and consent, first had and obtained in writing." It was not until 1855, when there had been an influx of New Englanders into Illinois, that a new law was enacted providing for common schools supported by public funds.[49]

In St. Louis, the Catholic Society of the Sacred Heart opened a convent and a school in 1827, in a fast-growing community of over 4,600 served by "a handful of Protestant pay-schools unable to satisfy the local demand." The new mayor had pointed out, in his inaugural address in 1823, that a free school was "more needed here than in any town of the same magnitude in the Union," but it would be 1838 before two public schools were opened, and these charged tuition except to families claiming poverty; it was not until 1847 that fees were abolished.[50]

The Sacred Heart sisters provided a boarding school for daughters of the middle class, and a free day school for poor children. As an indication of the inadequacy of public school provision of acceptable quality, "by 1834, at least one-third of all boarders were Protestant, the proportion rising to over half in 1844, and to a full two-thirds in 1846. Even during the surge in anti-Catholic nativism in the 1850s, Protestants made up a formidable one-third to one-half of the incoming boarders."[51]

The public common schools in St. Louis found it difficult to compete, since both middle class and poor parents had to be persuaded to send their children, the former because of the habit of using private schools, the latter because of resistance to public charity.[52] The latter, or at least the Catholics among them, may indeed have found it more natural to accept free schooling from the Sisters of the Sacred Heart. Whatever the reasons, the census of 1840 found that only one in five of St. Louis schoolchildren were in the public schools. A decade later, Catholic schools were still educating more children than the public schools, and the Missouri Synod Lutheran schools were also serving a growing number of pupils.[53]

Elsewhere on the frontier, the first California school law allowed religious schools to share in the state school fund, though it was repealed several years later as a result of nativist Protestant agitation; "Yankees and Southerners put aside their quarrels, including the slavery issue, to unite behind the Know-Nothing party and the Vigilance Committee of 1856 . . . in the fight against growing Irish political power."[54] The Texas legislature in 1856 designated all schools to which parents sent their children as "free public schools," entitled to receive a share of the state school fund.[55] Jorgenson cites research showing that public subsidies for private schools "actually increased until about 1820 and persisted in diminishing but still-significant amounts until well after the Civil War."[56]

Nor were the actual measures adopted effective, in most cases, in making schooling accessible by all. "In New York State, for example, even though school taxation was the rule in most local districts, the money raised in this manner paid for only 20 percent of teacher salaries. More than half of the total costs still had to come from 'rates' paid by the parents."[57] This helps to account for the curious phenomenon that "the expansion and consolidation of charity schooling did not result in a larger total percentage of urban children going to school . . . the percentage of children who were enrolled in public and private schools combined seems to have remained roughly constant in large cities, at least in the Northeast." How was that possible? It is important, Kaestle points out, not to "underestimate the vitality of independent schooling at the beginning of the century and assume that government support expanded the participation rates in urban schooling."[58]

Even with these measures, the effectiveness of schooling remained very much dependent upon local efforts, which of course varied depending upon many circumstances, and this pattern was characteristic in this period and indeed for decades beyond.

Southern states were even less committed to state support for schooling, though North Carolina (under Calvin Wiley) and Kentucky (under Robert Breckinridge) made more efforts than the others. Congress authorized public schools in the District of Columbia in 1820, but only two functioned before 1844, when a board of trustees was established that urged "[l]et ample means be provided to afford to all the [white] children of the city a sound public school education . . . in morality, virtue, and religion."[59] In Virginia, despite "prolonged and widespread agitation, at least three popular conventions on education, much public discussion, many bills in the legislature," there were only a few local districts by the outbreak of the Civil War that had provided the tax support to make schooling free.[60] An article sent to the *Common School Journal of the State of Pennsylvania* in 1844 reported sadly that:

This title ["Common School Education"] is rather a misnomer, as there is not in Virginia, strictly, any system of education by Common Schools, such as exist in Pennsylvania, and the states north and east of us. There is, however, an extended and somewhat successful plan . . . having for its object the education of *indigent* [white] *children at the public expense.*[61]

It was not until 1846 that Virginia enacted a law making it optional for counties to establish boards of school commissioners to provide free elementary schools for white children with some state financial support to supplement county taxes, but only a few counties took advantage of this opportunity.[62]

The state of Louisiana began, in 1818, to provide funds for the schooling of poor children, "but because of indifference, rural isolation, and an unwillingness of parents to submit to a pauper's oath, very few children were educated. Most of the state funds for education had been allotted to several public and private academies and colleges which, without exception, were failures."[63]

The first schools in Sumter County, South Carolina "emerged in connection with the churches. Even before the Revolution, the ministers of the Black River [Presbyterian] Church and St. Mark's [Anglican/Episcopal] Church conducted regular classes, and there is evidence of 'old-field schools' in abandoned log cabins." As the population increased,

> wealthier parents tended to have their children tutored at home, while poorer [white] parents desirous of schooling for their youngsters sent them to the public schools organized under the Free School Law of 1811. By 1826, Sumter District had forty-three such public schools enrolling 289 youngsters; by 1853, with a much larger white population, there were sixty-five public schools enrolling 442 youngsters. . . . In general, there was less schoolgoing among white children in Sumter District than in contemporary northern or midwestern communities, though not as much less as traditional historians of education have inferred by looking only at the records of public-school attendance.[64]

"Public schools" outside New England still had the connotation of charity schooling, and a number of private academies served Sumter County families not willing to send their children to such schools. Similarly, in North Carolina, the "gentry and yeoman farmers founded dozens of tuition-based schools and academies around the state in the first half of the nineteenth century—not in every county, to be sure, but in most," but "support for a uniform tax-supported public system languished."[65] Only North Carolina made a reasonably effective effort to provide public schools, though only for white children, before 1865.

Overall, at the end of the antebellum period, the average number of days of schooling a year for school-aged youth in the North ranged from 49.9 to 63.5, compared with 10.6 in the South.[66]

The federal Census of 1850 found a white illiteracy rate of 20.3 percent in the South, nearly 10 percent in the Midwest, 3 percent in the Middle Atlantic states, and 0.42 percent in New England. When the Civil War broke out, there were those northern educators convinced that the primary cause of Secession was the insufficiency of public schools in the South; one asked, rhetorically, "Would Virginia now be the scene of desolation if, like Massachusetts, she had always maintained common schools?"[67]

This does not mean that there was no demand for schooling in the South. Emigrants to the Mississippi frontier in the 1830s, we are told, felt keenly the lack of preaching and of schooling for their children, and provided for both as soon as they were settled. What was lacking was encouragement and support by state or local government. In 1839, only a little over 1 percent of the municipal budget of Richmond was for free schools and the orphan asylum. The situation was better in Lexington, Kentucky, where in 1833 there was a school

> which charged tuition at moderate rates but gave free tuition to those who could not pay. Twenty years later the town, with a population of 8,367, of whom 5,526 were white, was supporting four public schools, in three of which Latin and Greek were taught. The school term lasted for eleven months. The number of [white] children of school age in the town was 1,484, of whom 1,378 were enrolled in the public schools. . . . A committee of the city council adopted a uniform set of textbooks for all the city schools, among which were the famous "Peter Parley" readers prepared by Samuel Goodrich, a Northern man . . . The town spent approximately a fourth of its revenue . . . on operating the four public schools.[68]

The most notable exception was New Orleans, where an influential part of the population consisted of northerners settled there to engage in business or the professions. "Faced with public schools 'so worthless that no person[s] having a proper solicitude for their offspring would send their child to them,' a group of Northern-born merchants and professional men decided in 1840 to construct a public school system." One of them visited Horace Mann in Boston for advice about the best methods of establishing a public school system to serve their section of New Orleans. With passage of the necessary state legislation the following year, Mann recommended one of his Massachusetts allies to serve as the superintendent, and he in turn recruited teachers in the North. Soon a school system modelled on that of Boston was in operation, and each teacher was provided with a free subscription to Mann's *Common School Journal* "to make certain that the latest foreign and New England innovations in pedagogy would be available to the teaching staff."[69] New Orleans was an exception and, as noted, its schools were basically a New England transplant.

A similar pattern was followed in other port cities like Charleston, Savannah, and Mobile, where northern merchants and professional men promoted schooling on the New England model, but without having a stimulating effect on the interior sections of their states.

Even in the North, and after several decades of reform efforts, the situation was still far from satisfactory, at least in the view of those who sought to extend the State's leadership role. Although French visitor Alexis de Tocqueville had noted approvingly that "in New England, each citizen receives the elementary notions of human knowledge; in addition, he learns what the doctrines and the proofs of his religion are; he is made familiar with the history of his native country and the principal features of the constitution that governs it,"[70] the reality was much more uneven. Henry Barnard, later to be United States Commissioner of Education, wrote in 1839 about the dismal situation in Connecticut, pointing out

> the alarming number of children of the teachable age who are in no schools whatever, the still larger number who are in expensive private schools, the irregular attendance of those who are enrolled as pupils in the public schools, the thinly attended school meetings . . . and the unwillingness, not only of the public generally, but of that large class who are foremost in promoting other benevolent, patriotic, and religious enterprises, to make personal or pecuniary sacrifices to promote the increasing prosperity of common schools.[71]

In assessing these contrary accounts, one must keep in mind their contrasting purposes: for Barnard, it was to encourage Americans to greater efforts for the common schools, while for Tocqueville it was to shame his French compatriots into emulating the provisions for schooling in New England. For Barnard, the local control of schooling was a large part of the problem, while for Tocqueville it was precisely the great strength of New England. "I believe," he wrote in his second volume (1840), "the extreme centralization of political power in the end enervates society and thus at length weakens the government itself."[72]

Localism as both a blessing and a curse has been an ongoing theme of American education.

THE BLURRED PUBLIC/PRIVATE DISTINCTION

The distinction that—until the invention of the "charter school" in the late 1980s—seemed so fundamental and immutable between tuition-free "public" and tuition-charging "private" schools did not become clear in the United States until the decade before the Civil War.

> Indeed, when one considers the Pennsylvania and North Carolina constitutions [of 1776], it appears that their provisions for public schools and universities meant that they would be "public" in the British sense and that neither state intended to raise tax revenues to supply free education for its inhabitants. Rather, each state encouraged the formation of an extensive, tuition-based educational system.[73]

"Nonpublic" schools (to use an anachronistic term), either for profit or operated by benevolent foundations, existed side by side with "public" schools without the perception that there was a significant difference. Religious motivations were commonly at work in both private and public schools. Thus, in founding the Academy in Andover, Massachusetts, in 1778, Samuel Phillips urged the schoolmaster "early and diligently to inculcate upon [the pupils] the great and important scripture doctrines of . . . the fall of man, the depravity of human nature; the necessity of an atonement and of our being renewed in the spirit of our minds, the doctrines of repentance toward God and of faith toward our Lord Jesus Christ . . . and of justification by the free grace of God through the redemption that is in Jesus Christ."[74]

In the early Republic, such goals were unexceptional and would have characterized most "public" schools as well; the terms "public" and "private" had not acquired the specific and heavily laden significance that would develop in the twentieth century. Education was provided largely by local initiatives, including many schools sponsored by churches and many others operated by individual teachers as entrepreneurs. It is important to keep in mind, then, that "the terms 'public' and 'private' did not have their present connotations, and most schools did not fit neatly in either of our modern categories."[75] In fact, public schools in most states required parents to pay some tuition, either directly or through a supplemental tax, while many private schools received state or local funds. Despite the warnings about social-class sorting expressed by Horace Mann and others, "there was also no absolute class differentiation between the private and the public school populations."[76]

Private schools were a primary means of providing education at all levels in communities where population growth had outstripped the colonial arrangements. In the mid-Atlantic states, in particular, churches continued to provide most schooling well into the nineteenth century. Competition among religious denominations stimulated the provision of schooling, since "the competing sects increasingly used schools as agencies of missionary endeavor."[77] "In 1830, 217 of Pennsylvania's 274 Lutheran churches operated day schools. Despite the antebellum public school crusade, there were still about 100 Lutheran schools in 1850." Protestants and not Catholics were the first to provide extensive systems of what could be called "parochial schools," and

> immigrant resistance to common schooling was not restricted to Catholics or to cities. In southeast and central Pennsylvania, German Lutherans, Reformed Protestants, and Mennonites in small towns and rural districts resisted the introduction of free schools in the 1830s and 1840s.... German Pietists and other immigrant Protestants of Pennsylvania had supported their own schools long before the creation of public schools, and they had withstood efforts in the eighteenth century to assimilate their children through English-language charity schools.[78]

In many communities in the antebellum period, communities "ran a free 'public' school on funds from the state (usually derived from the federal land grants) until the cash ran out, then charged the parents tuition if they wanted their children to continue. Often free and tuition schools operated in the same building. In many places nuns taught with public funding and instructed in the Catholic religion; urban political machines sometimes deliberately blurred the public-private distinction to please their constituents."[79]

Public funds were provided to church-sponsored schools in Pennsylvania and elsewhere: to Catholic schools in Lowell, Massachusetts, in the 1830s and 1840s, in Milwaukee in the 1840s, in several Connecticut cities and in New Jersey in the 1860s, and in New York State even later.[80]

Nor were such arrangements considered in violation of the First Amendment, though they were often deplored on political and anti-immigrant grounds.

Such arrangements were fairly common until education reformers began to insist that schooling of future citizens should be provided under state authority, although that view gained wide support only gradually. Nonpublic schools were deplored by the generation of elite education reformers that included Horace Mann and Henry Barnard. Advocates of a system of schooling controlled entirely by local and state government were unenthusiastic about and sometimes openly hostile to the semipublic academies, which they saw as dangerous rivals. John Pierce, state Superintendent of Schools in Michigan, wrote in 1837 that

> wherever the liberality and enterprise of individuals have established flourishing private institutions, they have uniformly had a pernicious influence upon the common schools. Instead of being improved and elevated by their proximity to such institutions, they have lost their character and usefulness. In those towns where

private seminaries have been located and well sustained, the free schools are found, without exception, to be in a miserable condition.[81]

"Private schooling," Henry Barnard wrote in 1845 in a report on education in Rhode Island, "classifies society at the root; by assorting children according to the wealth, education, and outward circumstances of their parents into different schools, and educates children of the same neighborhood differently and unequally. These differences of culture as to manners, morals, and intellectual tastes and habits . . . open a real chasm between members of the same society, broad and deep, which equal laws and political theories cannot close."[82] Speaking at the dedication of the new public high school in his native Hartford, in 1849, Barnard "continued his battle with the private sector in education and showed his concern about the competitive founding of academies and colleges by corporations or religious bodies." Such institutions would not be under state control, he warned, and thus could not serve the primary function of schools, to create citizens.[83]

For others, though, it was precisely the diversity and competition allowed by the reliance upon academies that was among their chief virtues; they promoted "freedom from governmental interference with our literary institutions," and the right of parents to choose a school, wrote Edward Hitchcock, president of Amherst College from 1845 to 1854. A state system of secondary schools—a "treadmill system"—would be a "wretched substitute" for this richly diverse provision of schools.[84] In fact, it was not until the 1880s and 1890s that academies were replaced, in most cases, by public high schools, or converted to that status, while others evolved into what we now know as "independent schools." Throughout most of the nineteenth century, academies were the prevalent form of schooling beyond the 3 or 4 years typically provided by the common school. Academies

> came in every size, shape, and form, and under every variety of sponsorship. Many were chartered, many were not. Some were the ephemeral enterprises of particular teachers, some had corporate boards that transcended particular teachers. Some were tied to local communities, some to church assemblies, some to government agencies. Some were supported by endowments, some by taxes, some by subscriptions, some by tuition rates, and most by some combination of the four. . . . They seemed infinitely adaptable to particular needs and opportunities.[85]

Massachusetts made land grants in the interior parts of Maine (which did not become an independent state until 1820) to support academies, though—as was often the case on the sparsely settled frontiers of the United States as well as Canada—these did not provide a reliable-enough source of income to make much of a difference.[86] New York, Virginia, Louisiana, and other states similarly gave subsidies to academies under private control.

Ironically, the primary effect of the campaign to increase the enrolment share of the public schools was to cause nonpublic schools to become more and more socially elite as they served only those whose parents could afford to pay substantial tuition. "What occurred was not, then, a victory over separate elite schooling, as Mann would have liked, but a conversion of low-priced pay schools, local academies, and subscription schools . . . into town-controlled, tax-supported schools,"[87] while the more expensive private schools continued to flourish with a more socially restricted clientele.

Chapter Five

Schooling as Protection for Society

SCHOOLING FOR POOR CHILDREN

Before the massive immigration that began in the 1840s, efforts to provide schooling to children from families that could not afford tuition were sporadic and often dependent on initiatives by religious organizations. While rural communities usually made provision to include, in their schools, children whose parents could not afford to pay the tuition fees, the situation was more difficult in the growing urban areas, as we have seen in the case of Boston. Many children in these cities, in the 1780s and 1790s,

> were taught in independent pay schools. Most schoolmasters charged quarterly fees within the means of perhaps three-quarters of the population. Analysis of enrollment lists for New York City in the 1790s reveals that these pay schools were patronized by a wide variety of families. The only under-represented groups were day laborers, many of whom could not afford even the lowest tuition costs, and merchants and professionals, who may have patronized boarding schools or hired tutors.[1]

Basic schooling for children from families unable to pay tuition, if available at all, was provided by "charity schools" supported by individuals or groups of philanthropists, or by local churches, often subsidized by the state government. Legislatures in Pennsylvania, New Jersey, Delaware, Maryland, Virginia, Georgia, and South Carolina enacted arrangements to support with public funds children attending private schools from poor families, much like today's voucher programs in Milwaukee, Cleveland, and elsewhere. In contrast with New York and New England, other states did not require the maintenance of schools by local authorities.[2] "In the main, . . . the well-to-do in the few cities and larger towns sent their children to private schools and supported most meagerly a few charity schools through the churches."[3] In 1795, New York State adopted a program of aid to common schools, with an eligibility requirement of matching funds from counties, but the law expired in 1800; in New York City, at least, the existing "system" of schooling by nearly one hundred private schoolmasters and by church-supported charity schools seemed adequate . . . for a time.

New York City had six charity schools, all church-sponsored, in 1796, and when an elite group consisting predominantly of Quakers founded the New York Free School Society in 1805, its stated purpose was to supplement the educational work of churches through "extending the means of education to such poor children as do not belong to, or are not provided for by, any religious society," offering basic training in literacy and morality in order "to counteract the disadvantages resulting from the situation of their parents."[4] The following year it opened its first school, using the monitorial pedagogy developed by Joseph Lancaster, through which a single teacher orchestrated the drilling, by older pupils, of their younger classmates.[5] In 1809, it received a state subsidy to build a facility designed to accommodate 500 pupils in one room. Ravitch points out that "religious domination of schooling was so openly conceded that the Society asked permission to educate *only* those who were not in a religious school," but, this opening wedge gained, the Society was successful, in 1808, in gaining legislative support for serving *all* poor children.[6]

> The condition of this class is deplorable indeed [the Society wrote], reared up by parents who, from a variety of concurring circumstances, are become either indifferent to the best interests of their offspring, or, through intemperate lives, are rendered unable to defray the expense of their instruction, these miserable and almost friendless objects are ushered upon the stage of life, inheriting those vices which idleness and the bad example of their parents naturally produce.[7]

The subsequent history of New York's Public School Society would be stormy, as we will see. It was, however, from the publicly subsidized charity schools of this and other private groups that the public school system would eventually evolve.[8]

In Baltimore, as in other coastal cities during the first decades of the nineteenth century, charity schools were established by Episcopalians, Methodists, Catholics, and Quakers, and by the Irish Hibernian Society, but were able to serve only a relatively few children; similarly, the Sunday schools that were intended to reach children whose employment prevented them from attending regular schools found it difficult to attract pupils or to convince their parents that schooling was worthwhile.[9] Other voluntary efforts included the Benevolent Society for the Education of the Female Poor.[10] A close-knit coterie of New Englanders—merchants and professional men—agitated to create public schools on the Boston model.[11] In their campaign, which led to filing of state legislation in 1825 and appropriation of modest funding by the City Council in 1829 to support one or more monitorial schools, the advocates gave a greatly exaggerated account of the quality of the Boston public schools and their patronage, with the happiest results, by all social classes. They informed potential supporters that

> the schoolmasters of that city were all university graduates and a highly respected group in the community. Chosen by the School Committee, and paid by the city, these schoolmasters could remain impartial toward all students, even the children of the most influential members of the district. This vision of equal treatment of all pupils was an important part of the public school appeal, and school supporters expounded upon it at length. In Boston, they found "the most perfect republicanism, for here rich and poor literally meet together." In the public schools of that city, the son of a poor immigrant triumphed over the son of a respected and wealthy descendant of an original settler after numerous and difficult examinations. Honorary rewards were "distributed equally to children of day laborers and of the most accomplished statesman." Immune to the biases of class and religious affiliation, the public schools could draw out and reward the natural talents of its students. In this impartial institution, all could compete and achieve on terms not hindered by the artificialities of class and caste. Public school advocates anticipated the charge that children of respectable families might be morally tainted by associating with children of the lower classes. Again, referring to Boston, they assured Baltimoreans that the public schools "advance the moral standing of the poorer class of society and never have been found injurious to others." As proof of the harmlessness of this type of association, school supporters explained that "men of the largest wealth and still more . . . those of the most enlightened and religious character" sent their children to public schools. School proponents concluded their remarks with a call to establish a state-supported, "economical, well-organized" system of schools, such as could compare to the best that private schools offered.[12]

Opponents pointed out that there were empty seats in the free schools operated by the churches in Baltimore, but advocates of creating public schools insisted on the difference "between these charity schools and the public schools

in the eastern states," that is, New England. A supporter of legislation for
public schools wrote: "We do not want charity schools—we do not want free
schools—we want schools for freemen; such schools as the honest and independent mechanic and merchants of this city will send their children to."[13]

The evidence, in any case, is that such efforts in various communities
reached only a small proportion of the ever-increasing number of poor, and
especially immigrant, children and youth. Some historians have concluded
that "the public schools failed to attract or to hold their intended beneficiaries—the children of the poor. Working class parents often felt they could not
relinquish their youthful breadwinners to institutions whose instructional
program seemed irrelevant to the lives of the poor."[14] After all, literacy was
not a requirement or even an advantage for much of the employment that
was available at this stage in the development of the economy. For the elite
reformers, on the other hand, the provision of schooling for the children of
the poor—and especially of immigrants—had little or nothing to do with the
economic interests of those children or their families; it was concerned with
"the regulation of the feelings and dispositions, the extirpation of vicious pro-
pensities, the pre-occupation of the wilderness of the young heart with the
seeds and germs of moral beauty, and the formation of a lovely and virtuous
character by the habitual practice of cleanliness, delicacy, refinement, good
temper, gentleness, kindness, justice and truth."[15] Grave dangers threatened
American society, reformers warned, if these children could not be rescued
from the influence of their families.

The Pennsylvania *Constitution* of 1776, "generally recognized to be the most
radical and populist of the early state constitutions," instructed the Legislature
to establish schools in every county and to see that their teachers receive "such
salaries . . . paid by the public, as may enable them to instruct youth at low
prices." The more conservative 1790 *Constitution* did not continue this commitment to public support for a common school system and limited the mandate to requiring that instruction be provided "in such a manner that the poor
may be taught gratis."[16]

Pennsylvania state laws in 1802, 1804, and 1809 required that poor children
be taught free, but it was not until 1818 that five public schools were established for poor white children in Philadelphia, with a public school established
for black children in 1822.[17]

Apart from Philadelphia, virtually nothing was done to provide public
schooling for poor children in Pennsylvania, except by private and church initiative, until the 1830s. There was a Philadelphia Society for the Free Instruction
of Indigent Boys and the Philadelphia Directory of 1791 reported that: "almost
every religious society has one or more schools under its immediate direction,

for the education of its own youth of both sexes, as well of the rich, who are able to pay, as of the poor, who are taught and provided with books and stationery gratis; besides which there are a number of private schools . . . independent of any public body."[18]

The Quakers had an especially distinguished record of providing schooling, and not only to the children of their own community; other denominations, both English- and German-speaking, also maintained schools for their children. In Philadelphia there were at least 12 "charity schools" for poor children by 1810: Episcopalian, Presbyterian, Lutheran, Reformed, and Catholic;[19] several of these schools were maintained by black churches and organizations. In areas where the denominations were mixed together, there were often elementary schools and even secondary academies operated on what we would call an interdenominational basis, without any initiative or guidance from the state.

Pennsylvania laws were adopted in 1802 and subsequently required teachers of reading and writing in English or German to accept all poor pupils sent to them by the authorities, who would pay the usual tuition with public funds. The 1809 law required the county commissioners to inform parents who could not afford tuition at whatever schools were available locally "that they are at liberty to send them to the most convenient school, free of expense." The teacher of the school selected by the parents would then send in a bill to the county "agreeably to the usual rates of charging for tuition in said school."[20] In other words, it was what we would now call an education voucher.

It has been noted that "Not a single [public] school was established by these laws, but the private school became a thriving institution. Nevertheless the system was disliked by the teacher, it was offensive to those in smaller communities who had to send their children to schools attended by paupers, and it was hated by the beneficiaries of the system themselves." In 1829, it has been estimated, of 350,000 school-aged children in Pennsylvania, fewer than 5,000 were being schooled at state expense.[21]

A special law applying to Philadelphia was enacted in 1812 authorizing the County Commissioners to select and pay teachers for poor children. In fact, however, they continued to tuition those children into existing schools until 1818, when something that could be called a system of public schools was established by the decision of the legislature to establish the Board of Controllers for the charity schools in Philadelphia. In 1817, the Philadelphia Society for the Establishment and Support of Charity Schools had endorsed the monitorial system of organizing schools, pointing out that "when the rapid increase of our population is compared with the means of procuring Education, it is much to be feared, that at no distant period a large proportion of the people, in important sections of the United States, will be destitute of this important blessing, unless private benevolence or public provision should apply the remedy. The Lancastrian system ... presents the best mode yet discovered of spreading the benefits of Education."[22] The monitorial system of instruction was adopted for the charity schools, and Joseph Lancaster himself was attracted to the city to establish a model school for training teachers.

Washington, DC found another way to support free schooling for its poor (white) children; the city council, in 1803, adopted an ordinance that "so much of the net proceeds of taxes paid, or to be laid, on slaves, on dogs, on licenses for carriages and hacks, for ordinaries and taverns, for retailing of wines and spiritous liquors, for billiard tables, for theatrical and other public amusements, for hawkers and pedlars, be appropriated as the trustees may decide to be necessary for the education of the poor of the city."[23]

In many communities on the frontier that would become the Midwest, schools were established by German immigrants to teach in their own language and culture, usually with a strongly religious character. There were also German "freethinker" schools, something that would have been unlikely to appear among the Native American population, especially after the failed 1848 revolutions brought many radical exiles. In Milwaukee, St Louis, Chicago, and other frontier cities, up to half of the schoolchildren were in nonpublic schools, often partially supported with public funds or land grants.

In 1845, a cautious attitude toward poor families was expressed by the Boston School Committee, commenting on the difficulty of:

> taking children at random from a great city, undisciplined, uninstructed, often with inveterate forwardness and obstinacy, and with the inherited stupidity of centuries of ignorant ancestors; forming them from animals into intellectual beings; and, so far as a school can do it, from intellectual beings into spiritual beings; giving to many their first appreciation of what is wise, what is true, what is lovely, and what is pure; and not merely their first impressions, but what may possibly be their only impressions.[24]

By the 1840s, most cities had abandoned the practice of separate schools for children whose parents could not pay tuition, though Boston and other cities found ways to keep such pupils separate from those of middle-class families whose support for the system was considered essential.

Reisner points out that "as the transition from strictly private initiative in education to universal public provision of schools was mediated through the activities of the voluntary associations, the movement" of private and above all religious benevolence "has large significance in the evolution of a public school system."[25] "Public schooling"—schooling reaching out to a broad public and not limited to members of a particular religious community or to an economic elite—was often provided under private auspices. It was only in the years immediately before and after the Civil War, when gradually (much sooner in some states than in others) public elementary schools became tuition-free, that "the cheaper independent pay schools, previously patronized by ordinary families, declined."[26]

As poor children were increasingly brought into the same schools as the children of middle-class families, the latter often were withdrawn. The Boston school system, with its commitment to exercise an effective monopoly over schooling far in advance of most other urban systems, was particularly unwilling to experience this loss and became a pioneer in education "tracking" as in so much else. In 1861 John Philbrick, its superintendent, pointed out in his annual report that "there is in every large city a class of children, more or less numerous, which is too low down in the depths of vice, crime, and poverty, to be reached by the benefits of a system of public education." He recommended that "we need special industrial schools, where the children may be trained to habits of industry as well as of study . . . established and managed by benevolent individuals and associations, entirely apart from public schools." There would, he promised, be two advantages: "The multiplication of this description of schools would be a great blessing to the children of the 'perishing and dangerous classes' in the community, while it would at the same time tend to purify and elevate the character of the [other] public schools."[27]

The same prescription of "industrial education" would be the basis for the schooling provided to many freed slaves or their children at Hampton Institute, Tuskegee, and elsewhere in the South after the Civil War. The intention was to develop habits of self-discipline and hard work by combining physical with academic work, a model developed several decades earlier as the basis for schooling in the slums of Glasgow, Scotland, and considered a promising reform.[28]

THE IMMIGRANT THREAT

While in the first decades of the Republic the schooling of poor children had been an object of voluntary (usually religious) efforts with occasional public funding, by the 1840s the massive immigration from Ireland and Germany made it seem vitally necessary as a means of social control. Governor Henry Gardner—elected in the Know-Nothing landslide that took control of the Massachusetts government in January 1855—in his Inaugural Address stated that "the most prominent subject before our State and Nation at the present moment . . . concerns our foreign population;—the duties of republicanism toward them, its dangers from them." After an extended discussion of the importance of the need "to cultivate a living and energetic nationality—to develop a high and vital patriotism—to Americanize America—to keep entire the separation of church and state—to nationalize before we naturalize, and to educate before either," Gardner warned that "Every additional naturalization tends to denationalize, to Europeanize, America."

The people of Massachusetts (by which of course he meant those native-born of native parents), Gardner asserted, "distrust foreign influences nursed in customs and creeds antagonistical to republicanism." They were convinced that with the "Spiritual Despotism, a Fettered Bible, or, more probably, no Bible at all, and Sectarian Schools, our liberties would exist but in name, and very soon but in history." The first of the measures that the governor proposed to prevent those dangers was the enactment of a state constitutional amendment "prohibiting the diversion of the educational funds of the State to the establishment or support of sectarian schools."[29]

This provision, it should be noted, had nothing to do with interpretations of the First Amendment to the federal Constitution, and everything to do with the panic about Catholic immigration. Why this acute concern? One reason was undoubtedly that nerves were already on edge from bitter conflicts over slavery and threats of national dissolution, but the greater cause was the dramatic demographic changes in New England, which, unlike New York, Philadelphia, and Baltimore, had been quite homogeneous in population. Decades earlier, Josiah Quincy praised the people of Massachusetts for "their common principles, interests, hopes, and affection. . . . The fears and jealousies which in other countries separate classes of men, and make them hostile to each other, have here no influence, or a very limited one."[30] The population was changing rapidly, and fears and jealousies were no longer absent.

Even nationwide, there had been little foreign immigration during the first decades of the new nation: "only about 250,000 persons; while the original population increased almost threefold, or to nearly 10,000,000."[31] Such foreign immigration as there was came overwhelmingly directly or indirectly (via Canada and Newfoundland) from Europe; in 1820, for example, there were 8,385 immigrants, of whom 6,000 came from Britain or Ireland (many of the latter probably Scots–Irish Protestants), 968 from Germany, and 700 from elsewhere in Europe. There were five immigrants from all of Asia, one from Mexico, 209 from Canada, and 164 from the West Indies, most or all of whom were probably white.[32]

Before 1830, the number of immigrants arriving annually in Boston "never exceeded 2,000; before 1840 it reached 4,000 only once (1837). Distributed among many nativities [national origins], most were transients, westward-bound. . . . Thereafter arrivals increased rapidly from 3,936 in 1840 to 28,917 in 1849. The newcomers were overwhelmingly Irish" and settled in Boston and its vicinity.[33] By 1860, foreign-born parents for the first time since the seventeenth century produced more children in Massachusetts than did the native-born.[34]

It was the development of larger-scale manufacturing, often in what had been villages situated where a river could be readily exploited to produce power, like Pawtucket (1793) in Rhode Island, Fall River (1813), Waltham (1814), and Lowell (1823) in Massachusetts, and Nashua (1823) in New Hampshire, which made it possible for thousands of immigrants to find employment in New England, even as thousands of Yankees were moving West from worn-out farms. Nationwide, the urban population rose from 4.9 percent of the total to 6.7 percent in 1830, while the number of communities with over 8,000 residents increased from 11 to 24 . . . and this was just the beginning of a process which would gather momentum over the next decades, especially with the impetus given to manufacturing by the Civil War. Along with the spread of factories, of course, was a great increase in the number of industrial workers, seen as a new and unstable element in American life. Workers went on strike in Boston in 1825 and in Philadelphia in 1827, while the following year the Workingmen's Party Convention was held. For the evangelical reformers, a largely Catholic immigrant population represented a threat to the fundamental character of the country and its culture, while some of the demands articulated on behalf of workers by non-workers like Fanny Wright and Robert Dale Owen were especially alarming.

Between 1820 and 1860, the total population of the United States would grow by an astonishing 33 percent per decade, and that of residents of places of 2,500 or more by thrice as many. Boston would add more than 37,000 Irish immigrants to its population of 114,000 in 1847 alone. In 1820, only Philadelphia and New York City had over 50,000 residents; by 1860, there were 16 cities in that category.[35] Governor Gardner noted the "remarkable spectacle presented to the eyes of our people, naturally and wisely jealous of their nationality, of a foreign immigration in the ten years from 1840 to 1850 outnumbering the whole previous influx since the organization of the republic. . . . It is a great problem in statesmanship," he pointed out, "wisely to control the mingling of races into one nationality. The dominant race must regulate the incoming class. Such is political destiny, and history proves it."[36]

Under the pressure of this massive demographic change, the government institutions including schools established during the colonial period and the first years of independence simply could not cope. If there was a revolution in American education, it did not occur with the political revolution of the late eighteenth century, but in the second third of the nineteenth. New social realities came together with new ideas about the political and social function of schooling—influenced by European experience and debates—to transform all levels of American education in this period.

The issue was not—as it would become later, with the rise of immigration from southern and eastern Europe—cultural or linguistic differences, but the fact that a high proportion of the new immigrants were Catholic. This was, after all, a period when anti-Catholicism was still a respectable position among Protestants on both sides of the Atlantic . . . as indeed was anti-Protestantism among Catholics. The papal encyclical *Mirari vos* (1832), condemning positions taken by certain French Catholics in an effort to come to terms with nineteenth century political realities, "seemed to confirm the worst suspicions of American Protestants—that Catholicism threatened American liberty." Two years later, the General Association of the Congregational church of Massachusetts urged pastors to labor to save the "country from the degrading influence of Popery" and recommended that district associations "give the subject of Popery, in all its bearings, a serious and prayerful consideration."[37] Similarly, the founding of the American Protestant Association in 1843 was intended "to 'awaken' Americans to the 'assaults of Romanism.'"[38]

This changing attitude toward Catholicism as massive immigration made it a present reality rather than an abstraction was reflected in school textbooks. Elson points out that, in 1839 Samuel Goodrich ("Peter Parley"), in one of his widely used schoolbooks, "offers a pleasant picture of life in a convent, and a story of a monk offering his own great artistic talent to God. In 1853 the same author presents a violently biased picture of the Catholic Church."[39] Books used in Catholic schools, naturally, were as biased in the other direction.

Evangelical Protestants felt threatened—and saw America as threatened—by the rapidly growing Catholic immigration, primarily Irish in the eastern cities, German and Irish in the midwest. Some 30 Protestant newspapers were founded by 1827, all of which made warnings about the dangers to freedom as well as "pure religion" posed by Catholicism . . . even before the heavy Catholic immigration began.[40] Lyman Beecher wrote to his daughter Catharine in 1830, "the competition now is for that of preoccupancy in the education of the rising generation, in which Catholics and infidels have got the start of us."[41] The same year, an article in an orthodox Protestant publication pointed with concern to "the tide of infidelity and Romanism settling strongly into" the Mississippi Valley, and especially to the efforts of Catholic missionaries to establish "free schools, and female seminaries," in which "the most ruinous doctrines" would be taught.[42]

In his widely distributed fund-raising appeal, *A Plea for the West* (1835), Beecher warned that "three-fourths of the foreign emigrants whose accumulating tide is rolling in upon us, are, through the medium of their religion and priesthood, as entirely accessible to the control of the potentates of Europe as if they were an army of soldiers, enlisted and officered, and spreading over the land; then, indeed, should we have just occasion to apprehend danger to our liberties. It would be the union of church and state in the midst of us." As the only safe remedy, he urged "Let the Catholics mingle with most Americans and come with their children under the full action of our common schools and republican institutions and the various powers of assimilation, and we are prepared cheerfully to abide the consequences." After all, he told a Boston audience in an appeal for funds for Lane Seminary, only through "introducing the social and religious principles of New England" among the fast-growing western population, with their "limited means of education," could disaster be averted.[43]

The same year, Beecher's daughter Catharine's *Address on the Education of Female Teachers* (subsequently published in New York and Cincinnati) called for women teachers from the East to civilize the barbarous immigrants of the West. "Thousands and thousands of degraded foreigners and their ignorant families, are pouring into this nation at every avenue," she wrote, and the answer was "Moral and religious education [as] the foundation of national instruction."[44]

Similarly, a group of educators in Ohio expressed, in 1836, their concern with the "vast tide of immigration, yearly flowing in upon us, from all nations." The only answer was "to take their children . . . and educate them in the same schools with our own, and thus *amalgamate them* with our community."[45]

Nor was this concern limited to the West; the president of Middlebury College in Vermont asked, in 1849, "shall these adopted citizens become a part of the body politic, and firm supporters of liberal institutions, or will they prove to our republic what the Goths and Huns were to the Roman Empire? The answer to this question depends in a great degree upon the wisdom and fidelity of our teachers and associated influences."[46]

An editorial in *The Massachusetts Teacher* in 1851 complained that

> Our chief difficulty is with the Irish. The Germans, who are next in numbers, will give us no trouble. . . . But the poor Irish, the down-trodden, priest-ridden of centuries, come to us in another shape. . . . In too many instances the parents are unfit guardians of their own children. If left to their direction the young will be brought up in idle, dissolute, vagrant habits, which will make them worse members of society than their parents are. . . . the children must be gathered up and forced into

school, and those who resist or impede this plan, whether parents or priests, must be held accountable and punished.[47]

A rather different situation prevailed in the 1850s in Chicago, where the Catholic and public school systems grew up in parallel, and the establishment of parochial schools in immigrant neighborhoods was pressed much earlier and more vigorously than was the case in eastern cities.[48] The fact that a larger proportion of the Chicago immigrants were German, with an interest in schooling in their own language provided by some parochial schools, and that financial support was provided by Catholic organizations in Austria, helped to stimulate this development. Whereas in Boston, New York, and other cities in the East immigrants were mostly impoverished and their children were seen as an unwelcome problem for public schools, in Chicago public and Catholic schools competed for the patronage of immigrant families. "During the 1850s Chicago's public schools were actively working to overtake the Catholic schools in size and influence, and increasing their attendance from the city's large immigrant population was one obvious means to this end." This may in turn have made them more respectful toward and accommodating of the concerns of immigrant parents.[49]

Calvin Stowe, husband of Harriet Beecher, warned the citizens of Ohio in 1835 that "unless we educate our immigrants, they will be our ruin." Nor did this simply mean training in the skills required to work productively. After all,

> it is not merely from the ignorant and vicious foreigner that danger is to be apprehended. To sustain an extended republic like our own, there must be a national feeling, a national assimilation; and nothing could be more fatal to our prospects of future national prosperity than to have our population become a congeries of clans, congregating without coalescing, and condemned to contiguity without sympathy. . . . It is altogether essential to our national strength and peace, if not even to our national existence, that the foreigners who settle on our soil, should cease to be Europeans and become Americans; and as our national language is English, and as our literature, our manners, and our institutions are of English origin, and the whole foundation of out society English, it is essential that they become substantially Anglo-Americans. . . . The most effectual, and indeed the only effectual way, to produce this individuality and harmony of national feeling, is to bring our children into the same schools and have them educated together. The children of immigrants must be taught English and prepared for the common English schools, and the safety of the republic requires that destitute children should be sought out and made to attend the public schools.[50]

The remedy, he argued, was a state-led system of common schools based on the Prussian model, which he studied in person and described in a widely circulated report. Similarly, Horace Mann warned that "a foreign people, born and bred and dwarfed under the despotisms of the Old World, cannot be transformed into the full stature of American citizens merely by a voyage across the Atlantic";[51] they required the powerful influence of common schools. An article reprinted in Mann's *Common School Journal* from a Congregationalist quarterly stressed, typically,

> the importance of assimilating the people of this country,—of making them one in character and in spirit, and of the value of institutions and influences for this end; of which educational institutions and influences are most practical and powerful. This assimilation and unity of character and spirit are important in all nations, but especially in a nation politically free or self-governed. . . . As they come hither from all sections, nations and religions of Europe, it is important that their children should be neither uneducated, nor educated by themselves,—that they find here educational institutions for the *whole* people, which will command their confidence, and secure the attendance of their children. The children of this country, of whatever parentage, should, not wholly, but to a certain extent, be *educated together* . . . educated to be one harmonious people. This, the common school system, if wisely and liberally conducted, is well fitted, in part at least, to accomplish. . . . And it is with serious regret that we see it recommended, and zealously urged, to substitute for this common school system, a system of dividing children into sectarian schools for the avowed purpose of teaching them sectarian peculiarities,—a system which is fitted to lay deep in the impressible mind of childhood the foundations of divisions and alienations,—a system well fitted to drive the children of foreigners, and especially of Roman Catholics, into clans by themselves, where ignorance and prejudice respecting the native population and a spirit remote from the American, and hostile to the Protestant, will be fostered in them.[52]

Perhaps the most influential Protestant voice for the education of the children of immigrants in public schools was that of Horace Bushnell, theologian and Congregational pastor in Hartford. Bushnell delivered a "public fast day sermon" in 1853 on the role of the common school in relation to Catholic immigrants. Americans had been extremely generous, he told his audience of elected officials and leading citizens, in admitting immigrants to all the privileges of a free society, but "they are not content, but are just now returning our generosity by insisting that we must excuse them and their children from becoming wholly and properly American." The ungrateful Catholic immigrants wanted "ecclesiastical schools, whether German, French, or Irish, any kind of schools but such as are American, and will make Americans of their children." Bushnell warned that

> it has been clear for some years past, from the demonstrations of our Catholic clergy and their people, and particularly of the clergy, that they were preparing for an assault upon the common school system, hitherto in so great favor with our countrymen; complaining, first, of the Bible as a sectarian book in the schools, and then, as their complaints have begun to be accommodated by modifications that amount to a discontinuance, more or less complete, of religious instruction itself, of our "godless scheme of education" . . . Evidently the time has now come, and the issue of life or death to common schools is joined for trial. The ground is taken, the flag raised, and there is to be no cessation, till the question is forever decided, whether we are to have common schools in our country or not.

Ironically enough, it was because the author of *Discources on Christian Nurture* shared with Catholic educators the conviction that early education was of extreme importance, that Bushnell's opposition to their claims to educate the children of their denomination was particularly vehement.

Bushnell insisted that "this great institution, too, of common schools, is not only a part of the state, but is imperiously wanted as such, for the common training of so many classes and conditions of people." Overlooking conveniently how many private academies had long been receiving public funding—and including religious instruction in their programs—he drew a sharp distinction: "Common schools are nurseries thus of a free republic, private schools of factions, cabals, agrarian laws, and contests of force. . . The arrangement is not only unchristian, but it is thoroughly un-American, hostile at every point to our institutions themselves." Bushnell found it "a dark and rather mysterious providence, that we have thrown upon us, to be our fellow-citizens, such multitudes of people, depressed, for the most part, in character, instigated by prejudices so intense against our religion." It was his hope, however, that through the common school "we may be gradually melted into one homogeneous people."[53]

A powerful movement developed among native whites in a number of states in the early 1850s, organized on the basis of local lodges that admitted only native-born Protestant men "who were willing to cast off former party ties and take an oath to keep secret all lodge business, to vote for the party line, and to stand vigil against the enemies of the republic, chief among whom were the Pope and the immigrant." Officially known as the American Party, it was commonly referred to as the "Know-Nothings." "Certainly, burgeoning Catholicism and the hordes of Irish immigrants clustering into the cities and manufacturing towns of the state was an unsettling development for the Yankee Protestant majority."[54] In the Massachusetts state election of 1854, the American Party "managed the greatest election upset in the history of the state," gaining the entire congressional delegation, all 40 state senators, and all but three of the 379 representatives, as well as the statewide executive positions. The newly elected "Know-Nothing" governor, as we have seen, emphasized in his inaugural addresses in 1854 and again in 1855 that foreigners and the Catholic Church "posed the gravest and most immediate threat to American institutions." Without effective efforts to limit the influence of both, "liberty under democratic institutions will degenerate into anarchical licence or give place to slavish and bigoted superstition."[55]

The victorious Know-Nothings proposed, in 1855, the exclusion of Catholics from public office and of the foreign-born from office and the vote for 21 years after their arrival in the country; both proposals failed, but they were more successful in gaining approval of what is commonly called the "Anti-Aid Amendment" to the state Constitution (see Chapter Seven). This provided that state and local tax revenues for education could be "expended in, no other schools than those which are conducted according to law, under the order and superintendence of the authorities of the town or city in which the money is to be expended; and such moneys shall never be appropriated to any religious sect for the maintenance exclusively of its own schools." They also mandated the use of the King James translation of the Bible in public schools.[56]

SCHOOLING THE CHILDREN OF IMMIGRANTS IN NEW YORK CITY

As we have seen, schooling in the mid-Atlantic colonies and states in the colonial and early national period was usually provided by denominational and private initiatives rather than by town action, as in New England; "where there was great religious diversity, there was no impulse towards establishing communal schools for all."[57] Kaestle points out that, in New York City, "the impression that the city's pay schools were limited to the wealthy . . . is incorrect. . . . in a sense, the private pay schools, with the charity schools, were the public schools of New York City in the 1790s."[58] Funds appropriated by the state for the schooling of poor children, under laws enacted in 1795 and 1813, were granted directly to private and church-run charity schools. These included schools operated by the Free School Society (founded in 1805), as well as those of the Orphan Asylum Society, the Society of the Economical School in the City of New York (for children of white refugees from the West Indies), the African Free School, and "such incorporated religious societies in said city as now support or hereafter shall establish charity schools, who may apply for the same," although none did so until 1820.[59]

De Witt Clinton, frequent mayor of New York and later governor of the state, was speaker at the dedication of a new school opened in 1811 by the Free School Society, of which he was a prominent member. "True it is," he conceded, "that charity schools, entitled to eminent praise, were established in this city; but they were attached to particular sects, and did not embrace children of different persuasions. Add to this that some denominations were not provided with these establishments, and that children the most in want of instruction were necessarily excluded, by the irreligion of their parents, from the benefit of education." The Society, he reminded his auditors, had been established to provide "a free school for the education of poor children who do not belong to, or are not provided for by, any religious society."[60]

While the Free School Society was nondenominational, it by no means provided a secular program; in 1814, reported the Society, "the afternoon of every Tuesday . . . has been set aside for [religious instruction]; and the children have been instructed in the catechisms of the churches to which they respectively belong." The pupils in 1814 were enumerated as 271 Presbyterian, 186 Episcopalian, 172 Methodist, 119 Baptist, 41 Dutch Reformed, and 9 Roman Catholic.[61]

Nor was the religious emphasis confined to the instruction provided. In 1819, the Society informed poor parents that they had a duty to take their children to church every Sunday and "to omit no opportunity to instruct them early in the principles of the Christian religion, in order to bring them, in their youth, to a sense of the unspeakable love and infinite wisdom and power of their Almighty Creator." While the Society was concerned to "promote the improvement of the scholars [pupils] in school learning," they cared even more about the "more primary object of an education calculated to form habits of virtue and industry, and to inculcate the general principles of Christianity."[62]

There were those who objected to what Michael Katz calls the "paternalistic voluntarism" of the Free School Society, carrying out as it did "an important function of government, without a direct and immediate responsibility to the people." The Society took "exclusive control" of the pupils without allowing their parents, through the normal processes of democracy, any role in "the direction of the course of studies, the management of the schools or . . . the selection of teachers." Given the reality that schools are "culturally sensitive institutions" dealing with "areas of irreconcilable differences between denominations," conflict was inevitable. While in other parts of the state, as Benjamin Justice has shown, disagreement over the denominational character of schooling arose only rarely and was usually resolved without much difficulty, "simply because of the scale of its operation [the Free School Society] could never satisfy the various publics of New York City."[63]

At first the Free School Society by no means had a monopoly on education of poor children, or on the state funds for that purpose. A charity school for children of all faiths was opened by Bethel Baptist Church in 1820 and was supported from the common school fund, as were Catholic, Methodist, and Episcopalian schools serving the poor. Quite naturally, in New York City, as elsewhere, the "first impulse of state or city officials interested in subsidizing schooling for the poor was to give aid to existing institutions"[64] rather than to seek to create new ones.

These church-sponsored free schools often served pupils who were not of their denominations and thus competed with the Free School Society's schools. In response to a charge, by the Quaker-dominated Free School Society, that they were admitting non-Baptist children,

> the Baptists argued that the great economy with which they conducted their school was designed not to make a profit but to enable them to accommodate large numbers of poor children who were receiving no education at all. They insisted that their program was as nonsectarian as that of the Free School Society, since they used the same curriculum, relied upon the same Lancastrian methods, and employed the same nondenominational catechism for religious instruction that had recently been in use in the Society's schools. To the chief complaint against them, that they had admitted children of all denominations to their classes, the Baptists responded: "We supposed, innocently enough, indeed, that it was not very material by whose instrumentality the instruction was procured for the poor, whether by a society of Baptists or Friends."[65]

The Society had begun by urging that church-sponsored schools be allowed to enroll only children from their own congregations, but soon escalated its position to argue that no public funds should go to any school associated with a particular denomination, insisting that it could promote religious education *better* than could any of the church-sponsored schools that were receiving a share of the state funds. By 1825 the Society was arguing that "it is totally incompatible with our republican institutions, and a dangerous precedent" to allow any portion of the public money to be spent "by the clergy or church trustees for the support of sectarian education."[66] If the Legislature would grant it a monopoly on public funds, the Society argued, it would be possible "to preserve harmony and good feeling among the various religious sects, by removing all grounds for jealousy and contention." This would also make it possible to create "a uniform system in all the elementary schools of the city."

The instruction provided would still be profoundly religious, as was evident in a manual issued by the Society the next year, instructing teachers to tell their pupils that "the intention of this school is to teach you to be good and useful in this world, that you may be happy in the world to come." This was to be followed by a sort of catechism of moralistic teaching with a vaguely Protestant character.[67] This continued to be the case 15 years later when a special committee of the city's Board of Aldermen found that the program of the Society's schools was "well calculated to impress upon the minds of children, a distinct idea of the value of religion; the importance of the domestic and social duties; the existence of God, the creator of all things; the immortality of the soul; man's future accountability; present dependence upon a superintending providence; and other moral sentiments, which do not conflict with sectarian views and peculiarities."[68]

Kaestle suggests that "the Society objected to scattered denominational schools not as much because they were sectarian as because they made the Society's enrollment, and therefore their space requirements and financial aid, uncertain. They competed with the Society's schools, and the Society had decided that competition was not the best way to provide schooling."[69] Monopoly, in its competent and disinterested hands, would be much more efficient.

Seeking to resolve this controversy, the state legislature "directed the city's Common Council to take charge of the division of the common school fund within the city . . . the Common Council passed an ordinance in 1825 denying common school funds to any religious society."[70] No doubt this decision was strongly influenced by the elite membership of the Free School Society's board. Although it sought an effective monopoly of publicly supported schooling, the Society was insistent that it was a voluntary association of the most prominent citizens, not a branch of government, arguing that "all experience will demonstrate that public objects are better accomplished by these voluntary servants, than they are usually accomplished by persons chosen directly by the people."[71] Far from reducing "sectarian" tensions, the approval by the state Legislature of the renamed "Public School Society" (1826) would lead to a bitter conflict with the growing Catholic population of New York City.

Gradually, a number of denominational schools were turned over to the Society, relieving the churches and voluntary associations that had founded them of a financial burden. One sponsored by an Episcopalian parish became a "public" school in 1826, and in 1834 the Manumission Society surrendered the seven schools that it had created since 1785 to serve the children of free blacks; "this consolidation resulted at first in reduced attendance by Negro children because of the insensitivity of the Public School Society."[72]

The schools operated by the Public School Society "bore the stigma of their pauper origins." Though they sought to expand their clientele to children whose parents could afford to pay tuition, in the 1820s "for every child in the Society's schools there were three in private schools and another three in no school at all." Nevertheless, the enrolment continued to grow with the city's population; the Society expanded its network of schools, growing from 1,000 pupils in 1817 to 12,000 in 1834 and more than 20,000 in 1839.[73]

The Society was permitted to levy a local tax to support its schools, and Catholics and other religious groups sought public funding for their own schools in the name of fairness; in 1822, 1832, and in 1840 religious groups challenged the effective monopoly that the Society achieved on state funding for schooling, with Protestants as well as Catholics joining in the challenges. Catholic Bishop John Hughes charged, in 1840, that the administration of what now called itself the "Public School Society" was such that "parents or guardians of Catholic children cannot allow them to frequent such schools without doing violence to their rights of conscience." Parents should not be forced "to see their children brought up under a system of free-thinking and practical irreligion,"[74] and in fact "of about 12,000 Catholic children in the city in the late 1830s, only a few hundred were enrolled" in the Society's schools.

Ravitch comments that the primary concern of Catholics was not with removing "Protestant" elements from the instruction provided in the Society's schools, but rather with providing distinctively Catholic instruction. In fact, in 1840, "the Catholics offered to place their schools under the supervision of the Public School Society, in order to allay fears that public funds would be used for sectarian purposes. If they were given public funds, they promised all religious instruction would be offered after school hours." Although a Catholic publication charged that the schools of the Public School Society were "deist, sectarian, and anti-Catholic, . . . the clergy did not cooperate in editing biased material out of the books, because they knew that to do so would remove one of the best complaints they had against the schools of the Society."[75] The "controlling influence" on these schools, a Catholic petition charged, was that of Quakers,[76] with their emphasis on personal religious experience; indeed, Joseph Lancaster himself and many of his American supporters, like John Griscom, were Quakers. The petitioners wrote that, although the Public School Society was composed of men from different denominations,

> that denomination, Friends, which is believed to have the controlling influence . . . holds as a peculiar *sectarian principle* that any formal or official teaching of religion is, at best, unprofitable. And your petitioners have discovered that such of *their* children as have attended the public schools, are generally, and at an early age, imbued

with the same principle—that they become intractable, disobedient, and even con-temptuous toward their parents—unwilling to learn anything of religion—as if they had become illuminated, and could receive all the knowledge of religion necessary for them by instinct or inspiration.[77]

Drawing upon the Society's own publications, the petitioners argued that in fact the instructions provided in its schools were thoroughly and intentionally religious, asking sarcastically, "and yet in all these 'early religious instructions, religious impressions, and religious influences,' essentially anti-Catholic, your petitioners are to see nothing sectarian."[78] "To the [Society's] assertion that the schools had the confidence of all classes, [Bishop] Hughes countered that the Society has been so ineffective in overcoming the reluctance of poor parents to send their children to its schools that it had applied for a "legal enactment . . . to compel an attendance."[79] This compulsion included a decision by the city council, in 1832, that impoverished families that did not send their children to school would not be "entitled, in case of misfortune, to receive public favor,"[80] that is, relief payments.

Katz points out that "paternalistic voluntarism" as exemplified by the Public School Society was criticized, and not only by the Catholic hierarchy, because it

ignored the variety of American life and reflected an unacceptable cultural bias by imposing uniform services upon a diverse clientele. Although often couched in reli-gious terms, this criticism revealed a perception of important cultural differences of which religious doctrines served as symptoms. To the opponents of the Society, religious differences represented one form of cultural variation, towards which a democratic state had to remain neutral. Herein rested a dilemma: schools were cul-turally sensitive institutions; by definition they touched the areas of irreconcilable difference between denominations. The result was an inverse relation between the size of the school system and the degree of satisfaction it could offer its clientele.[81]

Governor William Seward attempted to head off sectarian conflict by recom-mending to the Legislature, in his 1840 Annual Message, that state funds be provided to support schools with "teachers speaking the same language with themselves, and professing the same faith." Only in this way, he argued, could the state ensure "the education of the entire rising generation in all the elements of knowledge we possess, and in that tongue which is the universal language of our countrymen."[82] Horace Mann and other crusaders for the common public school were deeply disturbed and publicly opposed this measure.[83] Protestant denominations that previously had sought and accepted public funding for their own charity schools suddenly discovered a principled objection to such subsidies. New York Methodists, for example, insisted "that the control of popular elementary education belonged to the state" and even "that attendance at these state schools [should] be made compulsory."[84]

Supporting the concerns of Catholics, New York Secretary of State John Spencer argued, in 1841, that "in a country where the great body of our fellow-citizens recognize the fundamental truths of Christianity, public sentiment would be shocked by the attempt to exclude all instruction of a religious nature from the public schools; and that any plan or schema of education, in which no reference whatever was had to moral principle founded on these truths, would be abandoned by all." Citing the First Amendment to the national Constitution, Spencer argued that the government had wisely abstained "from all legislation whatever on those subjects . . . connected with religious faith, profession, or instruction" by leaving it up to local communities to decide how religion would be treated in their schools.

The solution, Spencer proposed, was to be found in what Katz calls "democratic localism," leaving it up to each local community within New York City, as was already the case in the more rural parts of the state, to make decisions about what was taught in its schools, and on what basis. Thus, he wrote, "each district suits itself, by having such religious instruction in its school as is congenial to the opinions of its inhabitants." As a result, "the records of this department have been searched in vain for an instance of a complaint of any abuse of this authority, in any of the schools" outside of New York City. In a religiously diverse city like New York, however, finding a form of religious instruction that would satisfy all the different groups was impossible, and even the moderate degree of religious instruction that the Public School Society imparts must, therefore, be sectarian; that is, it must favor one set of opinions in

> opposition to another, or others; and it is believed that this always will be the result in any course of education that the wit of man can devise. . . . If that Society had charge of the children of one denomination only, there would be no difficulty. It is because it embraces children of all denominations, and seeks to supply to them all a species of instruction which is adapted only to a part, and which, from its nature, cannot be moulded to suit the views of all, that it fails, and ever must fail, to give satisfaction on a subject of all others the most vital and the most exciting.[85]

A recent exhaustive study of New York State records over most of the nineteenth century has confirmed Spencer's claim that there was little conflict over religious instruction in the smaller and more homogeneous communities.[86]

The position of the Public School Society, Spencer charged, also "calls for no action or cooperation on the part of those parents, other than the entire submission of their children to the government and guidance of others, probably strangers, and who are in no way accountable to these parents." The only solution for "the degree and kind" of religious instruction would be to leave it to the choice of parents in small homogeneous communities, in the city as in small towns. According to Spencer, "If it was the will of the people to have religious training in the public schools, then so be it."[87] Consistent with this prescription, the state legislature enacted, in 1842, a system of ward schools in New York City, managed by locally elected school boards as in smaller communities across the state, under the financial supervision of a citywide elected Board of Education with limited authority over the content of schooling. Under this arrangement, local ward committees were responsible for overseeing schools in their districts and could adjust their program to local and parental sensibilities. Spencer predicted that competition among the new school districts in New York City would improve school quality, since the funds would be allocated on the basis of enrolment.[88]

The Public School Society continued to receive public money for the schools it was already operating, but in 1853 turned over its remaining schools to the elected Board,[89] leaving to the city's school system a "legacy . . . of clearly defined hierarchy and standardization." In place of the previous disjointed provision of schooling, by the 1850s "the vertical extension of the system was complete. . . . students passed through it according to explicit, standard rules, in theory, at least." There was also a defined career path for employees of the system, from monitor up to superintendent, while "the moral mission of the schools reinforced the bureaucratic trend toward standardization. The schools became institutions set apart from, and, in some respects, opposed to the rest of the students' world."[90] What historian David Tyack (1974) has ironically named "The One Best System" was already coming into existence, with all its immediate strengths and ultimate weaknesses. "It is somewhat ironic," Kaestle comments, "that the schools became more conformist as the population became more diverse. . . . the public schools as a coordinated system were transformed into an instrument of great potential influence, for they were now amenable to uniform policy decisions."[91]

One historian interprets the conflict over funding of denominational and other alternative schools as merely one of the early examples of ongoing conflict between minorities and the dominant majority, more recently exemplified by the battles over the control of schools in the Ocean Hill–Brownsville section of Brooklyn between the New York public school system (and the teachers' union) and black community leaders. "To the opponents of the Society,"

Katz wrote, "religious differences represented one form of cultural variation toward which a democratic state had to remain neutral."[92] It would be more accurate, however, to put the conflict in New York City in the 1830s and 1840s in the context of contemporary issues in Europe: in country after country, governments were beginning to sponsor religiously neutral schools, and Catholic leaders were resisting, in terms very similar to those used by Bishop Hughes, what they saw as an infringement on the right of the church to determine the character of the instruction provided to Catholic children. The issue was not, in the United States or in Europe, what could accurately be called "cultural"; it had to do with which explicit worldview would be promoted by the schools, and whether a democratic society should support a pluralistic educational system or whether it was more important to seek to create a single model of citizenship based upon shared beliefs.

Orestes Brownson, who would in 1844 become a convert to Catholicism, and thereafter one of its most vigorous proponents, argued in 1839 that "a nonsectarian approach to education was impossible because religion or Christianity did not exist in the abstract; it resided in concrete historical communities with creeds and beliefs that were shared." In the common school urged by Horace Mann and other reformers, Brownson wrote, much could be taught in general, "but nothing in particular. No sect will be satisfied; all sects will be dissatisfied."[93] This should be no surprise, he suggested: "Mann knows nothing of the philosophy of Education because he knows nothing of the philosophy of human nature."[94]

The proponents of the common public school found this line of reasoning not only unconvincing but dangerous. The Rev Barnas Sears, Horace Mann's successor, wrote in the Massachusetts Board's Eighteenth Annual Report (1855) that some misguided persons had argued that "schools, having a distinctively religious character, should be established independently of the government," while others sought to banish religion altogether from the common school.

The zeal of the advocates of this theory went so far, that, in the regulations established by some school committees, even prayer was prohibited in the schools. Time, by giving opportunity for sober reflection and more careful observation, has done much towards correcting both these extreme views. The one class have become satisfied that nothing but public schools, vigorously supported, will prevent an alarming growth of the uneducated classes; that the children of emigrants, now swarming in our cities and manufacturing towns, will, unless brought into our public schools, soon form a dangerous part of our population; and that, while we are separating our children from each other in their education, in order to train them according to our several creeds, the very foundations of society will be rendered insecure, by the fearful amount of brute force that will be accumulating around us, breathing the spirit of riot and misrule.

The other class have come to see that a government cannot long perpetuate itself by means of mere secular education . . . that what is most needed in our country, at the present time, is a race of men of thorough-going and unbending integrity, such as can be found only where the law of God has been instilled into the mind as the rule of right; and that a reverence for divine things and for the Supreme Being, breathed by the conscientious teacher into the hearts of the young, especially of those who receive no such lessons at home, is indispensable for the preservation of social order among men.[95]

The following year, after the overwhelming victory of the "Know-Nothings" in Massachusetts elections, the Board's Nineteenth Annual Report warned about the degrading influence of "the presence of a foreign race of men" in even stronger terms, pointing out that "the domestics in our houses form a part of the circle in which our children are reared. Falsehood, deception, and petty frauds, practiced daily in the nursery and about our homes, by persons in our employ, will leave their effect on the tender susceptibilities of childhood." The foreign men working in gardens, farms, and workshops, "uttering words of profanity and of vulgarity, are acting most effectually in destroying the virtuous sensibilities of our sons, and in sowing the seeds of vice." Nor was that all:

The influx of a more intelligent class of foreigners, educated in the corrupt monarchies of the old world, brings with it other perilous influences, besieging the very citadel of our social virtues. The refined epicurism and infidelity. Imported largely at this time from countries where the popular religion [i.e. Catholicism] is a state trick or a farce, is in danger of being diffused in social circles by men of some literary and scientific pretension.[96]

In the midst of these controversies, the actual school enrollment of the poorest children languished. The shift of mission of New York City's Public School Society, toward serving the children of tuition-paying or at least moderately prosperous families as well as poor children, created pressure to exclude those among the poor who might discourage attendance by the more affluent. Requirements for dress, cleanliness, and regularity of attendance tended to exclude children from the most impoverished and disorganized families. "After 1850 this failure of the public schools to attract or admit the poorest students prompted renewed efforts by charitable societies to establish vocational and mission schools in the slums. In 1869 Matthew Smith wrote that there were 40,000 vagrant poor children, mostly of immigrant families, who are 'too dirty, too ragged, and carry too much vermin about them, to be admitted to the public schools.'" The Public School Society's first historian shifted the blame: "In proportion as the comfortably clad and cleanly and polished pupil makes his appearance, the opposite class shrink from contact." Whatever the precise dynamic, it was evident that schooling was not universal among the poor. In fact, Kaestle suggests, the provision of schooling for poor children in New York City was not notably more universal in the middle of the nineteenth century than it had been in the 1790s, during a period when the city's population had increased tenfold; "the most significant changes in this period were rather in the organization and purpose of the schools,"[97] as they became an instrument of public policy to transform the children of immigrants, rather than a religiously motivated effort to serve and save the poor.

It was, above all, the perceived need to achieve a uniform and effective socialization—what a later generation would call "Americanization"—of the children of immigrants that led to the creation of bureaucratically organized and centralized urban school systems in such contrast with the typical American pattern of dispersed and rather informal—but not less effective for that, as Tocqueville found—schooling initiatives. In the long run, the sensible and sensitive proposal by Secretary of State Spencer to allow immigrant communities in cities to control their schools as was the norm elsewhere in America could not allay the concern in elite circles about the use that "degraded" immigrant parents would make of the opportunity to decide about the education that their children should receive.

Chapter Six

Toward the Educator-State

As we have seen, schooling in the early Republic was overwhelmingly organized and controlled locally, often at the level of the one-room school. Reliance on local decision-making, though much attenuated in recent decades, has continued to be the basic American pattern, in contrast with comparable societies.[1] From more than 100,000 local districts in the early twentieth century, the number has been reduced through consolidation to about 15,000, but these continue to hire their administrators and teachers, open and close schools, and make countless other decisions within the framework of state and to some extent national legislation, regulations, and court decisions. This does not mean, it should be noted, that individual public *schools* in these districts enjoy significant autonomy, and frustration with the rigidity of local systems is a major factor in the rapid spread of public "charter schools."

For two centuries, the power of local decision-making has been deplored by those who saw popular schooling as an instrument of social transformation guided by the state. As Samuel Spear wrote in 1876, "[t]he State itself is a moral teacher. . . . The public school, as the instrumentality of an American State, whose creature it is and for whose purposes and by whose authority it exists, is sufficiently explained and justified by being patterned after the State."[2] Pioneer sociologist Lester F. Ward, in 1883, "proposed a planned society. Man had the obligation to sit in the driver's seat of life and *make* a better society, argued Ward. The only safe foundation for a progressive social order was the systematic education of the young. But universal education was not enough; a particular kind of education was needed that must provide the student with an understanding of his or her relation to society."[3] It was up to the state to guide this process, since, as economist Richard Ely (1886) wrote, "if there is anything divine on this earth, it is the state, the product of the same God-given instincts which led to the establishment of the church and the family."[4] With the eclipse of the latter (a point on which John Dewey insisted), it was evident to influential educators like Ellwood P. Cubberley (1909) that "each year the child is coming to belong more to the state, and less and less to the parent."[5]

Such claims would have been inconceivable when the model of local school organization was carried by settlers from New England into upstate New York and on into Ohio and the upper Midwest. This pattern of extreme decentralization is, according to one's perspective, either the major strength and glory of the American educational system or, rather, the principal barrier to effective standardization and accountability. State governments and even the national government were not altogether inactive in relation to schooling, but their role was primarily fiscal and even in that respect supplementary. The goals and methods of instruction were debated locally; the interventions of state government were hortatory rather than regulatory, as when the Massachusetts legislature passed its 1789 school law, urging all teachers, whether at Harvard College, in private academies, or in district schools,

> to take diligent care, and to impress upon the minds of children and youth, committed to their care and instruction, the principles of piety, justice, and a sacred regard for truth, love to their country, humanity, and universal benevolence, sobriety, industry and frugality, chastity, moderation and temperance, and those other virtues which are the ornament of human society, and the basis upon which the Republican Constitution is structured.[6]

The Vermont *Constitution* of 1777 stipulated that "a school or schools shall be established in every town, by the legislature, for the convenient instruction of youth, with such salaries to the masters paid by each town, making proper use of school lands in each town, thereby to enable them to instruct youth at low prices." The Pennsylvania *Constitution* of 1790 ordered that "the legislature shall, so soon as conveniently may be, provide, by law, for the establishment of schools throughout the State, in such manner that the poor may be taught *gratis*."[7] In nine other state constitutions as of 1800, however, there was no mention of education, nor has it ever been mentioned in the federal *Constitution*.

Not that the national government was altogether inactive with respect to schooling. In addition to efforts to promote schooling for Indians on the frontiers through subsidizing missionary organizations,[8] Congress provided support for schools through the management of lands in the West. The Northwest Ordinance, adopted by Congress in 1787 to provide a basis for the organization of territories west of Pennsylvania and New York, allocated land for the support of schools and of churches so that "Religion, morality, and knowledge being necessary to good government and the happiness of mankind, schools and the means of education shall forever be encouraged." Through the influence of a group of investors from New England who had formed the Ohio Company in 1786, the Ordinance provided that part of the land of each township in the new territories should be used as an endowment for schools, while another part was set aside for the promotion of religion.

> The original provision for the endowment of public schools out of the public domain came in direct response to the proposals of prospective New England settlers who desired to have schools in the wilderness to take the place of those they were planning to leave behind them. The government saw in the vast national domain a means of paying off the national debt if settlers could be induced to purchase land in the distant frontier country.[9]

While the Northwest Ordinance sought to attract settlers from New England for whom schools were essential, in turn "it was no less the increase of New England settlers and the gradual prevalence of the New England idea in education which caused the original legal impulse toward a public system of education to develop in the states of the Northwest Territory into a full-fledged state system of schools."[10] In 1803 Congress applied the same policy of public land endowment for education to the states to be formed out of the Mississippi Territory, and in 1826 it was also applied to the huge territory acquired through the Louisiana Purchase.

Although the federal government had no authority with respect to education (apart from its efforts to "civilize" the Cherokee and other native peoples)[11] it did have an influence at several crucial points through the resources which it provided to the states and they in turn to local schools, whether public or private. Federal reimbursements to Massachusetts for costs connected with the War of 1812 played an important role in promoting common schools . . . and a similar opportunity was missed in Virginia. The most important federal subsidy, however, was in the form of land grants designated for the support of schools, altogether more than 77 million acres over the course of the nineteenth century. The need to manage the sale or lease of these lands and distribute the (often rather disappointing) proceeds stimulated the development of rudimentary state administrative structures in touch with local communities on matters involving their schools. As the relationship developed by mid-century, in order to qualify for a share of the funds and of any funds appropriated by the states themselves, "local districts typically had to comply with certain minimal requirements, such as keeping schools open for a certain term, hiring only [locally] certified teachers, and submitting records to the state superintendent."[12]

Thus the state role in schooling—apart from the rhetoric of state constitutions—was long a matter of financial book-keeping rather than of determining how education would be provided and for what purposes.

Although the controversies over religion and schooling have tended to dominate historical writing about this period, it seems more accurate to say that—apart from New York City—these issues became acute only in the 1870s.

It was as government influence was extended into sensitive areas of local community life that conflicts over education—conflicts that have continued, in one form or another, down to the present—became a constant theme of American politics. There was, for example, ample precedent among the private academies in Massachusetts and Connecticut for the sort of liberal approach to Protestant beliefs that Mann sought to promote, but it had aroused no conflict beyond—very occasionally—the individual institution. Only when Mann attempted to use state-approved schoolbooks and the preparation of teachers under state auspices to influence local schools did orthodox Protestants and then Catholics began to object.

At first it was by no means clear that responsibility for assimilating immigrants and shaping them into Americans would be assumed by the state. The lead, as we have seen, had been taken by churches and church-related voluntary associations, and religious publications did a great deal to create a sense of urgency for the spread and improvement of schooling. Less explicitly religious—though by no means excluding religious appeals for popular schooling—were such publications as William Russell's *American Journal of Education* (founded in Boston in 1826 and continuing until 1831), Horace Mann's *Common School Journal*, and Henry Barnard's *American Journal of Education* (starting in 1855 and destined to exert a wide influence).

Local, state, regional, and national associations gave reformers an opportunity to share their experiences and then to return home to encourage their fellow-citizens to support the reform efforts. "The process by which educational improvement was accomplished was one of education of the people to desire better school conditions, to be willing to achieve such conditions for themselves, and to consent to putting some pressure, through legislation, on such of their fellow citizens as were somewhat slower in becoming educated." But that pressure could not be too strong, lest it evoke a reaction leading to repeal of the legislation, as happened in Connecticut, Michigan, and other states.

> Under such circumstances, the most effective agency of educational improvement was permissive legislation, which gave the more progressive communities the legal right to bring about desired changes, while the remainder of the state might be allowed to continue in old ways. Then, after a reasonable period in which the power of good example had had the opportunity of doing its work, and in which a safe majority of all the communities in the state had accepted the conditions of the permissive law, it could be made mandatory in its provisions. With a solid majority in its favor, pressure could safely be brought upon the recalcitrant communities to come up to the goal originally aimed at.[13]

The evangelical concern for moral and social reform was taken up by Americans who were not themselves evangelicals; its rhetorical style seemed to fit the mood of the day. Ralph Waldo Emerson commented sardonically about a lecture by Horace Mann in September 1839, that it was "full of the modern gloomy view of our democratical institutions, and hence the inference to the importance of schools."[14]

Nor were these efforts necessarily ineffective in the absence of state leadership and supervision of local schooling efforts; even in New England state government "made no provision during the period [before the mid-1830s] for the supervision by state educational officers of the efforts of the local authorities." Typical was a Massachusetts law enacted in 1826 which required towns to elect school committees that would have authority over the schools in the various districts of which the town was made up, thus transferring from the district to the town the responsibility for selecting textbooks and determining the qualifications of teachers.[15]

While this was an exercise of state authority over schooling, that authority was immediately delegated to local authorities. "Among the Americans," Tocqueville observed before Mann's efforts in education got under way, "the force that the state administers is less well regulated, less enlightened, less skillful, but a hundred times greater than in Europe. There is no country in the world where, after all is said and done, men make as many efforts to create social well-being. I do not know a people who has succeeded in establishing schools as numerous and as efficacious."[16]

Not that the states had ignored the need for popular schooling before Mann and his allies sought new means of extending the influence of state government and thereby of their own convictions about the nature of an appropriate education. Pennsylvania and North Carolina in 1776, Georgia and Vermont in

1777, and Massachusetts in 1780, "had made some broad provision for public education in their constitutions; however, the idea of general tax support
for schools, rather than parent-paid tuition, enjoyed little support anywhere"[17]
until the crisis over the Americanization of immigrant children. Governor
Caleb Strong of Massachusetts urged his legislature, in 1816, to require that
children working in mills be educated. Governor De Witt Clinton of New York
told his legislature, in 1822, that "The first duty of a state is to render its citizens virtuous by intellectual instruction and moral discipline, by enlightening
their minds, purifying their hearts, and teaching them their rights and their
obligations."[18] Examples could be multiplied, but effective measures continued to depend upon local rather than upon state initiatives throughout this
period.

Horace Mann set an example of aggressive state leadership after 1837, though
his efforts were by no means unique; it was a period when, parallel with and
to some extent inspired by the evangelical associations and other voluntary
efforts in support of social reform, there was a growing willingness to think in
terms of public action to promote "internal improvements," both physical and
social. "In his annual messages, [Massachusetts Governor] Levi Lincoln in one
breath could speak of the benefits accruing to the people of New York from the
Erie Canal, and in the next, laud the blessings Connecticut was bringing to its
citizens by supporting the work of Thomas Gallaudet with the deaf and dumb."
There was a growing belief that problems long considered an inevitable part
of human existence—poverty, disease, hunger, and ignorance—could now
be eradicated. The optimism overran class lines, cut across political loyalties,
and was shared by members of every religious denomination. Lincoln even
thought that education could be reformed radically by systematizing teaching
into a scientific pedagogy and had called upon the legislature to build a state
teachers seminary for this purpose.[19]

James Carter wrote in his influential *Essays on Popular Education* (1826)
that "[u]pon this topic of popular education, a *free* government must be *arbitrary*." The objective of educational action by government had little to do with
economic or egalitarian goals; it was to shape future citizens to a common pattern. Like Rousseau and educational theorists during the French Revolution,
Carter turned to the model of Sparta to illustrate what the State could and
should do. "If the Spartan could mold and transform a nation to suit his taste,
by means of an early education, why may not the same be done at the present
day?"[20] He was neither the first nor the last American to reach for this example; Samuel Adams, a generation earlier, had called upon Americans to show
the world "how to conciliate republicanism and virtue by founding their own
'Christian Sparta.'"[21] A few years after Carter, speaking at the dedication of a

state normal school, John Quincy Adams cited Sparta and Prussia as examples to follow.[22]

The 1827 Massachusetts law required that each town support its schools by taxation, in contrast with most other states, where that remained a voluntary decision until the 1870s and beyond, and added a provision that Horace Mann would later use as the basis for his efforts to modify the religious character of the common schools. Section 7 of the 1827 law required that the local school committee "shall never direct any school books to be purchased or used, in any of the schools under their superintendence, which are calculated to favour any particular religious sect or tenet."[23]

With Carter playing a key legislative role, Massachusetts created a School Fund in 1834 with part of the $2 million provided to the state by the federal government as compensation for militia who had served in the War of 1812. The following year, in a bill specifying how income from the Fund would be distributed, the reformers

> included a seemingly innocuous stipulation that only those towns which furnished detailed information on their schools to the legislature would receive state aid. The bill thus introduced a precedent for coercion by the state. Reformers also would make good use of information provided by the towns. Galvanized by the prospect of a windfall, 258 towns out of 301 immediately complied with the law; almost 100% would do so within a few years. Reformers therefore were provided with new data on town schools that they used as evidence of widespread departure from norms established by their own circle.[24]

This data was used effectively by Horace Mann in the series of annual reports which were his primary means of exercising influence and the basis of his effective advocacy with local officials.

HORACE MANN[25]

Perhaps the key to the influence exerted by Mann was the conviction with which he asserted the wonders that public schools could accomplish, a conviction that, if not borrowed from the Utopian reformers, was held no less passionately by Mann than by Robert Owen. "As an innovation upon all pre-existing policy and usages," Horace Mann wrote in 1846, "the establishment of Free Schools was the boldest ever promulgated, since the commencement of the Christian era." Massachusetts could be especially proud, he claimed in his *Tenth Annual Report of the Secretary of the Board of Education*, because "there is not at the present time, with the exception of New England and a few small localities elsewhere, a State or a community in Christendom, which maintains a system of Free Schools for the education of its children. Even in the State of New York, with all its noble endowments, the Schools are not Free."[26] In fact, he was being charitable; the neighbor-states Connecticut and Rhode Island did not have universally free public schools for another two decades.

Mann (1796–1859) is the best-known of the nineteenth-century educational reformers in the United States, and his annual reports were widely read in other states and in Europe and even Latin America. He was, however, never a schoolteacher, nor did he show much interest in schools until, as a successful attorney and Massachusetts Senate President, he began to deal with schooling as a sphere for State action.

Perhaps because his background was not in the classroom, Mann tended to speak and write about the possibilities of education in the most utopian terms. Though, as a legislator, he had refused appointment to the Committee on Education (choosing, instead, the more influential Judiciary Committee), he gave an early indication of how he would present education reform in a decisive speech during a Senate debate. "Sir," he said, "the folly of sitting still, while houses adjoining mine, on either side, are on fire, is not to be compared with the folly, in a government like ours, of neglecting the education of the young."[27] Five years later he concluded an Independence Day oration by warning that "licentiousness shall be the liberty; violence and chicanery shall be the law; superstition and craft shall be the religion; and the self-destructive indulgence of all sensual and unhallowed passions shall be the only happiness, of that people who neglect the education of their children."[28]

And education, despite the Puritan tradition of universal schooling, was being neglected, Mann charged when he became the first Massachusetts official with that responsibility. The reports which he received from local communities "told a story of neglect, parsimony, apathy, and sometimes even chaos."[29] Or so Mann concluded, though evidence suggests that "long before the common-school reform movement and the creation of state free-school systems, beginning at least as early as the late eighteenth century, the proportion of children attending school each year was rising, particularly among girls and particularly in the Northeast."[30]

A leading figure in the educational program of the French Third Republic at the end of the nineteenth century wrote about Mann that he had been "neither a philosopher of education, not a practitioner, but a militant, a tribune, a missionary who went from city to city, from village to village, peddling his ideas and his faith, a Peter the Hermit preaching a crusade against ignorance."[31] With the correction that Mann's "crusade" (an image he used himself) was not against ignorance so much as it was against unenlightened attitudes and beliefs, this is an accurate description. Mann and his allies had no direct authority over local schools, but they sought, through every means of influence, to have a powerful effect upon elementary classrooms and thus to shape the rising generation and the American future. "It may be an easy thing to make a Republic," Mann would write in his final report as Secretary of the Board, "but it is a very laborious thing to make Republicans.[32] Compare this to the often-quoted lament of Mann's Italian contemporary, Massimo d'Azeglio: "Unfortunately, we created Italy, but Italians were not created" (*purtroppo s'è fatta l'Italia, ma non si fanno gli Italiani*).[33]

Although Mann appreciated the role of voluntary associations in pressing for reforms, he grew convinced through his work for temperance reform that "the task of reformation was beyond the scope of sectarian and partisan groups and had gone beyond the control of public opinion and local law enforcement[;] it was therefore necessary to exert the superior authority of the Commonwealth."[34] One can see here the seeds of what have been continuing conflicts over education between state and national government—responsive to elite opinion and (more recently) to education professionals—and families, churches, and local government.

Mann made his initial reputation as a reformer, not with schools, but with the creation, through legislative action, of the first state insane asylum. "It was a time when men believed the deaf could be taught to 'hear,' the dumb to 'talk,' and the blind to 'see.' To an age that expressed a faith in science, progress, and the perfectibility of men, the insane were an ultimate challenge."[35] Like other Whigs, Mann admired "strong, paternalistic governments that assumed responsibility for the intellectual, moral, and physical welfare of their citizens. A wise statesman was 'like a father' to his people. . . . 'There is a science of moral economy, as well as a science of political economy.'"[36] For Whigs in the 1830s, "public schools represented a massive institutionalization of the Whig dedication to redeeming people. . . . The Whigs assumed that human nature was malleable. It could and should be shaped by schools, benevolent societies, reformatories, asylums."[37]

A crucial step was taken by the Massachusetts legislature in 1837, when it voted to create a state Board of Education to collect information about schools and to provide advice on how schools could be improved. Although several states had earlier given one of their officials responsibility for overseeing the distribution of the (limited) state funds provided to local schools and to academies, this was the first instance in which a state official made effective use of a charge to improve the quality of education.[38] The Massachusetts action was in response to a petition by the American Institute of Instruction (founded in

Boston in 1830 and destined to play a leading role in antebellum education reform) and a message from Governor Edward Everett,

> an admirer of the Prussian system of State oversight of schooling, who wrote to the legislature, While nothing can be farther from my purpose, than to disparage the common schools as they are, and while a deep sense of personal obligation to them will ever be cherished by me, it must yet be candidly admitted, that they are susceptible of great improvements. . . . The wealth of Massachusetts always has been, and always will be, the minds of her children.[39]

The new board was "granted no direct authority over the schools; its primary function was enlightenment,"[40] as Mann himself told a statewide education convention that year.[41] Everett appointed Mann to the Board, from which he soon resigned to take the paid position of Board Secretary, that is, its executive officer. "Having found the present generation composed of materials almost unmalleable," Mann wrote at the time, "I am about transferring my efforts to the next. Men are cast-iron, but children are wax. Strength expended upon the latter may be effectual which would make no impression on the former."[42] In the first issue of his *Common School Journal* (1838), through which he sought to influence public opinion as well as teachers, Mann wrote that "If we would have improved men, we must have improved means of educating children. . . . Of all the means in our possession, the common school has precedence, because of its universality." Even more boldly, in 1841, he claimed that "the Common School is the greatest discovery ever made by man. . . . Other social organizations are curative and remedial; this is preventive and an antidote. . . . Let the Common School be expanded to its capabilities, let it be worked with the efficiency of which it is susceptible, and nine tenths of the crimes in the penal code would become obsolete; the long catalogue of human ills would be abridged."[43]

Mann traveled tirelessly around Massachusetts to mobilize local elites in support of his vision of a centrally coordinated (though not centrally controlled) system of common schools; "he held up the common school as the only agency capable of moral education in an age of endemic sectarianism. . . . Basically, . . . its function was neither economical nor political, but moral."[44]

What could be accomplished through a state-directed system of schooling, Mann and his allies believed was almost unlimited. In its *Third Report* (1840), drafted by Mann, the Board of Education stressed that "the state, in its sovereign capacity, has the deepest interest in this matter" of popular enlightenment.

In this way, the state could "call into existence an order of men" who would be unlike any before.[45]

In his last report as Secretary of the Board of Education, Mann reported, on the basis of a survey of some of his fellow-reformers (as if they were impartial judges!),

> their belief, that, if all the children in the community, from the age of four years to that of sixteen, could be brought within the reformatory and elevating influences of good schools, the dark host of private vices and public crimes, which now embitter domestic peace and stain the civilization of the age, might, in ninety-nine cases of every hundred, be banished from the world. . . . without any miracle, without any extraordinary sacrifices, of costly effort, but only by working our existing Common School system with such a degree of vigor as can easily be put forth, and at such an expense as even the poorest community can easily bear.[46]

And he affirmed his own conviction that the Common School was "the most effective and benignant of all the forces of civilization," in large part because of the "universality of its operation." A few years earlier, writing privately to encourage his ally Henry Barnard, who was attempting to expand the state role in Rhode Island after losing his position in Connecticut, Mann predicted that "If Rhode Island passes that bill . . . in one generation it will regenerate the mass of her people."[47]

Mann lamented that many parents seemed to have little concern for the quality of schooling, while others who did have that concern were putting their children into the semi-public academies which had received significant state and local government support since the 1790s.

> Opposite to this class, who tolerate, from apathy, a depression in the common schools, there is another class who affix so high a value upon the culture of their children, and understand so well the necessity of a skillful preparation of means for its bestowment, that they turn away from the common schools, in their depressed state, and seek, elsewhere, the helps of a more enlarged and thorough education. . . . One party pays an adequate price, but has a poor school; the other has a good school, but at more than fourfold cost.

Those who were turning to the private academies, Mann conceded, were not only the wealthy, but "another portion, numerically much greater, who, whether rich or poor, have a true perception of the sources of their children's individual and domestic well-being." Mann admitted that "the patrons of the private school plead the moral necessity of sustaining it, because, they say, some of the children in the public school are so addicted to profanity or obscenity, so prone to trickishness or to vulgar and mischievous habits, as to render a removal of their own children from such contaminating influences an obligatory precaution." But this, he insisted, was shortsighted, arguing that those same watchful parents, by a commitment to the common public school, would swiftly overcome "these repellent causes." They should reflect that "after a few swift years, those children, whose welfare they now discard, and whose associations they deprecate" would constitute the adults to whom their own children would be "vulnerable at every point, and utterly incapable of finding a hiding-place for any earthly treasure." Instead, in the common school, "a general acquaintanceship should be formed between the children of the same neighborhood" to form "a stable possession to fraternal feelings, against the alienating competitions of subsequent life." Mann repeated this argument in similarly dramatic terms in his fourth annual report.[48]

Kaestle and Vinovskis observe that Mann and other reformers saw the defeat of private schooling as a high priority. In a long series of articles which he wrote for his *Common School Journal*, Mann urged "the professional men of Massachusetts" to put their own children in the common schools rather than in private academies, warning that, otherwise, "the distinctions of the dark ages, and of aristocratic governments, will be revived on these happy shores."[49]

In addition to this concern about social class distinctions, Mann was even more urgently opposed to schools representing a distinctive religious view-point, warning in his first annual report as Secretary of the Board that

> the tendency of the private school system is to assimilate our modes of education to those of England, where churchmen and dissenters . . . maintain separate schools, in which children are taught, from their tenderest years, to wield the sword of polemics with fatal dexterity; and where the gospel, instead of being a temple of peace, is converted into an armory of deadly weapons, for social, interminable warfare. Of such disastrous consequences, there is but one remedy and one preventive. It is the elevation of the common schools.[50]

Of course, he was wrong about England, where the maintenance, to this day, of publicly funded schools of various denominations has been accompanied by a high degree of secularization rather than by religious conflict. His next target in this vein, however, was even less a real threat: the little Shaker community of the rural community of Shirley, which refused to allow the town authorities to examine their teacher or inspect their school. Mann considered this a very dangerous precedent:

> If a difference of opinion, on collateral subjects [of course, the Shakers did not con-sider their religious beliefs "collateral"] were to lead to secession, and to exclusive educational establishments among us, it is obvious that all the multiplication of power which is now derived from union and concert of action would be lost. . . . if once the principle of secession be admitted, because of differences in religious opinion, all hope of sustaining the system itself must be abandoned. . . . our school system—alike the glory of the past, and the hope of the future—would be broken into fragments. . . . Civilization would counter-march, retracing its steps far more rapidly than it had ever advanced; . . . whoever would instigate desertion, or withdraw resources, from the common cause is laboring, either ignorantly or willfully, to shroud the land in the darkness of the middle ages, and to reconstruct those oppressive institutions of for-mer times, from which our fathers achieved the deliverance of this country.[51]

If this seems rather extreme language to apply to the desire of the world-shunning Shakers to be left alone to raise the foster children they had taken in, it is an indication of how much Mann believed was at stake when he insisted upon the importance of creating a single system of elementary education for all children under state supervision.

Mann had a special animus against private schools, and especially those with a distinctive religious character, but he was also very concerned that such beliefs not creep into the common public school. We have seen that he insisted repeatedly on the religious—indeed, the Christian—character and mission of common schools, but it was with a definition of Christianity which excluded most of the beliefs which are central to traditional Christianity, whether Protestant or Catholic. Such beliefs should be excluded strictly from the com-mon school. This theme recurs constantly in his reports and articles and Mann seems to attach to it an importance which—at least while the "sectarian" views against which he warns were merely those of different Protestant denomina-tions—seems out of proportion with any actual controversies of which we can find traces. After all, Methodists and Presbyterians and Baptists were quite able to cooperate at providing "union Sunday schools" or in sponsoring revivals; it is hard to believe that conflict among them would have doomed the common school in a Massachusetts village. Yet we find Mann insisting, in language he drafted for the third annual report of the Board, that

> any attempt to make the public schools . . . an instrument for advancing or depress-ing the opinions of any sect of christians, would meet what it would merit, the

prompt rebuke of every considerate citizen. Although it may not be easy theo-
retically, to draw the line between those views of religious truth and of christian
faith, which are common to all, and may, therefore, with propriety be inculcated
in school, and those which, being peculiar to individual sects, are therefore by law
excluded; still it is believed, that no practical difficulty occurs in the conduct of our
schools in this respect.[52]

While the new Board of Education had no direct authority over local schools,
Mann was ingenious at finding ways to extend state influence.[53] Using his
strong connections in the Legislature, Mann "composed drafts [of legislation]
to require school committees to keep records and present annual reports to
the Secretary of the Board of Education on buildings, attendance, and salary
expenditures. In addition, he attacked the division of towns into a myriad of
anemic school districts and urged the legislature to mandate consolidation.....
'Every recommendation and suggestion contained in the Reports have been
turned into laws,'" he boasted to an ally.[54]

To Mann and other elite reformers, "the district schools were far too
varied in quality and content. The academies were élitist and ignored the
agrarian and urban proletariat which needed education the most. The
philanthropic societies, lacking a sufficient financial base, could never
raise popular education above its pauper status. And parochial schools
would only perpetuate the religious antagonisms which had wracked the
European continent for centuries."[55] It was the common school, deeply
religious—indeed, Mann would have argued, *more* authentically religious
than "sectarian" schools—but religious in an optimistic mode with no
place for sin and redemption, that would usher in an age of unprecedented
social and personal felicity.

HENRY BARNARD

In 1834, a young lawyer, Henry Barnard, was invited to give the Fourth of July
oration in Hartford; he spoke about the importance of popular schooling to
the "enlargement of the understanding and the purification of the affections
of every individual voter, juror, witness, legislator, and judge of legislation." To
provide such education was "at once the only security, the highest interest &
the highest duty of the state & of individuals."[56] Barnard would play an important role in the development of the state role in schooling in Connecticut and
Rhode Island, and arguably an even more important role—over the next 50
years—as publicist for European models of government leadership in education and for pedagogy in the Pestalozzian tradition.

As in Massachusetts, schooling was already widespread in Connecticut before the 1830s, and reforms had long been in the air. A local association "for the Improvement of the Common Schools" had been founded in 1799, and the Connecticut Society for the Improvement of the Common Schools was organized in 1826; the following year, the governor called for a variety of measures to stimulate local efforts, both "public" and "private." There were various efforts to create popular support for strengthening local schools, but Barnard had not been involved. If such efforts produced only a limited response, it was because schooling was by tradition very much a local concern; in many communities, "schools may not have been very good, but they were as good as most of the population desired"[57] or as employment in a largely rural economy required. It was in the mercantile and growing industrial communities that more schooling was in demand, and local initiatives—some private, some by local government, some mixed—provided it.

In the 1830s, however, there was growing support, at least in elite circles, for a more active state role in promoting schooling across Connecticut. "The extension of the franchise in the 1820s had given a political voice to nearly all white males, and the emerging Democratic party provided a voice and a forum, and the means for political competition, especially in the bustling cities. The opposition Whig politicians and reformers hoped that their efforts would fortify the dikes of the past against an inexorable tide of the future." In 1838, a year after similar action in Massachusetts, the Whig-dominated Connecticut legislature adopted a bill creating a Board of Commissioners of the Common Schools and a Secretary of the Board. Barnard was appointed to that position. In his first *Report* to the legislature, a year later, he charged that a major weakness of the schools was "the lack of uniform standards; far too much was left to the discretion of the local committees."[58]

Over the next several years, though Barnard had limited authority over local schools, he exercised considerable influence because town and district officials turned to him with a wide variety of questions and controversies. "The net result of all of these requests to the state's education officer was the subtle strengthening of the role of the state in school matters." This role was resisted by the Democrats who, as in Massachusetts, supported popular schooling but opposed measures tending to limit the discretion of local governments to manage schools as they judged best. In 1842, the law establishing the Board was repealed. The following year, however, Rhode Island offered Barnard a position as its "agent" under a new law calling for a survey of the condition of schools in the state, and he had the opportunity to propose a comprehensive organization, "nothing more or less than a state system of education." Rhode Island would, through its agent, allocate partial funding to local districts, resolve disputes, and license teachers, with a goal of "uniformity in the administration of the system." The bill that he drafted—and which was enacted in October 1845— "created an embryonic state school system headed by an appointed bureaucrat who wielded considerable power."[59]

When, immediately after the Civil War, Barnard was appointed as Commissioner of a short-lived Department of Education in the national government, he developed an ambitious proposal for the schools of the District of Columbia, with governance "centralized under an incipient hierarchy of professionals."[60] Like many of his plans, this was never implemented, but it anticipated by a generation the models of school system administration which developed at the end of the century.

Barnard himself was not a success as an administrator, in part as a result of lack of sustained interest in the actual work of the various offices that he held. A newspaper report which foreshadowed the loss of his federal position, in 1868, mentioned "charges of gross mismanagement. . . . It is alleged that for a period of nearly two years he has been absent from Washington about two-thirds of his time; that he has used the clerical force of the department to assist him in editing a private journal at Hartford." Barnard's biographer notes that "of course all of this was absolutely true."[61] Soon he was back in private life, and devoted the next decades to what would be his greatest contribution to the development of American education, the publication of a journal that brought together reports on the progress of schooling in the United States and in Europe.

Barnard, Mann, and other common school reformers maintained an active correspondence and read each other's speeches and articles; they saw themselves as allies in a great movement of national regeneration through popular education. Calvin Wiley in North Carolina, Charles Fenton Mercer and Henry Ruffner in Virginia, William Perry in Alabama, Robert Breckinridge in Kentucky, and others less well known did their best to create adequate schooling in the South; in the Midwest, John Pierce and Isaac Crary of Michigan, Caleb Mills of Indiana, Samuel Lewis and Calvin Stowe of Ohio, John Mason Peck and Ninian Edwards of Illinois, and many others labored with rather more success. Many of the reformers were themselves transplanted New Englanders who sought to reproduce the model of schooling that they had known in Massachusetts or Connecticut.

PENNSYLVANIA: MODERATE REFORM

The State role was less prominent in Pennsylvania in the early nineteenth century than in New England and in the mid-Western states like Ohio and

Michigan settled from New England. J. P. Wickersham, the chief state school officer for a crucial period after the Civil War, wrote that

> the educational policy enforced in Pennsylvania for fifty years after the close of the Revolutionary war embraced two objects: first, the establishment in all parts of the State of endowed Academies, in which a small number of indigent pupils were to be taught gratuitously; and, second, the free instruction of poor children in the existing church or neighborhood schools.[62]

For decades the Pennsylvania state authorities sought to meet their constitutional obligation to provide for the schooling of those whose parents could not afford to pay tuition by providing what we would now call "vouchers" enabling them to attend existing non-public schools and academies, including church schools. This practice continued well into the 1840s. These schools were not called "common schools," for several reasons. The free schools in Philadelphia served *only* poor children, and thus did not provide the "shared schoolbench" that Horace Mann and others talked about; many of the local schools elsewhere in the state were under denominational or ethnic sponsorship, and thus were not "common" in another sense. And there is another reason: the phrase "common school" came to correspond to a specific and self-conscious program of reform of society through schooling. Local community schools that simply reflected the concern of parents to have their children taught were too haphazard, too responsive to local concerns, to suit the reformers.

A continuous and insistent theme of the debates and policies in Pennsylvania was that the system of universal education through elementary schools was a *local* responsibility, with almost all significant decisions made at the local level. The role of the state was to ensure that local government met its obligations, and to help with partial funding. Tocqueville had noted, during his visit in the early 1830s, that "one encounters no one among the inhabitants of New England . . . who recognizes in the government of the state the right to intervene in the direction of interests that are purely the township's," and the same spirit prevailed in other states.[63]

After long agitation by promoters of popular schooling, a 1834 Pennsylvania school law authorized—but did not require—local communities to establish common schools supported by local taxes. This new law aroused fierce opposition from those averse to state interference with what had been a local matter, as well as from many satisfied with the existing denominational provision of schooling; 32,000 citizens signed a petition for its repeal, and many state legislators who had voted for the 1834 law were defeated. The newly elected state Senate voted nearly two to one, in 1835, for "An Act Making Provision for the Education of the Poor Gratis" which essentially would have repealed the 1834 law, and there was a majority of 30 in support of this in the House. At this crucial juncture, Thaddeus Stevens (later, with Charles Sumner, leader of the Radical Republicans who supported the rights of freed slaves after the Civil War) successfully

> moved to substitute for the Senate bill another which greatly strengthened the Law of 1834, and upon the motion made a speech that electrified the House and saved the common school system from "ignominious defeat." In his speech Stevens said that "hereditary distinctions of rank are sufficiently odious; but that which is founded on poverty is infinitely more so," and declared that the Senate bill should be entitled "An act for branding and marking the poor, so that they may be known from the rich and proud." He appealed to his colleagues to cast their votes so that "the blessing of education shall be conferred upon every son of Pennsylvania—shall be carried home to the poorest child of the poorest inhabitant of the meanest hut of your mountains, so that even he may be prepared to act well his part in this land of freedom."[64]

Michael Katz comments that Stevens correctly saw that the question of a special category of "pauper schools"—in lieu of free or selectively free common schools—involved issues of "middle-class pride and status anxiety, touching what may have been many a very raw nerve" during a period of financial difficulty.

> Many people with children to be educated, Stevens pointed out, "may have seen better days—may have been unfortunate in life, and, by reason of their reduced situation and circumstances, may be unable to educate their families. Shall we . . . do nothing to allay the prejudice which persons in this condition, will almost surely entertain, against allowing their children to be educated in public schools?" By his very terminology Stevens reached the heart of the problem; only a radical reorganization could expunge the legacy of paternalistic voluntarism and divorce the concepts of public and pauper.[65]

Many years later, Stevens wrote proudly that an effect of his intervention had been that "there is now no obscure, barren spot within the broad limits of Pennsylvania, where the children of the rich and the poor do not meet in common schools on equal terms."[66] Whether many of the children of "the rich" were found in such obscure localities, or whether, in Philadelphia and other cities, they attended school with the children of the poor, we may doubt, but his sentiment is plain. Nothing in his speeches suggests that the state should take over responsibility from parents, however, or that uniformity should be imposed upon schools by government.

In his second speech on the subject during the legislative battles to sustain or repeal the 1834 law, Stevens placed a major stress on state endowments for the non-public academies which provided secondary education, so that poor children could attend them cheaply. In this respect, at least, he was moving away from direct state ownership and control.

The stronger 1836 Pennsylvania school law required that a vote be taken locally to determine whether to accept state funding for public schools, in which case a county tax would have to be levied amounting to at least twice the state contribution.[67] In other words, the major part of the cost of schools was to be paid locally, with the state funds used as an incentive and to supplement local effort. These state funds were not allocated on the basis of the wealth of local communities, and there is an indication from Wickersham's annual reports that poor and rural communities received less state funds to pay for their schools than did the larger and wealthier communities.

This law also allowed the local option of subsidizing non-public schools with public funds, provided that "such school shall be generally conducted in conformity with the common school system of the Commonwealth;" this provision was repealed in 1854 as part of the reaction, across the North, against the efforts to obtain public funding for Catholic schools.[68] Authority over public schools was to be vested in a local board elected by the people. As Wickersham summed up the situation before the Civil War,

> Let it be remembered that the management of the school system, during the early period of which we speak, was almost wholly in the hands of the district school boards. Little help came to them from Harrisburg, and none at all from any other quarter. They built their schoolhouses, examined their teachers, fixed the branches of study to be taught and the books to be used, made rules by which the schools were to be governed, as best they could, with no guide except their own limited experience in such matters.[69]

In response to the 1836 law, the Board of Controllers for the Philadelphia charity schools reorganized them to provide common schools for a socially heterogeneous enrollment, boasting that "the stigma of poverty, once the only title of admission to our public schools, has at the solicitation of the Controllers been erased from our statute books, and the schools of this city and county are now open to every child that draws the breath of life within our borders. What may not be accomplished by this mighty lever of universal education?"[70]

The Board had general oversight over the construction of school build-ings and setting salary levels for teachers, but its only direct control was over Central High School for Boys and Girls High School; there were local boards in each city ward and suburban township in Philadelphia County with author-ity to appoint or dismiss teachers and to determine the curriculum, and these boards elected the members of the Board of Controllers. This decentralized arrangement continued until 1905, except that a state law in 1867 gave the judges of the court of common pleas and the district court responsibility for appointing the members of the central board, thus making it more indepen-dent of local interests.

Nevertheless, as the superintendent of schools would note in 1904, "the Course of Instruction in the Elementary Schools was for many years deter-mined by the requirements for admittance into the Central High School." In fact, before the elaboration of extensive administrative mechanisms, Labaree notes, "issuing directives to the ward boards, as in a bureaucracy, would have been futile." Central High School "drew on the influence available to it because of its market power" derived from its ability to decide what qualification would be required by the highly competitive admission process.[71] Thus, as in many other instances in the nineteenth century (and indeed still today), informal influence took the place of direct control.

The education law passed in 1834 and revised in 1836 was the first con-crete effort to establish a system of common schools in Pennsylvania. But the Legislature at that time did not set out to create a uniform and equitable system of state-controlled schooling. Its ambitions were much more limited: to use modest state funding as a "carrot" to persuade local communities to establish, maintain and pay for common schools. In this, it was only gradually effective. "Of the 987 districts created by the law, 502 . . . accepted the system and elected school officers. There were 264 districts that rejected the law out and out, while 221 ignored it by taking no action." Communities in which education was provided by a church school were allowed, under later revisions of the law, to receive state funding for those schools.[72] Not until 1849 was it made mandatory to operate public schools, and Wickersham reports that the last communities did not come into compliance until 1873.

In his Report of 1871, Wickersham detailed the role of the State in rela-tion to Pennsylvania schools, and it is a very limited one: certification of the higher grades of teachers, advising school directors and providing a part of their pay from state appropriations, calling conventions for the election of county superintendents and publishing their reports, and not much else. The only sphere of direct control was with respect to the boarding schools for Civil War orphans.[73]

The Pennsylvania Constitution of 1874 took precisely the same view of the role of the state in mandating that the legislature "provide for the maintenance and support of a thorough and efficient system of public schools where all the children of this Commonwealth above the age of six years may be educated." It did not make schooling a direct function of the state; there was no fundamental shift on education in 1874, and the speeches of the delegates makes it clear that they saw themselves as placing a more solid foundation under the system of locally controlled schooling that already existed across the Commonwealth.

The state did not much concern itself with what was taught, or how it was taught. As Mulhern pointed out in 1933, Pennsylvania's "high school curriculum evolved without any effective direction by State educational authorities."[74] The same could be said of elementary curriculum and standards in the nineteenth century. Wickersham, writing in the 1880s, expresses shock at the daring of one of his predecessors as state superintendent who was "in favor of a uniform course of study and text-books throughout the State" and proposed a short list of recommended books (as did Horace Mann), commenting that "this daring step, which if taken by a State Superintendent at the present day, might subject him to fine and imprisonment, seems to have attracted little attention." Instructional leadership was clearly a local matter.[75]

The question of uniformity of textbooks entered largely into the debates over the education provisions of the *Constitution* of 1874, and the delegates explicitly repudiated attempts to make textbook selection a state responsibility. The following year an effort was made "by a kind of syndicate of book publishers and politicians," to enact a law which would have had that effect. This was successfully opposed by Wickersham as State Superintendent, and he commented later that "local control of school affairs is a fundamental principle of the Pennsylvania system of public education; and it seemed to him best to leave the selection of school books, as well as the building of schoolhouses and the employment of teachers, in the hands of the immediate neighbors and representatives of the people they serve."[76]

Legislators and school reformers in Pennsylvania sought to encourage local development of schools that taught what they called "the elementary branches of education" and were under some effective—and thus local—public supervision to ensure that they served "the common interests of society." They had in mind also schools that would serve any child without requiring that the parent either pay or declare himself a pauper, and were universally available. Finally, they described common schools as open to all children and teachers without regard to their religious convictions, though most assumed or insisted that common schools would be based upon and teach an ecumenical form of Protestant Christianity. "Common Schools universally established," wrote the

Joint Committee on Education in 1836, "will multiply the chances of success, perhaps of brilliant success, among those who may otherwise forever continue ignorant. It is the duty of the State to promote and foster such establishments"— but not to provide or control them.[77]

RESISTANCE TO STATE LEADERSHIP IN POPULAR SCHOOLING

The primary contribution of Horace Mann, Henry Barnard, and their allies in other states to American education was in the elaboration of new structures of state influence over local schools and the organisms of local government that actually managed them.[78] It was not, contrary to what Bernard Bailyn called "the history written by the educational missionaries of the turn of the [twentieth] century," to somehow invent the movement of educational reform associated with their names. In fact, "all aspects of the reform of the thirties, the demand for better teachers and school houses, the use of publicity and publication, even teachers' institutes, appeared in New England and the Midwest prior to the appointment" of either of them to their positions of state leadership.[79]

There can be no question, however, that the publicity which they gave to the achievements of popular schooling in German states—most notably, Prussia—where government took the lead in promoting and controlling its development, and the skillful use which they made of the collection and publication of data about schools, gave a new prominence to state action throughout the North. In a decisive shift of focus, the 1830s and 1840s saw legislation proposed and sometimes adopted in state after state that strengthened considerably the oversight of state government over local schools; indeed, "the common school revival should perhaps more accurately be titled state initiative or interference."[80] Not all politically active contemporaries welcomed this development, however, or were convinced that the State should take the lead in promoting and shaping the schooling of children.

In general, in the antebellum period it was Democrats who, while supporting the common school, opposed an expanded state oversight role. Historian Lawrence Cremin pointed out that the earlier account which represented "conservatives" as opposing state leadership of the common school movement had it exactly backwards: in Massachusetts, "it was a Whig governor, Edward Everett, who gave the Board life, and a Democratic governor, Marcus Morton, who in 1840 sought its elimination and a return to the 'democracy of the local district.'"[81] Morton was elected in a revolt against the elite reformers who, in addition to seeking to regulate and transform the local common school, adopted a law limiting the sale of liquor to quantities of at least 15 gallons. This was reform directed at the lower orders, who could not afford to lay in such large quantities and did their drinking retail in dramshops.[82]

Governor Morton, in his inaugural address (1840), insisted that schools should be the exclusive responsibility of local citizens without state supervision.

> To arouse that strong and universal interest in [the schools], which is so necessary to their utility and success, an interest that should pervade both parents and children, the responsibility of their management should rest upon the inhabitants of the towns. And the more immediately they are brought under the control of those for whose benefit they are established, and at whose expense they are supported, the more deep and active will be the feelings engendered in their favor, and the more certain and universal will be their beneficial agency. In the town and district meetings, those little pure democracies, where our citizens first learn the rudiments and the practical operation of free institutions, may safely and rightfully be placed the direction and the governance of these invaluable seminaries.[83]

The Massachusetts House Committee on Education supported a bill to abolish the Board and close the normal schools, having concluded that "the operations of the Board are incompatible with those principles upon which our Common Schools have been founded and maintained. . . If," they wrote, "the Board has any actual power, it is a dangerous power, touching directly upon the rights and duties of the Legislature; if it has no power why continue its existence . . . ?" What Mann and the Board were seeking to do, the legislators claimed, was to impose a Prussian model that was unsuited to American principles.[84] European countries like Prussia and France had imposed central control of schooling because of "the ignorance and incapacity of the administrators of local affairs," and, in compensation, the schools were all modeled "upon one plan, as uniform and exact as the discipline of an army." But such imposed uniformity was completely contrary to the American principle that the people should manage their own affairs. Indeed, the Committee pointed out, "De Tocqueville, whose work upon America has been so much admired, dwells at great length and with great emphasis, upon the advantages which New England derives from its excellent system of local authority; while he points out the want of public spirit in the countries of Europe." The French and Prussian systems, the Committee suggested, were more effective as means "of political influence, and strengthening the hands of the government, than as a mere means for the diffusion of knowledge." But

> in a country like this, where such diversity of sentiments exists, especially upon theological subjects, and where morality is considered a part of religion, and is, to

some extent, modified by sectarian views, the difficulty and danger of attempting to introduce these subjects into our schools, according to one fixed and settled plan, to be devised by a central Board, must be obvious. The right to mould the political, moral, and religious opinions of his children, is a right exclusively and jealously reserved by our laws to every parent; and for the government to attempt, directly or indirectly, as to these matters, to stand in the parent's place, is an undertaking of very questionable policy.[85]

The efforts of the Board, including its establishment of state normal schools to train teachers, would have the effect of undermining the essential element in the acknowledged success of schooling in Massachusetts, the participation of parents and other citizens in the control of their local schools. "Any attempt to form all our schools, and all our teachers, upon one model, would destroy all competition—all emulation, and even the spirit of improvement itself."[86]

Of course, the Committee was greatly exaggerating the authority that Horace Mann and the Board of Education possessed, though they summed up accurately enough the intentions of those who were developing state-directed systems of popular schooling in Prussia and France. Like Edmund Burke predicting, in early 1790, the turn the French Revolution would take several years later, the Committee on Education could be credited with a gift of prophecy for seeing, in such apparently innocent measures as the promotion of a set of schoolbooks that local committees were free to choose or reject and the establishment of normal schools that served only a handful of prospective teachers, the germ of what would become, in time, what its critics would call "The Blob" of interlocking interests seeking a monopoly of uniform, publicly funded schooling.

It was largely Democrats in the legislature and not the religiously orthodox as such who moved to abolish the Board of Education soon after Morton's 1840 address. "Horace Mann and the Whigs," Kaestle and Vinovskis observe, "never fully appreciated the depth of the fears of the Democrats that the creation of a state agency to do good might eventually result in a serious danger to freedom within the Republic."[87]

District schools [the Education Committee pointed out], in a republican government, need no police regulations, no system of state censorship, no checks of moral, religious, or political conservatism, to preserve either the morals, the religion, or the politics of the state. . . . Instead of consolidating the education interest of the Commonwealth in one grand central head, and that head the government, let us rather hold on to the good old principles of our ancestors, and diffuse and scatter this interest far and wide, divided and subdivided, not only into towns and districts but even into families and individuals. The moment this interest is surrendered to the government, and all responsibility is thrown upon civil power, farewell to the usefulness of common schools, the just pride, honor, and ornament of New England; farewell to religious liberty . . . farewell to political freedom.[88]

While there were no subsequent efforts to abolish the Board of Education, Morton returned to the theme of local control in his Inaugural Address when he returned to office (after a 2-year Whig intermission) in 1843. "Nothing," he insisted,

will so much promote their [the schools'] improvement, and the advancement of general education, as to excite the interest of the people in them. The best method to accomplish this object, is to devolve upon each school district the control and management of its own schools. Let the inhabitants realize that it is their own institution, that they alone are responsible for its success; that it is the child of their own little community, to prosper by their care, or pine through their neglect; and it would excite an interest, a pride, and an emulation, which would improve and benefit both parents and children.[89]

An eloquent spokesman for this view was Orestes Brownson (1803–1876), who urged—in anticipation of the principle of "subsidiarity" that would be given official status in Catholic social teaching by Pope Leo XIII in *Rerum Novarum* (1891) and then by the European Union in its founding Treaty of Maastricht (1992)—that individual school districts should remain "always paramount to the State." Each school should remain "under the control of a community composed merely of the number of families having children in it."[90] "Nothing desirable in matters of education," he wrote, "beyond what relates to the finances of the schools, comes within the province of the legislature. . . . Let the legislature provide ample funds for the support of as many schools as are needed for the best education possible for all the children of the community, and there let it stop." Government, Brownson insisted, "may found and endow schools, and pay the teachers, but it can not dictate or interfere with the education or discipline of the school. That would imply union of church and state, or, rather, subjection of the spiritual order to the secular." Brownson, one of the most penetrating and original thinkers about education and the state in nineteenth century America, argued that "the state has the right to enact compulsory education laws . . . and it has the obligation to assure [*sic*] the advancement of civilization by establishing, supporting, and maintaining schools. It cannot, however, educate and it must refrain from defining the curriculum."[91]

Commenting on Horace Mann's initiatives to extend the state role, Brownson argued that "the more exclusively the whole matter of the school is brought under the control of the families specially interested in it, the more efficient will the school be." In this he was, no doubt unconsciously, echoing Thomas Jefferson, who wrote, in 1816, "If it is believed that these elementary schools will be better managed by the Governor and Council . . . or any other general authority of the Government, than by the parents within each ward, it is a belief against all experience." Jefferson wrote again, in 1817, "If twelve or fifteen hundred schools are to be placed under one general administration, an attention so divided will amount to a dereliction of them to themselves. It is surely better, then, to place each school at once under the care of those most interested in its conduct."[92]

Brownson went on, "Government is not in this country, and cannot be, the educator of the people. In education, as in religion, we must rely mainly on the voluntary system. . . . Government here must be restricted to material interests and forbidden to concern itself with what belongs to the spiritual culture of the community. It has of right no control over our opinions, literary, moral, political, philosophical, or religious. Its province is to reflect, not to lead, nor to create the general will. It, therefore, must not be installed the educator of the people."[93] Brownson was especially critical of the state normal schools, with their focus upon methodology and their neglect of religion; he charged that "only those teachers whose political persuasion was acceptable to the board could be appointed" to instruct in the normal schools.[94]

Similar reservations about the state role in education were expressed by the editor of the *Philadelphia National Gazette*, in 1830, writing that education's "progress and wider diffusion will depend, not upon government, but on the public spirit, information, liberality and training of the citizens themselves, who may appreciate duly the value of the object as a national good, and as a personal benefit for their children."[95]

In a number of states, the public was reluctant to support an enhanced state role in overseeing the schooling provided—and largely paid for—at the local level. While efforts to abolish the state board failed in Massachusetts, they were successful for a time in Connecticut. "The Hartford *Times*, a Democratic paper, attacked the Whig centralizing reforms as 'despotic' and 'Prussian'";[96] "Illinois and Indiana did not have state superintendents or state secretaries or even state boards until 1854; Ohio, which had appointed its first state official in 1837, abolished the position in 1840, only reestablishing it again in 1853." In several states there was major controversy over legislative provisions allowing for local property tax support for schools. In Pennsylvania,

> these local communities did not oppose universal elementary schooling. They demanded only that they—the local communities—determine what was taught and

how it would be paid for. A unified, property-tax supported common schooling system had become anathema to them only because it meant that the majority would dictate its religion, its language, and its customs to the minority. Surely this smacked more of Old World established religious tyranny than New World democracy.[97]

Those who were successful in pushing through legislation for common schools in Pennsylvania, in 1834 and 1836, made clear that they repudiated the radical proposals of the Working Men's Party and their allies as "the fantastic scheme of forcing children from their parents to be placed under the guardianship of the State." Reformer Robert Vaux, in sending to Governor Wolf the Memorial of 1830 which had a decisive role in prompting later passage of public school legislation, expressed "his alarm at the dangerous, unconstitutional, and undemocratic notions on education" of the Working Men's Party. Pennsylvania lawmakers and reformers frequently insisted that they did not want to interfere in any way, as it was put in 1830, "with the rights of parents to educate their children according to their ideas of propriety, in private schools or in their own houses."[98]

> The Quakers, for example, did not believe in "mixed" or "indiscriminate" education but rather preferred what they called "guarded" education. . . . So did the Lutherans . . . who used guarded education to perpetuate a German paideia, with the German language at its core . . . the Mennonites and Moravians extended the notion of guardedness to the point of organizing their own communities in isolation from other religious and ethnic groups, in an effort to maintain their traditional patterns of life free of contamination by the presence of alternative modes.[99]

Under such conditions, there was little chance that the common public school could displace its rivals and indeed, as we have seen, those rivals were often publicly funded. In New York State a system of school administration was created by the legislature to actually exercise power over schools and local government, with a law enacted in 1841—just after the crisis over the Catholic demands in New York City—to establish the office of deputy superintendent of common schools for each county. Their responsibilities included examining and licensing teachers and supervising all schools to ensure compliance with the rules and regulations established by state authorities.[100]

Mann and other reformers were quick to dismiss any resistance to their attempts to systematize schooling under state leadership as either ignorant or malignant resistance to progress. "The rhetorical effect was to imply that if one was against centralization, supervision, new schoolhouses, teacher training, or graded schools, one must also be against morality, good order, intelligent citizenship, economic prosperity, fair opportunity, and a common American culture."[101] This strategy continues to be employed today, as opponents of any aspect of the agenda of the teacher unions are accused of being "enemies of education."

Mann's biographer concludes that "developing a bigotry of purpose, he worked toward his self-conceived goal. In studying this reform, one cannot escape the monomania at work in Mann, and its corollary, the total absence of self-doubt among the reformers. In fact, among them one finds the same hyper-certainty, narrowness of purpose, and adamancy which Mann utterly detested in his opponents" among evangelicals.[102]

> Although too politically astute to advocate immediate centralized control, Mann repeatedly referred to the necessity of an educational *system*. He was hypersensitive to any criticism of Prussianism, but tighter supervision and centralization were implied in much of what he attempted. Furthermore, he thought of children not as individuals but as masses of pupils or an entire generation needing to be trained. . . . Not individual learners with idiosyncratic interests, talents, and aspirations, they were to him young humanity—a humanity almost always understood in the abstract.[103]

Mann and his allies in the "Common School Crusade," "had fused the concept of public control with that of public support, two concepts which were never joined in the academies and the charity schools."[104]

In the long run, the growing anxiety about immigration produced broad political support for the common school under state supervision.[105] Connecticut, having abolished Henry Barnard's position as state superintendent in 1840, restored it in 1845 and "under a strongly nativist government in the 1850s, passed laws to strengthen consolidation and central supervision."[106]

Looking back over a quarter-century since the establishment of the first state normal schools, Samuel May (a Unitarian minister, as was his predecessor Cyrus Peirce) was able to assert, without apology, that "It is the duty which the State owes to its youthful members, as well as to its body politic, to take such children under its especial protection, from the families of the poor or the vile, and give to them the moral discipline and the literary instruction which they need, but which they fail to get at home."[107] For May and other reformers, the efforts of the benevolent associations were no longer sufficient.

State authority and its limits

The traditional view among historians of American popular education is that "by 1850 almost every northern state was well on the way to a permanent and systematic provision for common schools controlled by state officials and supported largely if not exclusively by public monies."[108]

Twenty-four of the thirty states had appointed a state official responsible for encouraging and overseeing local efforts to provide schools. In most cases, there was a state fund to supplement the efforts of local communities, and this in turn "hastened centralization of power by the states" since state legislatures could make compliance with their directives a condition for the receipt of this support. "States imposed requirements for participation in the funds, including the submission of statistical reports, the raising of local taxes, the hiring of only certified teachers, and the holding of school sessions for the term set by law."[109] Claims of effective state control of popular schooling are greatly exaggerated, however.

While it was the state legislature that had—and still has—ultimate legal authority over and responsibility for education, the rapid turn-over of representatives and their lack of staff and solid information about school conditions made much of the legislation adopted more statements of aspirations than concrete directives for the development of local schools. As a legislative committee in Michigan (perhaps the most advanced midwestern state in the promotion of education) complained, in 1841, the reports from local communities

> give us a few statistics. . . . But of the real character of these schools, and their success, nothing, literally nothing, is known. . . . Beyond the limits of each man's district or neighborhood, nothing is known, either to the people or to the legislature. The legislature cannot act intelligibly upon the subject, because they do not have the necessary information.[110]

Nowhere was control by state government at all extensive, and there is abundant evidence that schools continued to reflect local priorities. In New York City, for example, the decision of the state legislature in 1842 that the Public School Society be replaced with an elected Board of Education had the practical effect that schools were ". . . governed by elected trustees in each of the city's twenty-four wards. . . . each ward chose its own Bible, texts, teachers, principals, janitors, and curriculum. Since New York was already a city of ethnic neighborhoods, in Irish wards the Douay Bible was used while in others it was still the King James version."[111] When, toward the end of the century, this "urban localism" in the control of New York schools was dismantled, it was not because of an extension of state authority but because progressive reformers managed to centralize school governance in order to minimize the influence of immigrant-based political power.

In 1852, Massachusetts was the first of the states to adopt a compulsory school attendance law, requiring every child aged 8 to 14 to attend a public school "during at least twelve weeks," unless he had been "otherwise furnished with the means of education for a like period of time, or has already acquired those branches of learning which are taught in common schools," or had "a bodily or mental condition" preventing school attendance. The law also made exception for cases in which "the person having the control of such child, is not able, by reason of poverty, to send such child to school, or to furnish him with the means of education."[112] Other states were slow to adopt even such loose requirements; New York State, for example, made school attendance compulsory in 1874, and that did not occur in much of the South until the early twentieth century, with Mississippi the last of the states in 1918.

There was, in fact, considerable hesitation about extending government authority so far into the realm of family life. Horace Mann himself did not support compulsory attendance laws, "finding them out of harmony with the American idea of democracy."[113] Superintendent Wickersham wrote in his annual report for 1870 that "Pennsylvania must look in some other direction than that of a compulsory law to find the remedy we are seeking for the evil of non-attendance at school," and that "in the spirit of our institutions, I prefer to test voluntary action fully, fairly, and patiently, before resorting to force."[114]

Similarly, in the Pennsylvania Constitutional Convention of 1873, former state Superintendent Charles A. Black opposed an amendment giving the legislature authority to make schooling compulsory: "I can think of no measure," he said, "that could be presented to the people of the State which would be more unpopular. . . . The people claim the right, and they have the right, to regulate this matter for themselves, and we have no right to interfere with their prerogative. They claim the right to send their children to school or not, and the case of monarchical Prussia is no example for them."[115] As late as 1881 Pennsylvania Superintendent of Public Instruction E. E. Higbee expressed "very serious misgivings as to the propriety of any strictly compulsory law."[116]

This insistence upon parental and local rights lies behind the resistance that Horace Mann experienced (though he and generations of historians have chosen to interpret it as the last gasps of religious obscurantism), and explains why, despite his efforts and those of his allies, American education continued to be largely a local affair well into the twentieth century. Protestant theologian Charles Hodge, in 1846, saw clearly that the issue of the content of religious instruction in schools was tied to a structural issue.

> What right has the State, a majority of the people, or a mere clique, which in fact commonly control such matters, to say what shall be taught in schools which the

people sustain? What more right have they to say that no religion shall be taught, than they have to say that Popery shall be taught? Or what right have the people in one part, to control the wishes and convictions of those of another part of the State, as to the education of their own children? If the people of a particular district choose to have a school in which the Westminster or the Heidelberg catechism is taught, we cannot see on what principle of religious liberty the State has a right to interfere, and say it shall not be done; if you teach your religion, you shall not draw your own money from the public fund! This appears to us a strange doctrine in a free country . . . unjust and tyrannical, as well as infidel in its whole tendency.[117]

From this perspective, the issue was not one of free thought (represented by the common public school) against religious orthodoxy but rather resistance to the imposition of a new sort of orthodoxy, which denied a right to provide schooling based upon religious views—whether Protestant or Catholic—differing from those promoted by a liberal elite. Thus Frederick Packard, in one of a series of attacks upon Mann and the Board for its refusal to approve the books of the American Sunday School Union for use in the common schools, wrote "we protest against the interference of the government with the matter and manner of instruction, and especially against annexing any condition to its grants, that shall affect in the slightest degree the independence of the whole district or of the teacher whom they employ—and least of all on the subject of religious instruction."[118] Hodge, Packard, and others were not calling for state-imposed religion in public schools but for local freedom to provide orthodox (that is, Trinitarian Protestant) religious instruction in those areas where that reflected the desires of parents. Ironically, this was a central aspect of the Prussian system which its American admirers chose to overlook.[119]

While the northern states may have been taking the first steps toward what could fairly be called "systems"—though highly decentralized—of schooling by the 1850s, this was not the case in the South, where a patchwork of public schools and private academies provided very inadequate coverage, though arguably as much as an essentially rural population demanded. The failure in the South was in general not one of intentions at the legislative level, but of actual implementation. In what was then the frontier state of Georgia, in 1783, Governor Lyman Hall (not coincidentally a transplanted New Englander) urged upon the state legislature the importance of creating a system of schooling because many citizens led "profligate, and wicked lives," and schools would "restrain vice and encourage virtue." The General Assembly obediently passed several bills that encouraged the development of academies. Progress was slow, however; by 1800, six academies had received state charters, and another eleven received charters by 1810, even as the state's population grew from 25,000 in

1783 to 252,000 in 1810. "Critics of Georgia's educational policies in the 1830s noted that while academies received half the state's contribution to education, fewer than one tenth of the school-age children in the state attended these schools. Elementary level schooling received little state encouragement or support. Funding levels for all educational programs were minimal through the antebellum period. As late as the early 1850s the state contributed less than four percent of its budget to education, and state funds for elementary schooling were particularly lacking."[120]

Across the country, almost all the initiative and responsibility to provide schooling remained at the local level. Even toward the end of the nineteenth century, the state departments of education were, on average, staffed by the superintendent or commissioner and his clerk; the former "distributed money to districts from the common school fund, collected statistics, prepared annual reports, and gave speeches to arouse greater enthusiasm for the latest improvements in schooling. But even the most eminent superintendent had little direct power to regulate education."[121] Democratic localism provided and continues to provide the fundamental structure of American education, with communities enjoying broad discretion about how to manage their schools.

Despite rhetoric about the sacred mission of the state to shape its future citizens, it is certainly the case that "no legislature adopted the idea that children belonged to the state rather than their parents."[122] The idea that the State—and thus its schools—had ultimate authority over the shaping of children was dear to the nascent profession of "educators," whose role was thereby immeasurably dignified. Consistent with this view, "the Wisconsin Teachers' Association declared in 1865 that 'children are the property of the state.'"[123]

The first major encroachment on the control of parents and local voters came in the 1870s, as states enacted constitutional provisions seeking to remove decisions about the religious character of public schools from the discretion of local communities; Illinois, Pennsylvania, Missouri, Alabama, Nebraska, Colorado, Texas, Georgia, New Hampshire, Minnesota, California, and Louisiana did so in the 1870s, and others subsequently.[124] While these provisions were ostensibly designed to prevent religious conflict, they were in fact transparently aimed against Catholic schooling and did nothing to change the generically Protestant character of public schools. As we will see in Chapter Seven, the adoption of these so-called "state Blaine amendments" reflected a profound distrust of the educational pluralism which had flourished under the regime of local decision-making about the goals of schooling.

Chapter Seven

Religion as Source of Conflict

It was after the Civil War and the postwar focus on reconstruction—both of the devastated South and also of disrupted lives and families in the North—that what has usually been called "Church and State" controversies became virulent in the United States. The Protestant majority, so recently at war over slavery and secession, united to keep the Bible and prayer in public schools despite Catholic objections, and to insulate from the ordinary democratic process any efforts to obtain public funds for Catholic schools.

Before considering the details of these conflicts in the 1870s, it is necessary to consider why these questions had such resonance for the American public, both Protestant and Catholic.

THE PERCEIVED CATHOLIC MENACE

The social and political history of the United States in the nineteenth century is frequently written without reference to developments in Europe, but on this issue of Catholic schooling this would miss a connection of which contemporaries were very much aware. The 1870s and 1880s were, in Austria, Belgium, France, Germany, Italy, the Netherlands, and Spain a period of intense political conflict between the Catholic Church and the respective governments, with schooling more often than not the central issue. The Dutch *schoolstrijd* was the cause of the first mass political mobilizations in that country, as was the case in Belgium; the French Third Republic made banishing Catholic influence from popular schooling a central goal.

After some 15 years of self-absorption in run-up to and aftermath of the Civil War, Americans began to take notice of the conflicts that arose as European governments sought to use popular schooling to solidify control over the loyalty of their citizens and the Catholic Church sought to maintain its traditional role in schooling children it had baptized.[1] Catholic leaders in the United States were inevitably drawn into echoing the positions taken by the Papacy in these conflicts. They did so with confidence because the anti-immigrant hostility of the 1850s had been greatly reduced by the shared experience of war; indeed, many northern cities elected Irish mayors in the 1870s and 1880s.

While American observers were aware of these developments in Europe, and especially of the increasing insistence of the Catholic Church upon providing schooling under its auspices or supervision, they were especially interested in the measures taken by the government of Germany against the influence of the Catholic hierarchy. In the 1870s, having defeated France and established the German Empire through voluntary unification of German states, Chancellor Bismarck began to challenge the influence of the Catholic Church, especially in education, as a threat to that national project;[2] this *Kulturkampf* seemed to many in the United States an exemplary case of self-protection by a progressive government.

American Protestant leaders, as well as those indifferent to religion but concerned to promote the national unity for which a costly war had recently been fought, identified with the anticlerical efforts in Europe. James Garfield, the future president, told a gubernatorial campaign audience in 1875 that there was a common battle in both Europe and America against Catholic political demands: "Our fight in Ohio . . . is only a small portion of the battlefield," he told the voters.[3]

For American Protestants, as for French anticlerical Republicans, the Catholic Church, a large and ramifying organization and also a source of transcendent claims, seemed a menacing limitation upon national unity and progress; its opponents "hammered away at the idea that schools operated by the religious communities taught a perverted doctrine inimical to modem ideas and a hatred for laic society that must eventually prove fatal for the Republic."[4]

One result of the French defeat by Germany in 1870 was to strengthen the confrontation between the Papacy and many aspects of contemporary European culture and political life. With the withdrawal of French troops, Rome fell to the Italian army; this came to symbolize, for liberals and for many Protestants worldwide, "the victory of the progressive secular spirit, or indeed of free thought, in confrontation with the papal power considered as the very model of clerical obscurantism."[5] For the Catholic Church, by contrast, it was an almost unparalleled humiliation, leading to a compensating assertion of its spiritual authority. A papal encyclical in 1864 had condemned the pretension of governments to provide secular schooling to Catholic children. In the *Syllabus of Errors* attached to the 1864 encyclical, Pius IX condemned the assertion of the exclusive authority of the state over public schools, and the contention that

> the best theory of civil society requires that popular schools open to children of every class of the people, and, generally, all public institutes intended for instruction in letters and philosophical sciences and for carrying on the education of youth, should be freed from all ecclesiastical authority, control and interference, and should be fully subjected to the civil and political power at the pleasure of the rulers, and according to the standard of the prevalent opinions of the age.[6]

By also denouncing freedom of conscience and worship, Pius confirmed all the worst suspicions of liberals and Protestants in the United States as well as in Europe. In the political controversies in 1875–76, the *Syllabus* would often be cited, along with the claim of papal infallibility that followed in 1870, as occurred in Congress when the 'Blaine Amendment' was debated.[7]

It was widely believed, among the Protestant majority in the United States, that the very nature of Catholic schooling was contrary to fundamental principles of American life, aiming to produce adults unable to think for themselves and totally subordinate mentally and spiritually to their church. "Catholicism in this country depends for its life and progress upon two conditions: first, a large and continuous importation of foreign-born Catholics; second, home production, by educating the children of Catholics into the faith of their parents and the faith of the Church. . . . Ignorance and despotic control are historically the strongholds of Catholicism." There was a dangerous "inconsistency between what the Catholics desire and the whole genius and nature of our political institutions."[8]

As we have seen, Protestant theologian Horace Bushnell warned against the influence of Catholic schools, as a menace to society, their religious justification in fact no justification at all. In such schools, the children of immigrants "will be instructed mainly into the foreign prejudices and superstitions of their fathers, and the state, which proposes to be clear of all sectarian affinities in religion, will pay the bills!"[9]

While concerns in the 1840s (and again at the end of the nineteenth century) focused on the floods of immigrants and how their children could be made into real Americans, concerns in the 1870s, echoing the contemporary

European conflicts, focused more on the authority of the Catholic hierarchy over the minds of these new citizens who had begun to exercise political influence. "Even more than the Church's secular power, its assertions of theological authority seemed incompatible with freedom—especially with the individual independence and personal authority that were increasingly felt to be at the core of Protestant and American identity."[10]

This fear of the effects of Catholic schooling would continue for many decades. The National Education Association, in 1891, warned that parochial schools initiated the children of immigrants into foreign traditions that threatened "distinctive Americanism," and 30 years later a Methodist bishop in Detroit warned that "the parochial school is the most un-American institution in America, and must be closed."[11] It was this continuing and deeply rooted perception that Catholic schooling was a problem that led to the Oregon legislation struck down by *Pierce v. Society of Sisters* in 1925.

Nor has this theme been altogether abandoned, despite much recent research on the benefits of Catholic schooling for good citizenship. A contemporary professor of legal studies does not hesitate to assert (with no evidence) that religious schools harm children in all sorts of ways, producing not only intolerance but also "diminished self-esteem, extreme anxiety, and pronounced and sometimes life-long anger and resentment." Girls who attend Catholic school "find themselves unable as adults to act on desires, to take control of their sexual/reproductive lives, or to leave abusive marriages." Dwyer argues that "[e]ven students who are not presently inclined to question the religious beliefs they have been taught would have a greater total liberty if given the freedom to change their minds about religion." Public authorities should ignore "a child's expressed preference for a kind of schooling that includes the practices" of indoctrination and crippling of personality which the author claims characterize religious schools. Overriding the child's decision (not to mention that of her parents) "would be appropriate and even morally requisite."[12]

As with this contemporary example, nineteenth-century objections to public funding of parochial schools were not generally based upon abstract concerns about "separation of Church and State," but upon the presumed nefarious effect of Catholic schooling. Josiah Strong, in his widely read survey of the perils facing *Our Country* (1886, revised 1891), warned that

the Roman Catholic is not at liberty to weigh the Pope's judgment, to try his commands by his own conscience and the Word of God—to do this would be to become a Protestant. [To make matters worse,] he stands not alone, but with many millions more, who are bound by the most dreadful penalties to act as one man in obedience

to the will of a foreign potentate and in disregard of the laws of the land. *This,
I claim, is a very possible menace to the peace of society.*[13]

Not only was Catholic schooling considered dangerous in its effects, but
Republican leaders claimed to be concerned to avoid the conflict that would
be likely to arise (as in Europe) over efforts by Catholics to obtain a share of
the public funds for education through the political process. Typical of this
attitude was a long unsigned lead article reprinted from a Congregationalist
publication in Horace Mann's *Common School Journal,* extending over three
issues in 1848, entitled "Sectarian or 'Parochial' Schools." The author warned
that, with the proliferation of denominational schools, "the number of sects
would increase instead of diminishing . . . until they isolated every house from
every other house; until they ran through houses, indeed, separating man and
wife." The effect of this on educational provision would not be a healthy competition but would instead "destroy, if not the existence, certainly the prosperity of the public schools, taking away from them a considerable portion, and
probably the better portion of the pupils of the place, those best trained, by
example, precept and authority, at home, and with them the pecuniary support and earnest interest of their parents." It would be particularly unwise, by
extending public funding to denominational schools, to stimulate "the sectarian spirit . . . Better than this, it might be (are we not justified in saying *would*
be) to cast all the school funds to the bottom of the sea." Forgetting that almost
all popular schooling for the past 200 years had been provided by schools with
a distinct denominational character, the author asserted that only the nondenominational common school was "in accordance with the nature and necessities of our free institutions," and that the "influence of the church school
system . . . will be sectarian, divisive, narrow, clannish, anti-republican." Their
effect would be "to subvert our common schools, so beneficent for purposes of
unity and harmony, on the ground that they are not sufficiently sectarian."[14]

The conviction that schooling with a religious character was profoundly
dangerous to national unity and to social peace persisted over the course of
the nineteenth and twentieth centuries, and led to bitter struggles with parents—especially immigrants—who wanted the education of their children
to be within the framework of their Catholic or Lutheran or Reformed faith.
What Cavanaugh has called "the myth of religious violence"[15] continues to be
influential, as we see, for example, in Justice Stevens's dissent to the Supreme
Court's approval of school vouchers in Cleveland:

> I am convinced that the Court's decision is profoundly misguided. Admittedly, in
> reaching that conclusion I have been influenced by my understanding of the impact

of religious strife on the decisions of our forbears to migrate to this continent, and on the decisions of neighbors in the Balkans, Northern Ireland, and the Middle East to mistrust one another. Whenever we remove a brick from the wall that was designed to separate religion and government, we increase the risk of religious strife and weaken the foundation of our democracy.[16]

His colleague Justice Souter's dissent made similar reference to "sectarian religion's capacity for discord," while that of Justice Breyer stressed the urgency of "avoiding religiously based social conflict." None of the dissenting justices cited any examples of such conflict in the United States more recent than the mid-nineteenth century. The point is not, however, the cogency of their arguments, but the evidence they provide of the persistent conviction that there is something very dangerous about allowing schools to present to children different ways of understanding the nature of the Good Life and the purposes of education.

In fact, it was when Belgium and the Netherlands adopted laws giving parents equal access to public and private (mostly faith-based) schools through funding the latter based on the choices made by parents that social and political conflict based on religion subsided in those countries.[17]

What agitated many voters in the 1870s was fear that the Catholic Church was gaining political influence and advancing demands upon an educational system that rested in large part upon successful compromises among Protestants. "Must an American State change its essential nature to accommodate religious fanatics?" asked an author in 1876.[18] It was a period when politics were followed closely by the public—more than 80 percent of the eligible voters outside of the South participated in presidential elections from 1876 to 1900—and elections were often closely decided.[19] Anti-Catholicism was invoked often, and successfully, in these elections.

Faced with rapid social changes propelled by immigration and industrialization, and with an economic slump, the Protestant majority in the North was easily persuaded to transfer its concern from the situation of freed slaves in the South to the closer-at-hand "menace" of growing Catholic self-assertion. "By the early 1870s, the Republican Party officially adopted religion in public schools as a pet project." Nor was this an issue for only one election cycle; in Massachusetts, for example, religious conflict about schools dominated elections in 1888 and 1889. For several decades "the question of religion in the public schools . . . captured the imagination of rabid anti-Catholics, who warned of popish plots to take over American schools."[20]

As national politics became competitive again with revival of the fortunes of the Democratic Party, Senator Henry Wilson of Massachusetts, Chairman of the Republican National Committee, in a January 1871 article in the *Atlantic Monthly*, "outlined the new Republican strategy which called on the public school to become the centerpiece of a new Reconstruction of all of American society." The goals of preserving the Union and freeing the slaves had been met; now the party required a new mission.

> Concurrent with the miserable condition of the freedmen, he wrote, ignorant and illiterate immigrants from Europe were entering the country also to become voters. As never before, an unwanted cultural diversity characterized the voting class. . . . A genuine national unification through a national public school system was needed. . . . He held up the model of Prussian public education, organized from the center. . . . As Otto von Bismarck was centralizing a new German federation, the Republican Party was centralizing the American Union. As Prussia had invested heavily in primary education, the United States should do likewise.[21]

THE BIBLE IN PUBLIC SCHOOLS

As we have seen, the strong localism of schooling in the United States made it a simple matter in most cases to accommodate the religious loyalties of parents—in most communities Protestant, but in some Catholic—in daily practices and classroom instruction. This was a more difficult matter in cities where both Catholics and Protestants were strongly represented, and conflict sometimes broke out over whether the Bible should be read devotionally or used as part of instruction . . . and, if so, which version of the Bible should be chosen. It was to end such conflict that, in 1842, a public school system replacing the private Public School Society was established in New York City, allowing voters in each ward to determine to what extent their schools would have a Protestant or Catholic flavor.

Removing the Bible from public schools, Protestant leaders argued, would cripple their ability to train citizens, especially children from families that did not provide adequate moral instruction. As Calvin Stowe asserted confidently in 1844, in an address before the American Institute of Instruction, "[t]o the use of the Bible, then, as the text-book of religious instruction in our [public] schools, there can be no serious objection on the part of Christians of any sect; and even unbelievers very generally admit it to be a very good and useful book."[22] But resistance was already developing on the part of Catholics who saw the use of the Bible Church-sanctioned notes as a feature of distinctively Protestant education. "It is the priests of Romanism," one Protestant writer charged in 1854, "who would break up our common school system for sectarian purposes, and shut out the light and influence of the Word of God . . . putting the ban of sectarian ignominy upon it."[23]

While compromises were usually worked out at the local level, the issue of the use of the Bible in public schools could become a major political flashpoint. In Cincinnati, a conflict over this issue in 1869 attracted national attention and did much to define the political agenda of the Republican Party in the 1870s. Opposition to the Bible in public schools was reinterpreted as opposition to public schools as such, not because of a logical connection between the two but because Catholic spokesmen were identified with both.

> Public school advocates charged that support of their movement was the best lit-mus-paper test of true American nationalism. In the South, Ku Klux Klan terrorists were then burning public schools. Accordingly, these midnight criminals demon-strated their disloyalty to American nationalism. In the North, Roman Catholics sought to remove the Bible from the public schools. Therefore, these dissenters also revealed their contempt for the nation. . . . The powerful emotions of religion and patriotism mixed in the cauldron of Reconstruction politics around the symbol of the public school.[24]

The Cincinnati Board of Education had been negotiating with the Catholic Archbishop for an arrangement under which Catholic schools would become part of the public system, as occurred in a number of cities in New York State. The deal under consideration involved abandonment by the public schools of the common practice of starting each school day with a reading from the Bible and the singing of a hymn, while the Catholic teachers (if certified by the state) would be retained as public school teachers. The Church would use the build-ings for religious instruction on weekends.

When word of these terms leaked out, there was a strong reaction from Protestants, and the Archbishop promptly withdrew from the negotiations. "Angered over the Protestant reaction that had killed their negotiations, [the Board] voted to bar the Bible and hymn singing from Cincinnati's public schools independent of any deal." Within weeks, this was a national issue; "the logic of the anti-Catholic crusade portrayed the school board action as part of an international Jesuit conspiracy being played out not only in the United States but also in Germany, England, Italy, and Spain."[25]

Defending the use of the Bible in public schools was a basis for mobilization among a Protestant majority that was feeling beleaguered by the political gains of Catholics in cities across the North. Typical was an interdenominational rally in 1875 in the Broadway Tabernacle in New York City, at which the lead speaker told the crowd that "[t]he expulsion of the Bible is only the starting point . . . it means ultimately the elimination from public instruction of all that tends to the promulgation of the doctrines of true religion, or morality, and of the rights of free human worship. . . . It is time for the people of America to arouse, and, if there is no law or statute in the Constitution to specify what principle of religion or of faith shall be sustained, then it is necessary for the people to speak and amend the Constitution."[26] A leading Presbyterian publication insisted that all Protestants were concerned "that the Bible, the Lord's Prayer, the recognition and assertion of fundamental moral and religious truth shall not be prohibited in our public schools on any pretext whatsoever."[27]

As historian Robert Handy has pointed out, "at no point did the evangelical consensus which bridged denominational and theological gulfs show itself more clearly in action than in the common effort to maintain the public schools as part of the strategy for a Christian America."[28] One of the puzzling features of this episode is that Protestant political leaders and the voters who supported them found no conflict between insisting that public schools should continue to have a Protestant character while being equally adamant that "sectarian" schooling was unAmerican and to be opposed. For example, the new Colorado Constitution, adopted in 1876 in a successful bid to gain statehood, included a provision that "[n]o sectarian tenets or doctrines shall ever be taught in the public school" (article IX, section 8). The convention delegates were assured by Judge J. B. Belford that "fears that the cause of Protestantism will suffer from the exclusion of the Bible from the schools was chimerical. Ninety-nine percent of the teachers are Protestant; the books employed and the literature used have no smack of Catholicism about them. The associations of the children are largely in the same direction. The papers and magazines most read by them are anti-sectarian." In other words, the Protestant character of the public schools made them, by definition, non-sectarian. The following day a letter appeared in the *Rocky Mountain News*, signed "A Catholic," pointing out that Belford had shown "that the common schools were Protestant."[29] This made them, from the Catholic perspective, profoundly sectarian and unacceptable for Catholic children.

This term "sectarian," used so frequently in laws and political polemic, requires clarification. It is fair to say that no religious organization has used the word to describe itself or its own educational efforts. According to Richard Baer "[t]hroughout American history, 'sectarian' has been used to exclude and to ostracize. It is a term that is used to disparage and marginalize particular groups of Americans and particular kinds of thinking."[30] Calling a religious group "sectarian" was and is, in colloquial terms, a "put-down," implying narrowness and divisiveness. The term as applied to education, was not a synonym for "religious." A Protestant leader urged, in 1854, "not that our academies and colleges shall be made sectarian, but *religious*." Another, the following year, argued that "while it is essential to forbid sectarianism in the public schools, it is *as* essential to bring them under the teachings and power of true religion; that religion should not be driven out under cover of repelling sectarianism ... it is as clearly the right and duty of the State to instruct the children in religious as in secular truth."[31]

What was the religious teaching that public schools were expected to provide? William Kailer Dunn summarizes Horace Mann's understanding of it this way:

> The teachers were influenced towards inculcating a system of religion which amounted to an acceptance of the existence of God, His Providence and His preparation of a life beyond the grave. Mankind is to relate itself to God in this life by trying to practice the virtues extolled in the Bible, in emulation of the maxims and good deeds of Christ. Such good works will contribute to the preservation and enrichment of the democracy that is America and help the soul to a place in the life to come. Such a system of religion (and it should never be forgotten that such Mann conceived it to be and wanted it, *as religion*, in the common schools) comes close to being a summation of Unitarian theology. It is easy to see, then, how the traditional Protestants of his day regarded [Mann's] plan as a new brand of sectarianism, and it is hard to say that they were wrong.[32]

On the other hand, for most non-Catholic parents, this generic Protestantism, silent about the great drama of sin and salvation, seems to have been quite satisfactory, especially when accompanied with regular reading from the Bible and other devotional practices.

Catholics, accustomed to having their own schools denounced as "sectarian," turned the accusation back upon the public schools, as Senator Bogy (D-Missouri) put it during the debates over the proposed "Blaine Amendment" to the federal Constitution:

> The Catholics of the United States have been opposed to free schools ... as organized some years ago. And why? For the reason that they were sectarian. ... These schools were more or less sectarian and, this being so, there is nothing strange or astonishing or very remarkable that those who believed in their religion should not willingly sanction their children going where their religion was not only untaught but where they were really taught to believe it was not correct. There is nothing strange in that. Hence the Catholics have opposed throughout the United States the levying of public taxes for the purpose of maintaining public schools organized on sectarian principles, because they could not participate in the education conferred by them;

not that they were opposed to education, not that they were opposed to free schools, but only because they were opposed to paying taxes for sectarian schools.[33]

Indeed, as early as 1828 Bishop Fenwick of Boston had complained that "all the children educated in the common schools of the country are obliged to use books compiled by Protestants by which their minds are poisoned as it were from their infancy." In 1840, the Catholic bishops formally charged that "the purpose of public education in many parts of the country was to serve the interests of heresy."[34] As the Catholic population of the country grew dramatically through immigration, the demand for their own schools grew as well.

PUBLIC FUNDING FOR CATHOLIC SCHOOLS

As we have seen, it was not uncommon in the eighteenth and early nineteenth centuries for public funding to be provided to schools that we would now consider "private" and that had a religious character, in the great majority of cases Protestant but sometimes Catholic. These arrangements continued even as one state after another discontinued public funding support for their formerly established churches. In California, in 1870, the state legislature provided funding to schools operated by a Catholic teaching order, though this aroused considerable opposition.[35]

Prompted by the concern about Catholic intentions to obtain preeminence in the Midwest, a number of states (Wisconsin 1848, Michigan 1850, Indiana, and Ohio 1851) intended to forestall Catholic demands for a share of the funds derived from land sales to support schools. In the 1850s, the anti-immigrant American (or "Know-Nothing") Party swept the state elections in Massachusetts and promptly amended the state constitution to require that public funds could be "expended in no other schools than those which are conducted according to law, under the order and superintendence of the authorities of the town or city in which the money is to be expended; and such moneys shall never be appropriated to any religious sect for the maintenance exclusively of its own schools."

> As one member of the Constitutional Convention of 1853 bluntly put it, the Know-Nothings feared that "some new sect may outvote the Protestants, and claim the school fund." The Anti-Aid Amendment put the issue of who would provide elementary and secondary education in Massachusetts into the state's Constitution, its "organic law, something that cannot easily be changed."[36]

It is worth emphasizing that this anti-immigrant political movement thought it necessary to remove the question of funding of Catholic schools from the ordinary arena of politics in a democratic society, even though they obviously had the votes to block efforts to appropriate funds for that purpose. The message was that this was a matter of fundamental principle that could not be left subject to the vagaries of elections or entrusted to the wisdom of future voters. Massachusetts would make this even clearer in 1917, when another convention was called to remove the antireligious clause of the constitution and simply prohibit public funds to any institution "not publicly owned and under the exclusive control, order and superintendence" of the state or federal government. The same convention established a typical Progressive-era initiative process by which citizens could propose laws to be placed on a statewide ballot for approval by popular vote without legislative action, but included a prohibition against this process being used in the future "to repeal either the Anti-Aid Amendment, or the provision barring its use to repeal the Anti-Aid Amendment!"[37]

We will see that this unwillingness to trust the judgment of citizens in the normal process of democratic deliberation on the issue of funding Catholic schools was evident at the constitutional convention held in Colorado in 1876.

It was in the 1870s that such funding became a major political issue nationwide, for three reasons: the growing political strength of Irish and German Catholic voters in some highly visible cities, the conflicts in Europe between the Catholic Church and a number of national governments, and the need of the Republican Party for a new issue to mobilize voters and make them forget the financial scandals of the Grant Administration. Popular support for the "reconstruction" of the South and for schooling of freed slaves and their children had ebbed,[38] and in 1874 Republicans lost control of the House of Representatives and experienced serious losses in the Senate as well; "waving the bloody shirt" of the Civil War no longer ensured their political dominance. President Grant became concerned that the resurgent Democrats were monopolizing the issue of reform which the public was demanding. "'Realizing that the Republican Party had inherited a devotion to public education while the Democratic Party, thanks to its Southern conservative wing and its Catholic following in the North, had never been regarded as favoring free public schools, Grant sought to realign the party in favor of education.' Being in favor of free education made the Republicans appear moral and once again the party of reform."[39] Since in fact the federal government had no responsibility for schools, there were no practical measures that Grant could take, but in the context of the 1870s the surest way to be perceived as a friend of the traditional common public school, strongly marked by nondenominational Protestantism, was to warn against the Catholic menace. This perhaps came all the more naturally to President Grant because he had been a member of the Know-Nothing party in his younger years.[40]

In the 1870s, given the strong identification of urban immigrant Catholics as Democrats, Republican leaders found it easy to play upon the fear of many voters about the growing political power of the Catholic Church to seek to maintain their hold on the White House. In July 1875 the *New York Tribune* reported that both political parties were planning to use the issue of funding of Catholic schools to strengthen their positions. "Even the *St. Louis Republican* recently said: 'The signs of the times all indicate an intention on the part of the managers of the Republican party to institute a general war against the Catholic Church . . . Some new crusading cry thus becomes a necessity of existence, and it seems to be decided that the cry of "No popery" is likely to prove most available.'"[41] Similarly, *Harper's Weekly* announced that the Republicans had discovered a winning issue.[42]

As the opening move in this campaign, in a speech to Union veterans gathered in Des Moines, President Grant struck a chord that had immediate resonance in the press nationwide:

> Let us all labor to add all needful guarantees for the security of free thought, free speech, a free press, pure morals, unfettered religious sentiments, and of equal rights and privileges to all men irrespective of nationality, color, or religion. Encourage free schools, and resolve that not one dollar, appropriated for their support, shall be appropriated to the support of any sectarian schools. Resolve that neither the State nor Nation, nor both combined shall support institutions of learning other than those sufficient to afford to every child growing up in the land the opportunity of a good common school education, unmixed with sectarian, pagan, or atheistical dogmas. Leave the matter of religion to the family altar, the Church, and the private school, supported entirely by private contributions. Keep the Church and State forever separate. With these safeguards, I believe the battles which created the Army of the Tennessee will not have been fought in vain.[43]

While commentary in the "mainstream" press was generally highly favorable, Catholics saw Grant's summons as a politically motivated attack on their growing influence in many urban areas. In the subsequent debate over a constitutional amendment forbidding aid to "sectarian" schools, Senator Bogy (D-Missouri) told his colleagues:

> I think I know the motive and the animus which have prompted all this thing. I do not believe it is because of a great devotion to the principles of religious liberty. That great idea which is now moving the modern world is used merely as a cloak for the most unworthy partisan motives. The African race has played its part in this

country; the negro is for party purposes in a manner dead; and these gentlemen, knowing that this thing is played out, and that "the bloody shirt" can no longer call out the mad bull, another animal has to be brought forth by these matadores [sic] to engage the attention of the people in this great arena [the 1876 elections] in which we are all soon to be combatants. The Pope, the old Pope of Rome, is to be the great bull that we are all to attack.[44]

Grant's position was basically inconsistent; his administration had greatly increased the role of religious (i.e. "sectarian") organizations in carrying out federal responsibilities toward many Indian peoples, relying heavily upon denominational (including Catholic) organizations that it funded to provide schooling. The congressional appropriations in support of the "civilizing" work of religious organizations, which had begun with $10,000 in 1817, reached $100,000 by 1870, and in 1876 there were 54,473 Indians in publicly funded agencies supervised by Methodists, 40,800 supervised by Baptists, 38,069 by Presbyterians, 26,929 by Episcopalians, 24,322 by Quakers, 17,856 by Catholics, 14,476 by Congregationalists, and 21,974 by other denominations. The Commissioner of Indian Affairs expressed support for public funding of religious schools for Indians as late as 1882, writing in his annual report: "I am decidedly of the opinion that a liberal encouragement by the government to all religious denominations to extend their educational and missionary operations among the Indians would be of immense benefit. . . . No money spent for the civilization of the Indian will return a better dividend than that spent this way."[45]

In response to the growing opposition to Catholic schooling, however, policy-makers subsequently turned against Catholic schools for Indians. Hostility toward Catholic schooling was so strong in the late nineteenth century that leaders of Protestant denominations that had been accepting public funding for many decades for their own Indian schools decided to reject that funding in order to be consistent with their opposition to public funds for Catholic parochial as well as Indian schools.[46] In 1889, a Methodist minister and prominent anti-Catholic, Daniel Dorchester, was appointed Superintendent of Indian Education; he had been active in the public school controversy in Boston in 1888 and in that year published a book called *Romanism versus the Public School System*, attacking Catholic schooling. "Its crying defect," he wrote, "is that its teaching is not only un-American but anti-American, and will remove every one of its pupils, in their ideals, far from a proper mental condition for American citizenship, and enhance the already too difficult task of making them good citizens of a republic."[47]

THE "BLAINE AMENDMENTS"

No doubt encouraged by the wide attention paid to his speech to the veterans, President Grant included in his annual message to Congress, in December 1875, a call for an amendment to the national Constitution, already amended three times in the previous decade,

> making it the duty of each of the several States to establish and forever maintain free public schools adequate to the education of all the children in the rudimentary branches within their respective limits, irrespective of sex, color, birthplace, or religions; forbidding the teaching in said schools of religious, atheistic, or pagan tenets; and prohibiting the granting of any school funds or taxes, or any part thereof, either by the legislative, municipal, or other authority, for the benefit or in aid, directly or indirectly, of any religious sect or denomination, or in aid or for the benefit of any other object of any nature or kind whatever.[48]

Such an amendment, if enacted and ratified, would have revived an element that had been dropped from the 1875 Civil Rights Act, adopted as a last gasp of Republican dominance of Congress: the prohibition of racial discrimination in school admission. In addition to carrying forward this element of the Reconstruction agenda, however, the proposal added a crowd-pleasing new theme, a prohibition against public funding for Catholic schools. This was picked up immediately by an ambitious congressman from Maine, James G. Blaine, who introduced a bill calling for an amendment that dropped the racial provision, for which opposition had grown in the North as well as the South, and preserved only that aimed against Catholic schooling, disguised within an extension of the first clause of the First Amendment to the states:

> No State shall make any law respecting an establishment of religion, or prohibiting the free exercise thereof; and no money raised by taxation in any State, for the support of the public schools or derived from any public fund therefor, shall ever be under the control of any religious sect, nor shall any money so raised ever be divided between religious sects or denominations.[49]

It was no secret that this measure was directed against Catholic schooling; no one was concerned that a Quaker private school in Philadelphia or an Episcopalian private school in New York City might seek public funds. Behind the opposition to Catholic schooling was a conviction that Catholics sought to undermine the public school, as the long-serving Denver public school superintendent charged in 1878.[50] Senator Henry Blair (R.-N.H.) told the Senate in

1888 that "Jesuits . . . have come to our borders and they are among us to-day, and they understand that they are to secure the control of this continent by destroying the public-school system. They are engaged in that nefarious and wicked work."[51]

During the debate over the Blaine Amendment in 1876, Senator Morton (R-Indiana) warned

> My-friend says there is no danger. Well, Mr President, in my judgment there is danger. That cloud is looming above the horizon; it is larger than it was a few years ago . . . without giving names here tonight, . . . there is a large body of people in this country, sincere, earnest, and pious, I have no doubt, who believe that our public schools in which religion is not taught are infidel and wicked, and who are not in favor of any school that does not teach religion. Does he not know that the public-school system of this country has been condemned and interdicted? . . . there is a large and growing class of people in this country who are utterly opposed to our present system of common schools, and who are opposed to any school that does not teach their religion.[52]

A Catholic colleague, Senator Kernan (D-New York) protested that "when he expresses the idea that those to whom he alludes would take from Protestants the right to have their children educated just as they see fit, he does them great wrong . . . we only ask that we should be allowed to educate ours as we think best, in all kindness, without the slightest unkind feeling or dissent about it." But another Republican, Senator Edmunds (R-Vermont) returned to the attack, warning that "there is a feeling well-grounded . . . that there is a particular sect that believes, in all sincerity undoubtedly, that the public schools of this country as at present conducted, nonsectarian . . . are not justified by the principles of religion; that they are wrong, and that it is the duty of a well-ordered state to teach in the public institutions the particular tenets of a particular denomination." Edmunds had selections from the *Syllabus of Errors*, condemning the idea that civil authorities should provide schooling independent of the authority of the Catholic Church, read into the *Congressional Record*. Catholics, he insisted, were required to believe this, and thus to seek to "revolutionize our systems of public instruction."[53]

The proposed amendment passed in both the House and Senate, but fell short of the required two-thirds in the Senate. The real action, in fact, would be in the states, as one after another adopted similar language in their state constitutions over the next decades. In Colorado, a Constitutional Convention was at work for the aspirant state even as Congress considered Blaine's proposed amendment, and anti-aid language was debated and adopted in August 1876, with similar intent:

> Neither the general assembly, nor any county, city, town, township, school district or other public corporation, shall ever make any appropriation, or pay from any public fund or moneys whatever, anything in aid of any church or sectarian society, or for any sectarian purpose, or to help support or sustain any school, academy, seminary, college, university or other literary or scientific institution, controlled by any church or sectarian denomination whatsoever; nor shall any grant or donation of land, money or other personal property, ever be made by the state, or any such public corporation to any church, or for any sectarian purpose. (Article IX, section 7)

And, in another section of the Colorado Constitution, "No appropriation shall be made for charitable, industrial, educational or benevolent purposes to any person, corporation or community not under the absolute control of the state, nor to any denominational or sectarian institution or association" (Article V, section 34). In effect, these two sections employ different strategies to attain the same goal, denying public support to Catholic schools.

Colorado is an interesting example; unlike Boston, New York, or Philadelphia, it did not have the experience over decades of tension and even rioting between Catholics and Protestants, as in the Orange riots in New York City in 1870 and 1871 when more than 60 were killed in fighting between Irish Catholics and Irish Protestant marchers celebrating the anniversary of the Battle of the Boyne. Colorado had its own tensions, however, between "Mexicans" in the southern part of the territory and "Americans" which led to the so-called Trinidad War of 1867–68. Although about one in four of the residents of the territory was Catholic, including Irish railroad laborers, they were either not represented or minimally represented (historical sources differ) among the 39 delegates elected to the constitutional convention in October 1875, when Grant's speech to the veterans was still the subject of lively discussion in Colorado.

That prejudice existed among the Protestant majority there can be no doubt; the day before the convention began its deliberations, the *Rocky Mountain News* featured an article on the "thieving reputation" of Mexicans.[54] One of the debates in the convention was whether to tax church property, and the *Denver Daily Times* suggested that this was in retaliation against the Catholic position on the school questions. A former territorial governor who was lobbying for eleven Protestant churches seeking tax immunity wrote in a private letter that the Protestant ministers wanted to tax the Catholics while being exempted themselves. "It seems much like the Know–Nothing movement—the Republicans are going into secret societies against the Catholics . . . But I keep my hand covered while I stir them up."[55] A dissertation on the religious controversies surrounding this convention concludes that they "exemplified on a smaller scale the religious, social, and political currents of the United States as a whole," and review of debates and opinions reflected in the local press confirm that participants were very much aware of what was going on across the country and thought of themselves as participants in the same struggles. For example, the *Denver Daily Times* (September 5, 1875) gave detailed coverage to a controversy in New Jersey over public funding for Catholic schools.[56]

The newly formed Colorado Teachers' Association, meeting in December 1875, urged that the new constitution exclude "sectarianism" and prohibit the diversion of public funds for education to nonpublic schools.[57] In this respect, again, Colorado reflected closely what was occurring at the national level as well as the position of the National Educational Association, meeting that year in Minneapolis.[58]

Judge Belford addressed the convention at the end of December, warning that allowing public funding for religious schools would be a "denial of the right of the nation to provide a uniform system of education for its youth, and to compel its support."[59] As the convention debated the anti-aid ("Blaine") provision of the proposed Constitution, petitions came in on both sides of the question, though more supporting it than opposed; one petition suggested that failure to include such a provision could jeopardize congressional approval of Colorado statehood. Meanwhile, a vigorous discussion occurred in the press. A correspondent signing himself "A. Freeman" warned that the "antagonism of a certain church towards our American public school system, has been so bold, so defiant and so general as to leave no doubt its object . . . which, if achieved, would within a couple of generations, lay our vigorous young republic, bound with the iron fetters of superstition at the feet of a foreign despot, the declared foe of intellectual liberty and human progress."[60]

Two days later, an editorial and a letter to the *Rocky Mountain News* urged that, as a matter of prudence rather than of principle, the convention refrain from including a "Blaine" provision, lest that lead to Catholic opposition that might imperil the ratification of the Constitution by popular vote, and on January 29 the paper reiterated this position, while insisting that it would oppose any legislative attempt to fund sectarian schools. On February 2 this argument was made again:

> Were the passage of the constitution a foregone conclusion, it is perhaps unnecessary to say that this paper would hardly propose to, if only ostensibly, gainsay the

Blaine amendment to the federal constitution, or to even in appearance controvert the doctrines enumerated in the Des Moines speech of the president. Under the circumstances, however, The News regards it clearly the better part of wisdom for the constitutional convention to insert no clause in the constitution calculated to excite the opposition of any class in the community, even if such clause conspicuously contains sentiments of which the republican party particularly is the exponent . . . the legislature is fully competent to deal with the question, and the danger is far from conceivable of a majority in that body being in favor of any measure that would detract from the stability of the public school system as presently constituted. . . . there is every probability of an amendment to the constitution of the United States being passed, in no long time, which will put the matter to rest here in Colorado, without any local lifting of hands to bring about this consummation devoutly wished for by so many.[61]

On the other hand, an editorial in the *Boulder County News* asked rhetorically, "is it not enough that Rome dominates in Mexico and all of South America?" though a few days later the paper was also urging caution about offending Catholic voters.[62]

The Catholic position was asserted unmistakably by Apostolic Vicar Machebeuf, who insisted on the loyalty of Catholics to Colorado and lamented the absence of a Catholic voice in the deliberations of the convention. He argued that "sectarian, pagan and atheistic doctrines" were being taught in public schools, and that their "pervading air, their tone, and all these subtle and impalpable traits . . . are anti-Catholic," and accused some Protestant leaders of holding the hope of "grinding" Catholicism out of America's Catholic youth through the public schools.[63] On February 18, Machebeuf sent a message to the convention delegates, urging that the question of funding of denominational schools be left to the judgment of future legislators rather than locked into the Constitution, which would make it much more difficult for consideration through the ordinary process of deliberation. Machebeuf argued eloquently that

the question itself has never been fully and dispassionately discussed in this country, and can not be said to have been discussed at all in Colorado. We have had, so far as I am informed, nothing said on our side of the question in your honorable body. . . . So far, both in this country at large and in Colorado, the language of passion has been more often uttered than that of reason. . . . The present is no time for the exposition of the arguments in favor of denominational schools. But we look forward hopefully to the future. A day shall at last dawn—surely it shall—when the passions of this hour will have subsided; when the exigencies of partisan politics will no longer stand in the way of right and justice, and political and religious equality shall again seem the heritage of the American citizen.[64]

Despite Machebeuf's earlier threat that Catholics might be compelled to oppose the Constitution, the anti-aid language was included in the text approved by the Convention. The *Rocky Mountain News* concluded that "in taking the bull by the horns and grappling with the school fund question as it did, the convention showed the wisdom of the serpent, if not the harmlessness of the dove, for far more protestants can be got to vote for the constitution on account of this very clause than catholics for the same reason to vote against it, and many, no doubt, will vote for it for the sake of this clause alone . . . no doubt, but that the president's Des Moines speech and Mr. Blaine's amendment to the national constitution struck a chord in the average American breast that has not yet ceased vibrating. What at first seemed the weakest link in the constitutional chain, no doubt will prove a source of strength to all the others."[65] It seems there can be no question that the editorial was correct in assessing the public mood, for which opposition to Catholic schooling was an issue of paramount concern; the voters went on to ratify the Constitution overwhelmingly.

Were he alive today, Machebeuf would no doubt be surprised and disappointed to learn that (unlike other Western democracies, all of which fund faith-based schools) the United States still maintains barriers against reasoned deliberation about providing schooling that responds to the choices of parents. It is striking how, whether in Massachusetts, or Colorado, or in federal court litigation, opponents of making faith-based schooling available to parents without financial penalty seek to remove this issue from the sphere of democratic decision-making.

Unfortunately, across the United States, the adamant refusal to permit public funding for Catholic schools led to Catholic opposition to increased tax support for the public schools in those cities where that opposition had serious consequences. Political scientist Paul Peterson comments that "the public schools might have gained more in fiscal terms at an earlier date had they been more willing to work cooperatively with their fellow educators within the Catholic church."[66] But that would have required an openness rare in the nineteenth century, when so much anxiety was directed against the Catholic influence in public and even in private life, and when the common public schools were expected to fulfill a spiritually unifying role.

Chapter Eight

Redefining the Teacher

Other than in the higher-prestige academies and grammar schools, school-teaching was slow to emerge as a profession in the United States. For decades, "itinerant adventurers, drifters, young men seeking to avoid physical labor, chronic malcontents, and perhaps misfits who had failed at other enterprises most typically were claimants on teaching posts."[1]

Robert Coram of Delaware charged, in 1791, that "the teachers are generally foreigners, shamefully deficient in every qualification necessary to convey instruction to youth and not seldom addicted to gross vices."[2] Half a century later, the same concern was expressed by a school reformer in the Midwest, who claimed that "at least four-fifths of the teachers in the common schools of Illinois would not pass an examination in the rudiments of our English [let alone Latin] education, and most of them have taken to teaching because they haven't anything in particular to do."[3]

Even after the Civil War,

> 40 percent of teachers were new each year; the professional expectancy was only about three years; the sessions lasted only three, five, or seven months; . . . the majority of teachers were young women who hoped to teach for only a few sessions; and half the teachers were less than twenty-two years of age. How could a profession evolve from such conditions?[4]

What in fact evolved, as we will see, was a semi-profession more similar to a religious teaching order, informed by a fervent belief in its calling, than to an autonomous profession, based on specialized expertise and collegial discipline.

The unstable and undervalued situation of teachers continued, with some improvement, throughout the nineteenth century; at its close, the typical elementary school teacher "had less than the equivalent of a high school education. By 1922, the same was still true of approximately one-fourth of all teachers working in the primary grades," and a decade later only 10 or 12 percent of them had earned a bachelor's degree.[5] Not only had elementary school teachers in 1931 received little formal training, but the "training of faculty members of the teacher-training institutions was also singularly unimpressive; over fifty percent of the faculty members of state teacher colleges and normal schools had one year or less of graduate work, and most of them had no personal experience in elementary education."[6]

Schoolteaching was, in fact, not an occupation with great attractions for those who had other options in an expanding economy, which is why it increasingly came to be dominated by women. Men who taught were generally doing so for a year or so until something better came along; others suffered from physical handicaps. Their situation was often difficult, like that of a Mr Harris, a school teacher in New Orleans, who had not been paid for his work, had contracted malaria, and was dependent on charity for simple survival.[7]

Unlike Prussia, whose normal schools were so much admired by American reformers, in antebellum America there was never "a body of professional schoolmasters at all adequate to the demands of the rapidly increasing and expanding population, and the deficiency had to be supplied with casual teachers who taught in the intervals of other occupation or as a stop-gap in their careers."[8] In 1859, the average teaching career lasted less than 2 years, and very few continued to teach for more than 5 years. The status of teachers was in fact in decline during the early years of the new republic[9]:

In the early 1800's, the coming of the teacher was a special event and families spared no effort to make him comfortable and serve him the best from their larder. But not in 1837. Boarding the teacher was simply an economy measure which reduced their individual taxes. . . . the young Henry Thoreau, fresh from Harvard, was finding that conditions in his classroom made it impossible to try out his educational ideas. After a two-week trial, he gave up. . . . Meanwhile at the other end of the state . . . Herman Melville stuck it out for the winter season, then left, thoroughly disgusted.[10]

Horace Bushnell—later an eloquent spokesman for the role of the common school in assimilating the children of immigrants—tried his hand at teaching "undisciplined" and "ungrateful" pupils and concluded that being a teacher would "freeze the heart and dissipate the mind of the best man living."[11]

Some teachers were—like Thoreau—recent college graduates taking a school while looking for a better position, or college students on their long vacation; "several New England colleges arranged their winter vacations so that students could take advantage of them to keep school."[12]

REDEFINING THE ROLE OF WOMEN

The rapid development of popular schooling across the northern states with minimal effective state intervention—and none at all from the federal government—cannot be understood apart from the changing role of women, providing teachers for tens of thousands of schools in a nation whose dynamic economy delayed the development of a stable teaching profession. It was in the antebellum decades that teaching at the elementary level came to be seen as a natural occupation for women before or in lieu of marriage.

The gender transition was gradual. In the first decades of the nineteenth century, "women ordinarily taught during the summer when the older school boys and girls and the more rambunctious teenagers stayed on the farm or at home working with their parents or hiring out as seasonal laborers,"[13] while men taught during the winter months when schools had more fee-paying pupils. By the 1840s, however, this haphazard pattern of school staffing had largely vanished in New England and mid-Atlantic region and was vanishing in the Midwest.

Catharine Beecher concluded that, as she wrote her father in 1823, "there seems to be no very extensive sphere of usefulness for a single woman but that which can be found in the limits of a school-room."[14] Similarly, English visitor Harrier Martineau commented, in the 1830s, that

> the lot of poor women is sad. Before the opening of the factories, there were but three resources: teaching, needle-work, and keeping boarding-houses or hotels. . . . For women who shrink from the lot of the needle-woman . . . there is little resource but pretension to teach. . . . Teaching and training children is, to a few, a very few, a delightful employment, notwithstanding all its toils and cares. Except to these few it is irksome; and when accompanied with poverty and mortification, intolerable.[15]

Beecher and others set out to change this situation. She gave early evidence of her energy and executive ability by establishing, in 1823, the Hartford Female Seminary, which offered young women an education comparable to that which young men could receive in college. This was by no means just a finishing school; she told her students that "A lady should study, not to shine, but to act," and "that they had no right to spend their time in idleness, fashion and folly, but they as individuals were bound to be useful in Society after they had finished their education, and that as teachers single women could be more useful in this than in any other way."[16]

Although her school was a considerable success, by 1831 she left it to give her own desire for activity greater scope. Her father Lyman Beecher became President of Lane Theological Seminary in Cincinnati, founded to train Presbyterian ministers for the expanding frontier; his widely distributed book *A Plea for the West*, expanded from his fund-raising lectures, stressed the urgency of Protestant efforts to reproduce the educational and religious institutions of New England to protect against Catholic schemes to dominate the Ohio Valley. Catharine reinforced this message with her own *Essay on the Education of Female Teachers* (1835), which warned that "The education of the lower classes is deteriorating, as it respects moral and religious restraints. . . . and at the same time thousands and thousands of degraded foreigners, and their ignorant families, are pouring into this nation at every avenue."[17] She called for sending well-prepared women to teach on the frontier and thus claim it for Protestantism and civilization. Her essay also proposed a network of teacher training establishments at key locations in the West, endowed from the East, and offering "a curriculum equal in character and quality to the colleges for men, with special emphasis on moral and undenominational religious instruction," and with model schools attached to demonstrate the best teaching methods.[18]

In a succession of widely read books, including *The Moral Instructor for Schools and Families: Containing Lessons on the Duties of Life* (1838), *Treatise on Domestic Economy for the Use of Young Ladies at Home and at School* (1843), *The Duty of American Women to Their Country* (1845), *The Evils Suffered by American Women and American Children: The Causes and the Remedy* (1846), and *The True Remedy for the Wrongs of Women* (1851), Beecher promoted a view of women as uniquely fitted to be the moral guides of society and teachers of children. This required, she wrote in 1851, that "teaching should become a profession for women, as honorable and as lucrative for her as the legal, medical, and theological professions are for men,"[19] and that women receive an education comparable to that of men. A profession was to be created for women, Beecher wrote in 1846:

> To marry for an establishment, for a position, or for something to do, is a deplorable wrong. But how many women, for want of a high and honorable profession to engage their time, are led to this melancholy course. . . . *The education of children,*

that is the true and noble profession of a woman—*that* is what is worthy of the noblest powers and affections of the noblest minds.[20]

It was women who possessed the "noblest minds" and, in an early form of "difference feminism" designed to create a sphere for activity by women outside of the home, Beecher and others stressed a parallel between the role of mothers within their own families and the role of women as school teachers. "Mothers have as powerful an influence over the welfare of future generations as all other earthly causes combined," they argued. Emma Willard emphasized the key function of women in ensuring the welfare of the country. "[America's] prosperity," she stressed, "will depend on the character of its citizens. The characters of these will be formed by their mothers; and it is through the mothers, that the government can control the characters of its future citizens, to form them such as will ensure their country's prosperity."[21] Although teaching was considered "the most wearying drudgery, and few resort to it except from necessity," Beecher said, it should be elevated into a "true and noble" calling, the special "profession of a woman."[22]

Supporting the call which her father had issued to export New England culture to the West, Beecher was instrumental, in the 1840s and 1850s, in recruiting and raising funds to send hundreds of young unmarried women to the frontier as teachers, in an effort anticipating the similar movement of New England women into the South to educate freed slaves in the 1860s. In 1847 she recruited and sent out 70 young women, more than half of them to Illinois and Indiana, where "most of them lived in primitive surroundings and faced daily obstacles, not the least of which [in some cases] was local hostility to religion in public schools." Beecher, however, insisted on the importance of religious teaching to provide guidance on how "to live to do good," because of the breakdown of social controls on the expanding frontier, where the "education of the lower classes is deteriorating, as it respects moral and religious restraints."[23] Her ally Emma Willard advocated "systems of morality, enforced by the sanctions of religion," and opposed teachers "who would not teach religion and morality, both by their example, and by leading the minds of the pupils to perceive, that these constitute the true end of all education."[24]

It has been suggested that,

Under the guise of 'woman's role,' the wily Catharine Beecher was staking out a new territory for women. They were to be trained for their work, as men were trained for theirs; women were to become teachers; they were to leave their families, and friends to travel alone to frontier lands, and by their own efforts, to support themselves.[25]

If hundreds of women went west to teach, thousands staffed the schools of New England: by 1834, women were 56.3 percent of the teaching force in Massachusetts, a proportion that increased to 77.8 percent by 1860 and 80 percent by 1861. The 80 percent mark was reached in New Hampshire in 1864, in Connecticut in 1865, and in 1866 in Rhode Island, though the more rural Vermont and Maine didn't reach 80 percent women teachers until 1880 and 1890, respectively. Nationwide, the number of women working in schools rose from 84,500 in 1870[26] to 325,500 in 1900, when they out-numbered men three-to-one.[27]

Most teaching careers were short and ended with marriage; thus, it has been estimated that already before the Civil War about one out of every five women in Massachusetts served as a school teacher at some point in her life, and this may have risen to one out of four of those native-born.[28]

This situation emerged as "a rapidly expanding population demanded more teachers, but a rapidly developing economy had relatively fewer males available for nonindustrial or noncommercial work." Catharine Beecher sought to create career possibilities for single women, "the road to honourable independence and extensive usefulness where she need not outstep the prescribed boundaries of feminine modesty,"[29] and stressed the characteristics which, she argued, made women especially fitted to be elementary teachers. As Beecher articulated her case in 1837, "first the character of women should be highly differentiated from the character of men in order to allow women to exemplify domestic virtues; and second, women should permeate the nation with their special character through their influence as teachers in public schools."[30] A few years later she pointed out that "wherever education is most prosperous, there woman is employed more than man. In Massachusetts, where education is highest, five out of seven of the teachers are women; while in Kentucky, where education is so much lower, five out of six of the teachers are men."[31]

Beecher's biographer notes that

> Several forces converged in the 1830s and the 1840s to form a matrix of support for Catharine Beecher's ideas. These were the creation of a leisured middle class of women, the institution of tax-supported common schools, the expansion of population in the West and its need for new schools, and the glorification of female qualities of nurture throughout the United States.[31]

As a result of these forces, and the willingness of single women—without career alternatives—to work for very low salaries, by 1888, 85 percent of the teachers in the United States were women, and this rose to 90 percent in cities.[32]

While teaching did not guarantee a middle-class income, it did square with middle-class gender ideology while also allowing women a degree of independence. . . . Unlike working-class women generally, teachers were better positioned to "marry up" as a consequence of their greater visibility, geographic mobility, and genteel image.[33]

It was commonly said that by

> returning to the classrooms they had so recently departed as graduates, . . . young unmarried women were simply anticipating the domestic happiness and personal fulfillment that matrimony would later confer. For widows and spinsters, the rewards of teaching would serve in part to compensate them for their unhappy fate.[34]

Horace Mann, Henry Barnard, and other common school reformers were eager to promote the hiring of women to make it possible to expand the supply of schooling without a corresponding increase in cost. For the elite reformers, Beecher's widely read books on the emerging role of women were a godsend. Her argument that women were uniquely fitted to be the instructors of youth, in a natural extension of their biological destiny as mothers, became a staple of the case for hiring women to replace more expensive men. Her accompanying argument for collegiate-level education for women was largely ignored and the efforts of the reformers went instead into creating "normal schools" which focused almost exclusively on preparing young women to teach the elementary-school curriculum.

When Beecher wrote her final appeal for the appropriate recognition of female teachers in *Woman's Suffrage and Woman's Profession,* published in 1872, female teachers in Massachusetts were still earning less than 40 percent of male teachers' wages. Other female educational leaders who advocated the feminization of teaching made liberal use of Beecher's arguments about women's moral superiority and the responsibilities issuing therefrom. Mary Lyon proposed that women's mission, that of teaching, necessitated higher institutions of learning for women. She also advanced the idea, as did Beecher, that female teachers had a special role in taming the West. A student of Lyon's was informed, as she reported in her journal, that women who teach in the public schools "would do more for the great West than all the colleges and academies." Emma Willard likewise garnered support for Troy Seminary by framing her appeals with the assertion that women are "the natural instructors of youth." Both Lyon and Willard, however, invoked domestic ideology to a much lesser degree than did Beecher, choosing instead to stress women's right to equal education.[35]

For Catharine Beecher and other would-be reformers of society, schools could have the hoped-for impact only if they were staffed by a new sort of teacher, for whom the moral content of instruction was at least as significant as the traditional academic skills. Horace Mann insisted that it was in the normal school, with its strong emphasis on the teaching of morality and on an atmosphere of liberal piety, that the teachers would be formed upon whom the hopes of the education reformers rested. The journal kept by Cyrus Pierce as the first normal school got under way, in 1839, and the journal of Mary Swift, one of his first group of students, alike testify to how seriously this moral mission of teacher education was taken.[36] This was not, it should be noted, what Catharine Beecher, Mary Lyon, and Emma Willard were calling for in the education of women; they sought a liberal arts education of the sort that Mount Holyoke came to exemplify. A few years later, the same tension would emerge over the sort of advanced education to give to freed slaves and their children, between the training of rural teachers and craftsmen in the Hampton/Tuskegee model favored by white philanthropists, on the one hand, and the liberal arts education provided in the colleges established by African American churches, on the other.[37]

Mann agreed with Beecher that women were uniquely suited for teaching because of their natural qualities, pointing out that women were "more mild and gentle . . . with stronger parental impulses . . . [and] of purer morals," and that they were "less intent and scheming for future honors or emoluments" for themselves than were men. For women, he wrote, "the sphere of hope and of effort is narrower, and the whole forces of the mind are more readily concentrated upon present duties," and this single-mindedness was an asset for teaching. His concept of the education that women required to be teachers differed radically from that of Beecher, Lyon, and Willard, however. State normal schools would deliver woman from "that shameful sentence of degradation by which she has been so dishonored" by preparing her for to be a common school teacher. "Yet never in Mann's vision were women to achieve equality with men; indeed he considered that proposition anathema, a position he would later elaborate in *A Few Thoughts on the Powers and Duties of Woman: Two Lectures* [1853]."[38]

A pioneer of the training of women as teachers was Zilpah Grant, whose Seminary for Female Teachers in Ipswich, Massachusetts, was founded in 1829, and included as her assistant principal Mary Lyon, who would go on to found Mount Holyoke Female Seminary, the first institution to provide college-level instruction to women, in 1837. The catalogue of the Ipswich school promised instruction "on the manner of communicating knowledge to children and youth of different capacities, and in different stages of improvement, and also on the manner of correcting their faults, and improving their dispositions," as well as "on the manner of awakening attention, of exciting inquiry, of arousing the indolent, of encouraging the diffident, of humbling the self-confident, of cultivating the conscience, of regulating the conduct, and of improving the whole character."

The private academies for young women ("female seminaries") founded by Emma Willard, Mary Lyon, Catharine Beecher, and other enterprising women were preparing teachers years before Horace Mann established the first state normal schools. In 1819, Willard submitted a plan to the governor of New York State to create a state-supported system of secondary institutions ("seminaries") to train women as teachers, arguing that "the education begun in the home by mothers educated in state seminaries must continue in state-established primary schools, where the most apt and available teachers would be women, not men."[40] That proposal being unsuccessful, she responded to an invitation from the municipal authorities in Troy, New York, to move her private academy there in 1821 as what became the Troy Female Seminary, which would train many women for teaching and other roles.

An analysis of the policy of state funding of female academies in New York State suggests that

> efforts to standardize teacher education ... actually *undercut* standards of female education. Standardization of teacher education occurred during the reform era of the 1830s and 1840s. The increased moral and political significance attributed to teaching in this era represented the fulfillment of one aspect of Willard's vision. Educated to think of their lives in terms of the larger, public purpose of educating others, female students could find challenges equal to their ambitions as leaders of educational reform. At the same time, however, as the increased importance of schooling enlarged the educated woman's field of labor in some respects, the standardization of teacher certification compromised the liberal character of her education in others.

In 1849, the state reduced certification requirements from 3 years to 4 months of study, reduced the required age of admission for young women from 16 to 14, and dropped the requirement of completing a full curriculum to one in which the only required subject was "principles of teaching." In short, "state regulation trivialized the vocation which female educators had carved out for women as worthy of their talents and dedication, and as requiring the full development of their minds."[41]

THE STATE AND THE TRAINING OF TEACHERS

Most teacher training throughout the antebellum period was in private institutions and as a supplement to their primary function. Benjamin Franklin had
suggested, in 1750, that the proposed Philadelphia Academy could prepare "a
number of the poorer Sort . . . to act as Schoolmasters." The Rev. Samuel Hall
(a striking proportion of those engaged in training teachers were clergymen)
opened a "seminary for teacher training" in Vermont in 1823, and in 1830
moved it to Phillips Academy in Andover, where he "attempted to incorporate
courses in pedagogy into the curriculum, but soon found his classes filled with
nothing but the dregs of the student body"; over 12 years he was able to train
fewer than a hundred young men as teachers.[42]

As early as 1789, Elisha Tichnor had published an article calling for the
creation of specialized institutions for training teachers, and in 1816 Denison
Olmsted gave an oration at Yale on "The State of Education in Connecticut,"
which argued the need for an Academy for Schoolmasters. Over the next two
decades, the need for better prepared teachers was a constant theme, and it
seemed increasingly evident to the reformers that this required professional
preparation of the sort that had been available in Prussia for several decades
and was promoted by the French government from the early 1830s. In 1825,
Thomas Gallaudet outlined in some detail how such an institution might
function, and asked, "Why not make this department of human exertion a
profession as well as those of divinity, law and medicine? Why not have an
Institution for the training up of Instructors for their sphere of labor, as well
as institutions to prepare young men for the duties of the divine, the lawyer,
or the physician?" The following year, Governor Clinton asked the New York
State legislature to authorize and support a public "seminary" to train teachers, but in vain. Nevertheless, a private benefactor, Stephen van Rensselaer,
founded and endowed the Rensselaer Institute that year, offering free tuition
to young men who would "go out to the world as an army of Teachers for at
least one year."[43]

There was a growing concern in Massachusetts, as well, for professional
training of teachers, beyond what could be provided by the periodic "teacher
institutes" that brought together hundreds of otherwise isolated teachers for a
few days of lectures on "school-keeping." The promotion of higher standards
in teaching in the period before the Civil War occurred largely through these
institutes that "operated as a kind of revival agency."

> Prayers and hymns not only were incorporated into the actual proceedings but usu-
> ally began and concluded the main exercises and lectures of an institute. It was

often more than a matter of convenience that institutes were held in churches. . . . Numerous expressions, such as "filled with the spirit," "the holiness of the work," the "vocation" of teaching, being "called," "fixing attention," and, of course, "awakening" itself, bore striking similarities to the rhetoric of the religious revivals. Most of all, the institute, like the revival, proposed to transform a congregation of individuals into a conscious moral body with its own special tone and spiritual goal, the two essential elements of awakening and professionalization.[44]

Far more teachers were reached by these institutes than passed through normal schools or other academic institutions for teacher preparation in the antebellum period: "in 1849, 36 percent of the teachers in Maine, in 1859, about 20 percent of the teachers in Wisconsin, and also in the late 1850s, approximately 15 percent of the teachers in Michigan attended institutes."[45] The early meetings of what became the National Education Association (NEA), founded in 1857, had many of the same characteristics, with prayers before and after sessions and regular discussion of the role of the Bible in public schools.[46]

In a series of articles published in the *Boston Patriot* in 1824–25, however, James Carter called for a more systematic approach to popular education, based on a thorough training of teachers. "The character of the schools," he wrote, "and of course their political, moral and religious influence depends, almost solely, upon the character of the teachers. Thus

> an institution for the education of teachers . . . would form a part, and a very important part, of the free-school system. It would be, moreover, precisely that portion of the system which should be under the direction of the State . . . An institution for this purpose would become, by its influence on society, and particularly on the young, an engine to sway the public sentiment, the public morals, and the public religion, more powerful than any other in the possession of government, it should, therefore, be responsible immediately to them. . . . It should be emphatically the State's institution.

Carter went on to warn his fellow reformers, "If it be not undertaken by the public and for public purposes, it will be undertaken by individuals for private purposes."[47] But what invidious private purposes can Carter have been thinking of? Private academies had been training teachers for some years without noticeably negative effects, and in fact Carter himself would attempt to operate a private teacher training institution a few years later. It seems likely that his concern was with the potentially "sectarian" character of teacher training not under state control. His own efforts would not be sectarian, of course, to his own Unitarian way of thinking, but having claimed the tremendous power of teacher training to "sway the public sentiment, the public morals, and the public religion," he must have seen that it would be in the interest of the churches to influence the "engine" that promised to take over so much of their traditional role. To Carter and other reformers, "the church was viewed with suspicion, but not the State."[48]

A further impulse for the creation of state teacher-training institutions was given by a series of reports on the importance of *Lehrerseminaren*, established in the beginning of 1819, in making the Prussian system of popular schooling the envy of reformers in other countries.[49] Particularly influential was the report by a French philosopher, Victor Cousin, published in Paris in 1833 and the English translation in London in 1834 and in New York in 1835; Cousin placed special emphasis on the provisions, in Prussia, for teacher training, since "the state has done nothing for popular education, if it does not watch that those who devote themselves to teaching be well prepared."[50] Cousin's report was widely influential; the Massachusetts and New Jersey legislatures had it reprinted and distributed to schools. It was followed by Calvin Stowe's descriptions of German teacher-training institutions, especially for teachers in the common schools, in a report presented first to the Ohio state legislature and subsequently published and reprinted by the legislatures of Kentucky, Tennessee, Pennsylvania, New York, and Massachusetts. In 1839, Stowe followed up with a detailed plan for teachers' education.[51]

In 1837, the leading association of "friends of education," the American Institute of Instruction (founded in 1830 by Hall and others) called for the establishment of several state teacher-training seminaries as well as for establishment of a state board of education in Massachusetts. It was Unitarian Minister Charles Brooks, however, who pressed the Prussian example most vigorously: "over and over again," he wrote, the Prussians "proved that elementary education cannot be fully attained without purposely-prepared teachers. . . . we are confident that teachers thoroughly prepared, as they are in Prussia, would put a new face on elementary education, and produce through our State an era of light and of love."[52] Brooks insisted that "school instructors should be as fully prepared for their duties as is the clergyman for his. Teachers, teachers, yes I say teachers, have an inconceivable and paramount agency in shaping the destinies of the world."[53]

Naturally enough, when later that year Horace Mann became Secretary of the new Board, he wrote in its *First Annual Report* that

> the subject of the education of teachers has been more than once brought before the Legislature, and is of the very highest importance in connection with the improvement of our schools. That there are all degrees of skill and success on the part of

teachers, is matter of too familiar observation to need repetition; and that this must depend, in no small degree, on the experience of the teacher and in his formation under a good discipline and method of instructions in early life, may be admitted without derogating, in any measure, from the importance of natural gifts and aptitude, in fitting men for this as for other duties of society.[54]

This led inescapably to the conclusion, the reformers pointed out, that

institutions for the formation of teachers must be established among us, before the all-important work of forming the minds of our children can be performed in the best possible manner, and with the greatest attainable success.[55]

At the dedication of a building for the state Normal School at Bridgewater, Mann proclaimed

I believe Normal Schools to be a new instrumentality in the advancement of the [human] race. . . . Neither the art of printing, nor the trial by jury, nor a free press, nor free suffrage, can long exist, to any beneficial and salutary purpose, without schools for the training of teachers. . . . Coiled up in this institution, as in a spring, there is a vigor whose uncoiling may wheel the spheres."[56]

Bringing the training of teachers under direct state control seemed, to Mann and other education reformers, an effective way of avoiding the problems that a direct assault upon local control of schools would have caused; it made it possible to argue, in all sincerity, that the common schools were under direct oversight of local school committees elected by parents and their neighbors and frequently chaired by a Protestant clergyman. The real content of public education, the reformers expected, would be determined by the teachers trained by state normal schools in shared values and perspectives that would counter local particularisms. Governor Edward Everett, under whose aegis the Massachusetts Board of Education had been established, speaking at the opening of the state Normal School in Barre, in 1839, explained the origin of the name:

Schools of this character were called normal schools, on their establishment in France, either because they were destined to serve in themselves as the model or rule by which other schools should be organized and instructed, or because their object was to teach the rules and methods of instructing and governing a school.[57]

In this manner, although the state had no direct control over the common schools, it was in a position to shape a growing proportion of the teachers in those schools according to the ideas of the education reformers. This strategy did not escape the notice of opponents of an expanded state role, including Orestes Brownson, who warned in 1839 that "as soon as they can get their Normal Schools into successful operation, they will so arrange it, if they can, that no public school shall be permitted to employ a teacher" not trained in one. Then, goodbye to "all liberty of instruction; . . . Adieu then to republicanism, to social progress."[58] Similarly, the Massachusetts legislative committee recommending, in 1840, the abolition of the Board of Education

> dismissed normal schools as European institutions unsuited to a free society and destructive of the progress that came from academies and high schools rivaling each other to produce the best teachers for common schools. To this the Committee added scorn of the whole idea of professional instruction for teachers; "every person, who has himself undergone a process of instruction, must acquire, by that very process, the art of instructing others," and teachers needed special schools no more than mechanics. Nor was it desirable to raise the job of school teaching into a "distinct and separate profession," given that schools were open only 3 or 4 months a year. "We may as well have a religion established by law," wrote Brownson, "as a system of education [so established], and the government educate and appoint the pastors of our churches, as well as the instructors of our children."[59]

Despite fears that state-sponsored teacher preparation could lead to a monopoly on the formation of citizens, there was a growing concern about the uneven quality of those appointed to teach in many local communities; the state-sponsored normal school, imitated from Prussia and France, seemed to reformers the key to educational progress.

The actual effect of state normal schools on the supply of well-prepared teachers was disappointing. Cyrus Peirce, the Unitarian minister who headed the first normal school, in Lexington (opened in July 1839 with three students), was discouraged to find that he "could not count on a regular flow of applicants graduating from some lower institution. Instead, he would gather in academy dropouts, a few high school graduates, and numerous bright persons who had no more than an elementary education."[60] initially he was the only staff member, teaching 17 different subjects and supervising a model school for practice teaching. Here and at the other two normal schools (Barre established in September 1839 and Bridgewater in August 1840), "while Mann assumed most normalites would complete a two-year course of study, he grossly overestimated their previous education and their thirst for additional learning. For most of them, a thorough review of elementary arithmetic and English grammar was necessary."[61] Pierce complained that they lacked "the power of generalization and of communication"; in fact, they were in need of learning the subjects taught in elementary schools before they could learn how to teach them.[62] Not until the end of the nineteenth century was it necessary to graduate from high school before being admitted to a normal school in Massachusetts, and requirements in other states lagged behind.[63] In 1895, only 14 percent of a nation-wide sample of normal schools required a high school diploma, and this had increased to only 22 percent by 1905.[64] Attendance at a normal school was often an alternative to high school, while many high schools offered a normal school program. The proportion of "normalites" who had completed high school varied greatly from one region to another, and even within states.[65]

Public normal schools (later developed into state teachers' colleges) only very gradually imposed themselves as the primary source of elementary school teachers. By 1850, there were seven of them, three in Massachusetts and the others in Albany (1845), Philadelphia (1848), New Britain, Connecticut (1849), and Ypsilanti, Michigan (1850).[66] Immediately after the Civil War, however, there was a rush of new state normal schools, and by 1870 there were 35, in 16 different states.[67]

Mann's biographer concludes that his ambitions for the normal schools were ultimately disappointed. "Although he did not understand it at the time, the teacher élites he hoped would come forth to staff the schools never appeared, but in their stead came an educational bureaucracy of the [sic] hoi polloi."[68] Although Mann and his allies regarded teacher training through normal schools as the key to the reform of the common school and to the state's influence over those schools, the desirability of this state role was by no means universally accepted. There was "just as much reason for asking the State to instruct young men in making shoes and hats," suggested the *Hartford Times* in 1850, "as to require it to fit them for teaching."[69]

Nor were the states able to establish a monopoly on teacher preparation, as Carter and Mann had recommended. Pennsylvania, New York, Wisconsin, and Indiana found it appropriate to provide subsidies to private academies and normal schools for teacher training.[70] After the Civil War, northern religious organizations established normal schools to train black teachers across the South, with Boston's American Missionary Association still supporting 43 such institutions in 1900.[71]

Despite the efforts of Mann and others, the United States lagged behind France, not to mention Prussia, in the provision of institutions dedicated to the preparation of teachers. The lag, contemporary observers pointed out, was attributable in large part to the different economic conditions on the two continents. In Prussia, a position in a government-regulated career, even at the lower ranks, was highly desirable, and young men who obtained normal school training were likely to remain in the teaching career for life. With the much more dynamic opportunities in American society, schoolteaching tended to be a short-term job for young women before marriage. Attendance at a normal school was not a necessary preparation for these fugitive careers, while for many who did attend that was simply a convenient way of continuing their schooling for a year or two longer with no intention of teaching. Experience was to show that few of the normal school students (especially among the men) were interested in making a life-long commitment to teaching.

> The normal schools served the young people of Massachusetts' farming areas and small towns as vocational training centers. They prepared their students for temporary employment in the schools or future nonfarming careers elsewhere. . . . The normal schools did not thereby accomplish their original purpose of aiding the rural schools. . . . The normalites were on the move both socially and geographically, and only few stayed or returned to play the role of country schoolmaster or schoolmistress.[72]

Even in Massachusetts, normal schools were slow to realize Mann's ambitions; by 1900, 60 years after the launching of the first three, only about 40 percent of the public school teachers in the Commonwealth had a normal school training.[73] On the other hand, the spread of state normal schools and of high schools with teacher preparation programs gradually forced most of the academies that had provided so much of the teacher preparation to become either public high schools or elite private secondary schools. By the 1890s, there were about 135 normal schools under state or city sponsorship nationwide competing with about 40 under private or denominational sponsorship.[74]

The standardization of teacher preparation which ensued from the gradual spread of state normal schools had its down side, as the experience in New York State demonstrated. "Different educational visions thrived for a time within the academy system because each institution enjoyed independent corporate legal status and government, and because no institution was completely dependent on one source of support. Once the state had incorporated the majority of academies into a tax-supported common system, however, that foundation of independence was seriously threatened, and the drive for integration and standardization could not be resisted except by moving outside the dominant system,"[75] as only those institutions with generous private benefactors—like Vassar—could do.

Formal teacher training was not limited to state and private normal schools; colleges and state universities began to see this as a promising market. In Virginia, Randolph-Macon College established a teacher-training program in

1839, and Brown University followed suit in 1850, only to suspend the program 4 years later. Normal (teacher-training) departments were established at
a number of mid-Western state universities.[76] By 1900, some 114 colleges and
universities, or more than one in four, were offering teacher training, though
of questionable quality and low prestige: "what they offered more often than
not was an entirely separate course of instruction, pitched not much above the
secondary level, and for students who might not otherwise have qualified for
regular admission."[77] The great majority of teachers, however, did not receive
training at even that level, if indeed they received any at all.

DEVELOPMENT OF PROFESSIONAL NORMS AND ROLE

In the long run, teacher institutes, private and public normal schools, teachers'
colleges, and teacher-training programs based in colleges and universities were
significant, not so much for imparting skills and knowledge to future teachers, as for advancing a set of ideas about the role of the teacher and the goals
of education. They promoted a spirit of consecration and confidence that the
teacher had it in her hands to shape a better world, while nurturing a succession of educational fads, from phrenology (Horace Mann's favorite) down to
the more recent enthusiasms for Constructivism and Multiple Intelligences.

Training of teachers under state supervision and direct control was the key
to Horace Mann's strategy for influencing the common schools and—through
them—the rising generation of Americans. In normal schools, permeated by
a liberal Protestant spirit indistinguishable from Unitarianism, future teachers
would imbibe that "pure religion of heaven upon which all good men agree,"
making them fit agents of a strategy committed to overcoming the cultural and
religious diversity that Mann and his allies found so threatening to America's
future. In an address at the opening of one of the first state normal schools,
in 1839, Mann's ally Massachusetts Governor Edward Everett explained that
its program should include "the important subject of the governance of the
school ... that is, of exercising such a moral influence in it as is most favorable
to the improvement of the pupils. [This includes] the all-important subject of
direct instruction in morals and religion. . . ."[78]

While, as we have seen, only a small minority of teachers had received formal training before the Civil War, and the proportion increased only gradually subsequently, it was to a considerable extent in normal schools and the
teachers' colleges that replaced them that a set of distinctive ideas about the
goals and methods of education and the role of the teacher was nurtured; these
came to constitute the shared norms and self-concept of educators as exercising a higher calling, a sort of sacred ministry, despite their modest status

and pay. This set of ideas—a distinctive ideology—was also promoted through the teacher institutes that served many as a substitute for academic training, and through the professional organizations that brought together educational leaders and, increasingly, rank-and-file teachers.

The normal school movement "created an idealized and imbalanced vision of teachers' role in the community. While they heaped a tremendous number of responsibilities on teachers, they also implied that teachers had a great deal of power."[79] A compensatory consolation for low status and pay would become the basis for what Rushdoony later called the "messianic character of American education," the attribution to public schools of something approaching salvific character.

> Even though normal schools existed because nature produced no teachers, the notion that a poet wrote with divine fire, a preacher preached with divine inspiration, and a teacher taught by means of innate powers would not die. . . . In spite of the actuality of low status, mean pay, and dim prospects, the teacher was accorded an unctuous recognition in sermons and orations. . . . Speakers were fond of magnifying the sacredness, nobility, and dignity of the teacher's work.[80]

One is reminded of how, within the Catholic Church before Vatican II, those committed to "the religious life" were accorded a special status (and a security of life) that compensated them for their vows of poverty, chastity, and obedience.

Although during the nineteenth century only a minority of teachers went through a period of structured professional training in a full-time "normal school," those institutions reflected faithfully the exalted meanings that were being assigned to the role of common school teacher. "Heaven's approval . . . came from employment 'in a heavenly mission.'"[81] Most of the first normal school principals were clergymen, and the rules for students commonly required that they attend a local church on Sundays; prayers were a daily routine. The French normal schools upon which those in the United States were modeled gave a similar priority to shaping the future teacher's sense of mission in contrast with professional competence, though in the French context of struggle against the influence of the Catholic Church it was through promoting a sort of secular religion. As a result of this strong emphasis upon moral formation, "young people emerged from the [French normal] School penetrated with the idea that a secular teacher had a mission to fulfill. . . . They were much less sure to have received an appropriate pedagogical education."[82] French teachers-in-training who read Emile Durkheim's book on moral education were left with the conviction that they had a more significant role than did parents in the formation of future citizens. "The center of gravity of moral life, formerly in the family, tends increasingly to shift away from it. The family is now becoming an agency secondary to the state." After all, Durkheim assured them, "the teacher . . . must believe, not perhaps in himself or in the superior quality of his intelligence or will, but in his task and the greatness of that task. . . . Just as the priest is the interpreter of God, he is the interpreter of the great moral ideas of his time and country."[83]

A milestone in the development of the special position—more symbolic than practical—of public school teachers was the founding of the National Teachers' Association, later renamed the NEA, in 1858. From the start, the mission and status of teachers was its central concern:

> Teaching must become a profession, one in which its own members set the standards and passed upon the applications of candidates for admission. . . . Temporary and incompetent teachers must be weeded out by raising the standards of the profession, thus revealing the great gap between unqualified incumbents and successful teachers. . . . "Our cause is good, and it requires wisdom, zeal, high purpose, forgetfulness of self, unanimity and a true devotion to our high calling."[84]

Horace Mann told the gathered members of the new association that "A brighter day is dawning, and education is its day-star. The honor of ushering in this day is reserved for those who train up children in the way they should go."[85]

This theme would be renewed late in the nineteenth century and would continue in the twentieth century as immigration from eastern and southern Europe came to be seen as a threat to the character of American society. For educators this was an opportunity to remind the public of the essential role that public schools could play in weaning the children of immigrants from the unacceptable ways of their parents. "At the 1920 NEA convention, there were six speeches about the need for Americanization, one speaker insisting that 'Americanization must be to us a political religion and teachers are the preachers of this gospel.'"[86]

Just as Horace Mann was fond of religious imagery in describing the role of schools and teachers, so this became a standard way of expressing an exalted view of the teacher's role, in parallel with other "guides of humanity" such as poets and preachers. A word frequently used in connection with the life and character of a true teacher was Consecration.

The use of such religious vocabulary could be dismissed as a tactical maneuver to gain support, but it went deeper than that and reflected the evolution over time of an alternative "secular religion" of which teachers were the selfless acolytes and educational theorists like John Dewey would be the high priests.

Dewey himself wrote a short book entitled *A Common Faith* (1934), insisting that "[i]t remains to make it explicit and militant."[87] The idea was not original with Dewey; Ferdinand Buisson, a key figure in the development of the modern French school system, had published *La foi laïque* in 1912, and Auguste Comte was only the most prominent of a series of promoters of a secular "religion" in France in the nineteenth century.[88]

More even than France and other countries where the relationship of the Catholic Church and those promoting the expanding role of the State was often conflictual,

> America remained dominated by patterns of religious thought. . . . Most were implicit, shaping ideas that seemed to be about secular matters. . . . the subsequent secularization of modern culture has obscured the importance of religion in forming the minds even of the most secular thinkers.[89]

Thus, for example, "[d]emocracy for Dewey was not mere governmental machinery, but 'a spiritual fact,' the 'means by which the revelation of truth is carried on.'"[90] In what he did not hesitate to entitle "My Pedagogic Creed" (1897), Dewey wrote that "the teacher always is the prophet of the true God and the usherer in of the true kingdom of God."[91] A decade later he would write about the "positive creed of life implicit in democracy and in science," and the need to "work for the transformation of all practical instrumentalities of education till they are in harmony with these ideas."[92] One of his biographers writes that "at each stage in his intellectual development, Dewey's philosophy culminates with a theory of religious experience and faith that completes his vision of the way to unification of the ideal and the real."[93]

Such claims for the power of education, properly implemented, achieved a wider resonance in American society as part of general optimism about progress. In 1858, *Harper's Weekly* told its readers that

> Teachers are God's workmen. Parents may pay them; States may pay them; but Heaven claims them and their office. Teachers, too, are always the safest reformers. If they would combine and take hold of the heart of the American people, they could soon elevate the tone of Education.[94]

This theme continued to be expressed after the Civil War; in 1896, pioneer sociologist Albion Small urged that teachers should "not rate themselves as leaders of children but as makers of society."[95]

The NEA's centennial historian noted that the "almost pathological interest in proving that teaching was a profession received continuous attention during the first decades of the association."[96] This required insisting that teachers and school administrators possessed essential knowledge distinguishing them from everyone else in society who thought that they knew something about education. Horace Mann and Henry Barnard had been lawyers, Charles Brooks, Calvin Stowe, and many other pioneers in promoting public education systems had been ministers, but educators must now come out from under the shadow of laymen.

> Efforts to achieve professional status involved opposition to the educational pretensions of preachers, lawyers, and other public figures. Even at educational meetings these presumptuous laymen occupied the center of the stage and crowded the principal or superintendent into the background. The same editor had previously admonished: "Let the physician stick to his physic, the clergyman to his divinity and the lawyer to his law books," but only persons trained in education should be placed in charge of school systems.[97]

In this effort to raise the status of educators, the normal schools and their successor institutions played an important role. Those few who attended them in the antebellum period left "with little knowledge of educational theory and a tenuous grasp of the teaching enterprise, but a very firm sense that they had a mission."[98] Theory would soon follow, since it offered essential support to the definition of teaching as a craft requiring knowledge not shared by parents or elected officials or attainable by common sense and experience. In addition to inspiration, normal schools and the teachers' colleges and other institutions that gradually replaced them sought to offer the latest pedagogical theories. In the antebellum period, the influence of Pestalozzi was vigorously promoted by Henry Barnard and others, and after the Civil War the Oswego Training School in New York State became the center from which the idea of "object teaching" spread nationwide. "Object teaching offered a template for teaching virtually any subject, and thus was potentially a theory to impart to future teachers"[99] as a mark of their distinctive competence.

This process began in the mid-nineteenth century on a small scale, since relatively few teachers underwent the socialization provided by normal schools or took part in the meetings of the National Teachers' Association, and it would gather force in the twentieth.

> The new profession increasingly saw its members as specialists with their own language who could not easily communicate with laypeople. As more and more teachers graduated from 4-year teacher preparation programs, they brought to the schools a new outlook, one which made them more independent of the communities they

served, but one that also distanced them from parents and other voters. For example, Waukegan parents must have been dismayed to read articles, written by teachers for the local newspaper that argued that parents might actually harm their children if they tried to teach them reading or number skills. As Lawrence Cremin has pointed out, the new professionalism which increased the distance between school personnel and the general public, turned out to be "a supreme political blunder" because it led to the erosion of lay support that became so evident in the 1950s.[100]

This differentiation in support of a claim to professional status had begun half a century before, with the increasing emphasis among those defining norms for education on methods and goals that were contrary to what most parents and the general public expected from the schools. For example, the Child Study movement told teachers-in-training that their efforts should focus not upon the subject matter of a prescribed curriculum, but upon "the child waiting to be taught," whose needs and possibilities they were trained to understand better than could unenlightened parents. Through careful observation of the psychology of children, in their differences as well as their similarities, "any desired traits or attributes could be developed within learners by means of a simple conditioning or shaping process."[101] In the 1920s, there would be an effort to apply "scientific methods" to curriculum.

> The method involved compiling the qualities of a good citizen, collecting the opinions of selected groups, listing the daily activities of typical workers, analyzing the contents of selected books and magazines, counting the preferences and interests of selected groups of children, listing the legal difficulties of a chosen sample of the population, making job analyses of various occupations, and making specific quantitative data which would indicate the topics, problems, and issues that children should study in school. The resulting curriculum would, it was assumed, be realistic, functional, and socially useful.[102]

Through this pseudoscientific process (which in fact was replete with value choices), the centennial history of the NEA noted approvingly, the

> guidance of tradition, the influence of abstract principles, the weight of authority, and the enumeration of opinions gradually lost favor and were replaced by studies of the social setting, the principles of learning, and student capacities. Old, inert portions were discarded from all subjects, and the remaining portions were reorganized. The fixed course of study was replaced by a changing, growing body of information, enriched and expanded by a great variety of meaningful activities. While

basic skills and minimum information were never slighted, they were put into more appealing contexts.[103]

Such ideas about the educational process came to enjoy unquestioned authority among educators.

Another element in carving out a sphere of independence and status for educators, and cultivating group solidarity, was the conviction that they—and thus the public school itself—were under attack from a variety of opponents. Horace Mann and others in the first generation of elite reformers warned against forces working against what otherwise would be the triumph of social and moral progress through the Common School. In what would become a continuing theme of the NEA, speakers at the very first meeting expressed concerns about private and parochial schools as damaging to the country. Over subsequent decades, members would often be urged that "the entire profession must be alerted and mobilized to counter the 'attacks' of education's 'enemies'" who criticized or offered alternatives to the public schools.[104]

Among the most important functions of teacher associations (the NEA was joined by the American Federation of Teachers in 1916) was to offer protection against demands for reform from outside the "profession." But while "professionalism assured teachers some autonomy, . . . it also placed them under the mandate of centralized control."[105] This autonomy, however, has been not only from the attempted interventions of reformers, but also from the concerns of parents and local tax-payers.

> What was needed was an ideology that separated teachers from the community, reinforcing their differences from the communities they came from and making them the hirelings of a new superintendent of schools who alone would determine their success in education . . . instilling a sense of loyalty not to the community, but to the school principal, superintendent, and educational professoriate.[106]

The development of the self-understanding of American teachers led to belief that following a consecrated calling gave teachers legitimate authority to resist the direction of both individual parents and of society as a whole in the form of government mandates. It is, in this view, only the teacher and the corporate body of educators who understand what is truly in the best interest of children; John Dewey's constant invocation of the word "Democracy" in writing about education does not reflect any respect for the results of elections and other forms of democratic decision making. In a later work he would write, "[t]here is no sanctity in universal suffrage, frequent elections, majority rule, congressional and cabinet government."[107] Consistent with this casual attitude toward the mechanisms by which a democratic system actually functions, Dewey insisted that "[t]eachers may be appointed by school boards and boards of trustees," as his biographer notes, "but teachers are first and foremost responsible to 'their moral employer,' the public. They are 'the servants of the community, of the whole community, and not of any particular class interest within it.' Their 'primary loyalty is to an idea, to a function and calling,' which is 'the pursuit and expression of truth,' and they have a responsibility and right to organize to insure that they and their institutions carry out this social function."[108] Thus, we find Dewey's disciple and popularizer William Heard Kilpatrick writing in 1923,

> [s]hall the people who vote the taxes decide what shall be taught in our schools? So stated, the answer may to some seem obvious. How else, they will ask, could a democracy run its schools? But if Democracy answers the question in this fashion, Progress takes an opposed view. Progress asks: How can we get ahead if we decide truth by majority vote? Or how can we expect people who know to teach what they don't believe? There seems here a head-on conflict between majority rule and progress.[109]

This belief in a mission superseding that of the family has continued to prevail among educators. Those who train future teachers (now mostly in universities) tend to communicate a set of beliefs about education that are unapologetically at variance with those held by most parents and by the general public. In a survey of professors in teacher training institutions, 79 percent of 900 respondents agreed that "the general public has outmoded and mistaken beliefs about what good teaching means," and communication with parents was considered important, not to learn what parents wanted for the education of their children, but so they could be "educated or reeducated about how learning ought to happen in today's classroom."[110]

In a phenomenon that has become increasingly evident, public school teachers have become hierarchical subordinates in bureaucratic organizations, rather than representatives of a local community and especially of parents.[111] Of course, this is much more true in large cities than in small towns, but detachment from the concerns of parents seems almost universal. While teachers submit docilely to the administrative requirements of their employers, sociologist Dan Lortie noted in his classic study, they strongly resist interference with their teaching, or external evaluation of its effectiveness. As a result, "that which is most central and unique to schools—instruction—is least controlled by specific and literally enforced rules and regulation," and this continues to be true even in the face of No Child Left Behind and other accountability efforts.

Working alone, the individual teacher selects behavior from the flux of classroom activity which she takes as evidence of learning. Cultural and psychological differences among teachers may produce dissimilar selections. . . . One teacher will assert the importance of written tests in assessing student performance; another will argue that it is the quality of discussion which really tells whether students are learning. Many teachers apparently believe that the "good teacher" relies primarily on her own observations and uses her own conception of desirable outcomes in monitoring her teaching behavior.[112]

Lortie reports on a study of how elementary school teachers—all teachers at this level participated—in Dade County (Miami) believed that teaching effectiveness should be measured: 60.4 percent relied upon "general observations of students in light of the teacher's conception of what should be learned," 13.9 percent on "results of objective examinations and various other tests," and only 1.7 percent on the "reactions of students' parents."[113] The continuing insistence of teachers, and their unions, that the most important aspects of their work cannot be measured is in effect a demand upon parents to trust them, something that parents have in general been willing to do—the public image of elementary teachers is very positive—even as American public education has been mired in mediocrity.

Nothing has blocked the emergence of a true profession of schoolteaching more than this insistence on substituting the soft evidence of each teacher's satisfaction with the results of her efforts for the hard evidence of measurable outcomes, increases in the skills and knowledge of students, and their readiness for the next challenges in education and life.

Chapter Nine

The Educators Find Their Prophet

We conclude by considering John Dewey, usually thought of as a harbinger of "Progressive Education" in the twentieth century but also the culmination of nineteenth-century developments in thinking about education and educators. It was Dewey who provided a theoretical rationale for understanding education as the primary means of creating an improved humanity, not through the promotion of skills and knowledge but through a process of quasi-religious conversion. Like Horace Mann, Dewey rejected the Calvinistic faith in which he was raised but not the conviction that, what he called (in one of his book titles), "a common faith" was essential to the educational enterprise and thus to social progress.

Historian Lawrence Cremin tells us that, in 1916, "when [Dewey's] *Democracy and Education* appeared, it was immediately hailed in some quarters as the most notable contribution to pedagogy since Rousseau's *Émile*."[1] To the reader, it lacks the often beguiling details of Rousseau's book, the concrete examples that Rousseau handles so well were not a feature of Dewey's style. Even the occasional examples that he offers don't stick in the memory like the anecdotes with which Rousseau advances his argument. Few of us would read any of Dewey's books for pleasure. Canadian Hilda Neatby puts it best:

> It is well . . . to skirt Dewey's philosophy lightly, not through irreverence, but rather through godly fear. He has been looked upon as the fountain at which every novice must drink; in truth he is no fountain, he is rather a marsh, a bog where armies of school teachers have sunk, and, one might add, many of them have never risen, but

speak with muffled accents from the depths. . . . not the least of his sins has been to pass on to his disciples the dreary obscurities of his own style.[2]

Why, then, has Dewey had so great an influence? Not because he provides a blueprint for American education; Dewey's books "were chronically described as impenetrably difficult. Indeed, readers today would often be hard put to it to decide just what their implications are for the organization of schools and the content of their syllabi." They offer "less a theory of education and more a theory of the place of education in the politics of modern society,"[3] and a passionate argument that schools should not seek to adjust their pupils to the present realities and requirements of society, but seek, through classroom activities, to refashion those pupils and thus prepare a better society for the future.

Dewey makes the claim that the pedagogy we employ will determine the sort of society we have:

> [t]o organize education so that natural active tendencies shall be fully enlisted in doing something, while seeing to it that the doing requires observation, the acquisition of information, and the use of a constructive imagination, is what most needs to be done to improve social conditions.[4]

It's not difficult to see why educators would welcome Dewey's validation of the importance of their work to building a better world, not through more widespread literacy and numeracy, or the prevocational skills that might be learned, or even instruction in civic virtues, but something like a transformation of personality. In this respect Dewey is in substantial agreement with Rousseau, who has the same confidence that a different sort of human being can be molded by the right form of education. Dewey's "view of the problem of education and democracy was not economic or sociological, or even political, except in the broadest sense of that term; it was largely psychological or social-psychological. In Dewey's theory, the ends of democratic education are to be served by the socialization of the child, who is to be made into a co-operative rather than a competitive being and 'saturated' with the spirit of service."[5] In one of his first essays on education, in 1897, Dewey insisted on socialization as the heart of education: "the individual is always a social individual. He has no existence by himself. He lives in, for, and by society. . . ."[6]

Because he was convinced that schools could and should remake society by their effect upon personality and values, Dewey disparaged curriculum content that did not grow out of actual classroom experience. He would complain that "schools tend to be pipe-lines and delivery wagons," with "learning a synonym for taking in and reproducing what other persons have already found out." Dewey charged that "[t]o oscillate between drill exercises that strive to attain efficiency in outward doing without the use of intelligence, and an accumulation of knowledge that is supposed to be an ultimate end in itself, means that education accepts the present social conditions as final, and thereby takes upon itself the responsibility for perpetuating them."[7]

A critic of Progressive Education in the 1950s noted the astonishing "implication that 'subject matter' cannot contribute to 'life and personality.'" After all,

> [f]rom every age we have acquired some precious bits of intellectual and moral and esthetic insight. . . . until recently, nearly all men believed that they were parts of a mosaic which, with continued effort to cleanse them of their encrustations, would give us an ever-growing body of truth. Not an exclusive or complete or sectarian body, but one composed of minimum elements upon which all men of good will could agree and act, even while they sought to enlarge the mosaic. The pragmatist says in effect: throw out most of those bits; the human race was working on the wrong mosaic until about 1900.[8]

For Dewey, however, as summarized by Stephen Rockefeller, "the overriding concern of education is growth itself, the process of growing, and not any particular end. Growth is an inclusive end which comprehends all the particular intellectual, aesthetic, social and moral ends that expand, enlighten, and enrich experience. . . . there are no fixed or final ends toward which human growth is evolving."[9] While bits and pieces of past traditions might, after critical examination, prove useful, there was no reason to privilege them in the educational process.

It's important to follow Dewey's strategy closely, here. He was not simply arguing for "relevant" curriculum—dropping Latin, for example, and substituting a modern foreign language—but for making the whole question of curriculum content distinctly secondary. "Purposeful activity" would be the new slogan, and that activity could be exercised in relation to any subject matter that posed a problem around which classroom projects could be organized. This is true even of traditional subjects such as history. "The present," Dewey wrote, "generates the problems which lead us to search the past for suggestion, and which supplies meaning to what we find when we search." The implication is that we are not to be concerned with determining the *truth* about an historical occurrence or process, but only what we can use from the past as a storehouse of examples. Ironically, this is very close to the sort of "moralizing" history of nineteenth-century schoolbooks that Dewey scorned. Instruction should stress economic history, which Dewey characterized as "more human, more democratic, and hence more liberalizing than political history."[10] Egan points out the irony that

> when children showed little interest in liberalizing economic history and much more interest in the heroic activities and vivid personalities of political history, Dewey's response was . . . [that] . . . child-centeredness extended only to the threshold of . . . ideological convictions. When children's pleasure conflicts with the theorists' convictions, so much the worse for pleasure.[11]

Where does the child fit into this scheme? Is it really the child's interests, as Dewey seems to suggest and as Progressive educators have insisted, that should be the starting point for learning? And are the actual interests of children consistent with the direction that Dewey believes education—and society—should take? It is always a good question, whether educational theorists have reckoned with (or even know) children as they actually are.

Plato had no sympathy for childhood, Locke was unmarried and childless, Rousseau sent his five children to the foundling hospital, where they almost certainly died in infancy, Mill was childless and unkind to his siblings, Russell's advice to parents was that they should take care what sorts of servants they hired to look after their children, and Mme. Montessori had an illegitimate child she had to place for adoption.[12]

In Dewey's case, the emphasis is not "a *child*-centered education so much as a *social*-centered child."[13] This leads to Hofstadter's criticism of the vagueness of the educational goals proposed by Dewey.

> The child's impulses should be guided "forward"—but in which direction? Such a set of criteria presupposes an educational goal, an adult prevision of what the child should know and what he should be. "Let the child's nature fulfill its own destiny," Dewey urged, but the suggestion that the child has a destiny implied an end or goal somewhat removed in time and not envisaged by the child.[14]

This is fundamentally different from a stress on determining the curriculum by what the child's vocational and other needs will be as an adult. Dewey sought to create a new kind of society through the stimulation, in schoolchildren, of cooperative habits and goals. "Progressive communities," Dewey tells us, "endeavour to shape the experiences of the young so that instead of reproducing current habits, better habits shall be formed, and thus the future adult society be better than their own." This points us toward Dewey's concept of "democracy," which he describes as "primarily a mode of associated living, of conjoint communicated experience," whatever that means. The classroom experience is to provide the model and develop the habits and attitudes that will transform society.[15] Or, as his ally and popularizer William H. Kilpatrick would put it, "the school [must] become more truly a place of actual experiencing, for only in and from such experiencing can the child get the inherent close-to-life kind of education formerly given by his home and community,"[16] which were no longer able to provide such experiences and must be largely superseded by the school.

This assertion leads to Dewey's insistence on "the reconstruction of social habits and institutions by means of wide stimulation arising from equitably distributed interests."[17] It is worth pausing over this word "reconstruction." Dewey was fond of the word, which no doubt had for him some echo of the (abortive) transformation of the South after the Civil War, during Dewey's adolescence. It seems to express for him a root-and-branch transformation which can occur when we are purposeful—"mindful"—about some situation or problem. There is usually a sense of a fundamental break with the past. The word also became a favorite with Kilpatrick, who wrote, characteristically, that "our basic theory of education must be . . . reconstructed."[18]

The word became central to Dewey's prescriptions as early as 1894, when he still retained his connections with Liberal Protestantism, in the form of radical optimism about human possibilities, guided by the "informed intelligence" of those like himself. "Because science represents a method of truth to which, so far as we can discover, no limits whatsoever can be put," he wrote at that time, "it is necessary for the church to reconstruct its doctrines of revelation and inspiration, and for the individual to reconstruct, within his own religious life, his conception of what spiritual truth is and the nature of its authority over him."[19] In other words, traditional Christian beliefs in realities external to this world should be abandoned and what remained of value in the "Christian message" should be stated in terms consistent with the new secular morality to which science was pointing the way.

Or, as Dewey put it in *Reconstruction in Philosophy* (1920), a quarter-century later, the "mission" of philosophy was "to extract the essential moral kernel out of the threatened traditional beliefs of the past."[20] There can be no question about what he is calling for when he uses the term "reconstruction" in *Democracy and Education*: it is a really fundamental change in the nature and authority of "social habits and institutions," not simply their improvement or adjustment.

You will mostly look in vain, in Dewey's voluminous writing on education, for references to "family" or "parent" or "mother" or "father," but it seems very likely that families as well as churches and other traditional sources of meaning and authority are among the "social habits and institutions" that are to be "reconstructed" in order to create a "democratic society" to Dewey's taste. Thus in his article "Impressions of Soviet Russia, IV: What Are the Russian Schools Doing?" (1928) Dewey wrote that, in Russia, "the great task of the school is to counteract and transform those domestic and neighborhood tendencies that are still so strong, even in a nominally collectivistic regime." After all, he told his American readers,

> to anyone who looks at the matter cold-bloodedly, free from sentimental associations clustering about the historic family institution, a most interesting sociological experimentation is taking place, the effect of which should do something to determine how far the bonds that hold the traditional family together are intrinsic and how far due to extraneous causes; and how far the family in its accustomed form is a truly socializing agency and how far a breeder of non-social interests.

Implicitly accepting the latter assumption, Dewey noted how the Soviet authorities had promoted "the role of the schools in building up forces and factors whose natural effect is to undermine the importance and uniqueness of family life," and observed with apparent approval that "we have here a striking exemplification of the conscious and systematic utilization of the school in behalf of a definite social policy."[21]

Every moral situation, Dewey argued, is unique and the right and wrong that apply to it are derived from the application of informed intelligence. Thus, he came to assert that all the controversies of the past about what is right and wrong could simply be put aside. After all, "the transfer of the burden of the moral life from following rules or pursuing fixed ends over to the detection of the ills that need remedy in a special case and the formation of plans and methods for dealing with them, eliminates the causes which have kept moral theory controversial," while "the theory of fixed ends," such as those deriving from traditional moral codes and divine revelations, "inevitably leads thought into the bog of disputes that cannot be settled." With a confidence in the universal applicability of the scientific method that now seems quaint, Dewey urged that "inquiry, discovery take the same place in morals that they have come to occupy in sciences of nature";[22] indeed, morality itself should become a form of scientific inquiry, not "retarded by the false notion of fixed antecedent truths," such as those of religion.[23]

Just as morality, come of age, can do without "fixed antecedent truths," so Dewey concludes that "education as such has no aims. Only persons, parents, teachers, etc., have aims, not an abstract idea like education. And consequently their purposes are indefinitely varied."[24] Certainly no aims external to the educational process itself will be considered, nor would Dewey agree with his contemporary, British philosopher Alfred North Whitehead, that "a certain ruthless definiteness is essential in education. I am sure that one secret of a successful teacher is that he has formulated quite clearly in his mind what the pupil has got to know in precise fashion."[25]

But it turns out that there *are* some aims that characterize good education, according to Dewey. The first—anticipatory shades of Howard Gardner!—is that it be based upon "the specific powers and requirements of an individual." The second is that it be designed to "liberate and organize" the "capacities" of those being educated. Here we should pause again, since it is too easy simply to accept the verbs that Dewey is here proposing. Let us—unlike Dewey—take a specific example. Imagine a student who is to be taught to play the clarinet, or to solve geometrical problems, or to run the hurdles. Would the teacher or coach "liberate and organize" that student's capacities, or would she instead—to pick another couple of verbs—"develop and discipline" them? But if she did, would she, in helping her students learn actually to play the clarinet, be adopting a "rigid aim," an "externally imposed end," that ought to be avoided? Would the students be "confused by the conflict between the aims which are natural to their own experience at the time and those in which they are taught to acquiesce?"[26] Or is Dewey simply using the word "liberate" disingenuously?

This was not a new theme for Dewey. In *The Child and the Curriculum* (1902), he had written that "Guidance is not external imposition. *It is freeing the life-process for its own most adequate fulfilment.*"[27] Like Rousseau, Dewey is proposing that the liberation of the child requires the educator's superior judgement, even manipulation.

While seemingly spontaneous, much of what went on in a progressive classroom was, in fact, determined well ahead of time. A major difference between the progressive classroom and a conventional classroom was, therefore, that in the former the guidance was hidden. This could leave children with a vague feeling that although they were supposedly making their own choices, they were not really doing what they wanted to do. Similarly, in the future society that Dewey sought to achieve through this pedagogical approach, "constraints would not be eliminated but they would be replaced by a hidden form of social control."[28]

Experienced teachers realize, however, that they cannot make everything that they teach "worthwhile in its own immediate having." Of course, they try their best to make everything interesting and "relevant," but sometimes their students need to take on faith that what their teachers are insisting that they learn is important as a basis for what they will learn later. Sugg argues that Dewey's

> pragmatist theory of knowledge militated against prescription of subject matter, against respect for the logic of subject matter, and against all fixed principles except that of growth. For all his emphasis on social values in education, his influence told against the common schooling because the "psychologizing" of subject matter meant in practice that there was no guarantee, though there was a naive expectation, that a maximal number of pupils would learn any given things in any given order. . . . [His] temperamental and philosophical commitment to growth and democracy prevented him from defining a common curriculum, so he weakened his assertions with vagueness. A school should arrive at least at "some significant subject-matters." It was only "some" organization of subject matter that was necessary to encourage "real" individuality in students. . . . Out of multifarious unspecifiable and unpredictable projects, differing not only from one school to another but within a given school and from one year to the next, all supposedly founded in the atomistic initiatives of pupils, he expected teachers so to manipulate the situation that pupils should learn particular, though ever unparticularized, subject matter. I am not aware that he ever got down to cases and specified subject matter and the proper sequence of it in relation to the maturation of pupils. Nor, so far as I know, did he ever discuss teaching method in relation to the logic of subject matter rather than in relation to "finding the conditions which call out self-educative activity"—as if initiation into the logic of subject matter might not do this!—and "cooperating with the activities of the pupils so that they have learning as their consequence."[29]

It is a striking illustration of the meaning Dewey attaches to the word "democracy" that he rates "the ability to produce and to enjoy art, capacity for recreation, the significant utilization of leisure" as *more* central to "social efficiency" than what he calls "elements conventionally associated oftentimes with citizenship." This is in line with his lack of enthusiasm for the ordinary mechanisms of political life in a democracy, his scorn for school boards and other elected officials.[30] Dewey lamented, in 1902, that progressive reform of education was blocked because the conservative

> was there not only as a teacher in the classroom but he was in the board of education, he was there because he was still in the heart and mind of the parent, because he still possessed and controlled the intellectual and moral standards and expectations of the community.[31]

Dewey places a strong emphasis on "interest" as a factor in education, and identifies it with "activity." He seems to suggest that anything to which the activity of the students can be directed is thereby of interest and, correspondingly, those curriculum contents that cannot be connected to "purposes and present power" had better be left aside. In fact, he points out, what will be of interest to one student at one time will not be to another, which seems to make impossible any sort of coherent curriculum content.[32]

This creates a daunting challenge for teachers, "finding material which will engage a person in specific activities having an aim or purpose of moment or interest to him." It leads to the project method popularized by Kilpatrick but anticipated in Dewey's discussion of the need to discover "typical modes of activity, whether play or useful occupations, in which individuals are concerned, in whose outcome they recognize they have something at stake, and which cannot be carried through without reflection and use of judgment to select material of observation and recollection...."[33]

Social conditions will be improved if schooling makes pupils active problem-solvers, Dewey is saying, and indeed he contends that this is more important than—say—any political or economic changes that might be proposed, presumably because it will create a new mental disposition and spirit of cooperation in the population. Failure to employ these active methods of education will be the surest way to prevent beneficent social change, and will represent a deliberate decision to do so. The challenge could not be put more directly.

How do we assess this claim? The idea that there is a one-to-one correspondence between educational experience—not the content of one's education, but how it is taught—and the way that one faces the challenges of later life has a certain immediate plausibility, but it may not stand up to the test of experience. After all, Hofstadter asks,

> [w]as it necessarily true that education founded upon authority invariably produces a conformist mind, and that there is a one-to-one relationship between the style of an educational system and the nature of its products? There hardly seems to be any place in Dewey's idea of the educational process for the fact that Voltaire was schooled by the Jesuits, or that the strong authoritative structure of the Puritan family should have yielded a personal type so important to the development of modern democracy.[34]

Or, if we think that Dewey's theory is plausible, we might ask whether it is ethical: that is, whether educators have a right to attempt to change human nature? It may be, as Dewey claims, that "progressive societies" do so, though it is not clear what examples he had in mind when he wrote *Democracy in Education*; within a few years, however, he was able to express his admiration for how the Bolsheviks who had come to power in Russia were "creating, by means of education, a new mentality in the Russian people" and "substituting a collective mentality for the individualistic psychology" inherited from the past.[35] He seems not to have noticed the threat to freedom of such manipulation in the name of changing fundamental human nature.

> A major difference between the progressive classroom and a conventional classroom was . . . that in the former the guidance was hidden. This could leave children with a vague feeling that although they were supposedly making their own choices, they were not really doing what they wanted to do. The hand of authority was there but so disguised that it could not be readily recognized. Moreover, in Dewey's vision of the reformed community that was the ultimate goal of his philosophy of education, the need for coercion would be reduced because individuals would be taught to want to act for the common good. In these communities constraints would not be eliminated but they would be replaced by a hidden form of social control. Over time we have come to recognize how dangerous this can be. As Henry May has pointed out, "[o]nly by painful experience have we learned to fear, even more than the old-fashioned visible tyrant, the pressures against which it is unthinkable to rebel."[36]

Already in 1916, a review of *Democracy and Education* in *The Nation* pointed out that "in the Deweyan social system there is no room for any individual who wishes to lead his own life in the privacy of reflective self-consciousness. . . . in spite of Mr Dewey's fine defense of individualism, his moral ideal is really that of the 'good mixer.'"[37]

Without a familial or societal mandate (what Dewey would call "external aims"), are educators as a profession entitled to use their privileged access to children to seek to "reconstruct" their values, habits, beliefs? Dewey sought a social transformation that society itself was not clamoring for, and a change in children from individual to collective motivations that most parents were not seeking when they sent them off to school. The year before he published *Democracy in Education*, Dewey wrote in a private letter, "I am interested in the question of social control—a method which will do practically for our human associations what physical science has done for control of nature or 'matter.'"[38]

Despite the title word "democracy," there is no discussion, in this book, of democracy as a system of government through which the majority rules; the words "election," "legislature," "board," "committee," and "voter" make no appearance. In fact, throughout Dewey's collected works there is a good deal of hesitation about endorsing the actual system of democratic government, which Dewey saw as corrupted by special interests and by the ignorance of the public: "until the dead hand of the businessman was removed from the schools and the control of education placed with the teachers, where it belonged, it was folly to talk about liberating intelligence or reforming the curriculum."[39] Dewey's concern was, rather, with the formation, through schools, of a set of habits and attitudes that would lead to the creation of what would more accurately be called "guided democracy," based upon rational deliberation informed by expert judgement. Dewey stated frequently that educators should take the lead in building a new social order—and, beginning in the 1930s, a new economic order—through the schools, but he was always rather cautious about how this might occur.

Dewey's concern is about formation for democratic living, for what he considers the necessary conditions of a democratic society. To begin with, then, he makes a rather traditional argument for the school as the instrument by which the diverse population of the United States, even more profoundly influenced by immigration in 1916 than it is today, could be unified and enabled to live together. Then he goes on to make a rather more distinctive claim:

> The school has the function also of coördinating within the disposition of each individual the diverse influences of the various social environments into which he enters. . . [The individual is] in danger of being split into a being having different standards of judgment and emotion for different occasions. This danger imposes upon the school a steadying and integrating office.[40]

Sociologists have made us familiar with the concept of the "plural life-worlds" that many of us inhabit, moving between the workplace and the family and (perhaps) the religious or ethnic or avocational association, each with different ways of understanding the world. Dewey reminds us that one of the tasks we must each accomplish is to work out how to balance these sometimes contrary perspectives. At the same time, we might feel a prickle of caution at two assumptions evident in this passage.

One is that it is necessary or at least desirable to eliminate these differences. We might feel that we can live quite happily with "different standards of judgment and emotion for different occasions." Part of the richness of life derives from the fact that our experiences are kaleidoscopic, and a healthy personality is able to bring to bear the appropriate "standards of judgment and emotion" for different occasions.

The other reservation we might have relates to the assumption that the school should play the crucial role in enabling us to achieve psychological and perspectival integration. Does this have the effect of inviting the school to mediate among the different "standards of judgement and emotion" that children bring from their particular family backgrounds, perhaps approving some and disapproving others? Wouldn't it be more appropriate as well as realistic to say that the school is one of "various social environments" which shape the child's experience, not the one that stands in judgement over the influence of the others and somehow reconciles them?

Dewey writes that "progressive communities . . . endeavor to shape the experiences of the young so that instead of reproducing current habits, better habits shall be formed, and thus the future adult society be an improvement on their own."[41] On one level this statement is completely unexceptional; we always hope that our children will go farther and reach higher than we have done. On another, though, it continues the theme of the school's privileged position as the arbiter of what human beings should become.

Democracy and Education was written at a time when America was caught up in a wave of enthusiasm about "progress," and about the possibility of building a better society through application of the techniques being perfected in the manufacturing process and in science. Education was a particular target of those who believed in rational planning and organization. Raymond Callahan described "the cult of efficiency" in education, David Tyack the effort to create "the one best system" of education. The result "was to be a standardized, modernized 'community' in which leadership came from the professionals."[42]

Dewey was himself not immune to the idea that has proved so seductive to "experts" in modern times, that society should be planned and run by "intelligence," that is, by experts like themselves: "the problem of an educational use of science is then to create an intelligence pregnant with belief in the possibility of the direction of human affairs by itself." This theme would become much stronger in his writing during the Depression, when his concern for the "socialization of the economy" would lead to rather chilling statements about the right of "organized intelligence" to crush the opposition to "social experimentation leading to great social change."[43] Or, again, "the experimental method" of social and economic change "cannot be made an effective reality in its full adequacy except in a certain kind of society. . . . The objective precondition of the complete and free use of the method of intelligence is a society in which class interests that recoil from social experimentation are abolished."[44] Abolishing "class interests" could, one assumes, occur only through the abolition of private property as well as all sources of resistance to the "social engineers" who would undertake as well as judge the results of the experimentation.

The word "experience" is key to understanding the educational project that Dewey advanced in many books and articles; by my count, he uses the word

485 times in *Democracy and Education*. He distinguishes his understanding of
the role of experience in education from that of Plato and also from that of the
eighteenth century.

> Experience is no longer a mere summarizing of what has been done in a more or
> less chance way in the past; it is a deliberate control of what is done with refer-
> ence to making what happens to us and what we do to things as fertile as possible
> of suggestions (of suggested meanings) and a means for trying out the validity of
> the suggestions. When trying, or experimenting, ceases to be blinded by impulse
> or custom, when it is guided by an aim and conducted by measure and method, it
> becomes reasonable—rational.[45]

In other words, the emphasis in the classroom should be upon providing
opportunities for actual experience and interaction with objects and with fellow classmates in such a way that the pupil tries things out and reflects upon
the consequences much as a scientist might. This is how learning occurs outside the school as well, Dewey points out, but the difference is the purpose-
fulness of experience within the school. "Purposive education or schooling
should present such an environment that this interaction will effect acquisition
of those meanings which are so important that they become, in turn, instruments of further learnings."

The pupil, in Dewey's account, is not described as being taught but as having "learning experiences." "In order to make sure these occurred, a great deal
of stage-managing was obviously necessary on the part of teachers. Dewey
apparently never worried about the manipulative aspect of his program, which
seems as egregious in its way as the drill it was supposed to replace."[46] One
is reminded of Rousseau's advice in *Emile*: "Let him always believe he is the
master, and let it always be you who are. There is no subjection so perfect
as that which keeps the appearance of freedom. Thus the will itself is made
captive."[47] Mortimer Smith would later point out the paradox at the heart of
the Progressive Education agenda: "while they have been insisting on 'freeing
the child's personality' by lessening the pressure of the individual authority of
the teacher, they have been exalting the authority of the social mass" of other
pupils in the classroom "society."[48]

If there was often uncertainty about what precise form the "new education"
should take, there was wide agreement, in progressive circles, about what must
be replaced. Traditional

> [e]ducation was static and reactionary, emphasizing revealed truth as found in
> Aristotle or the Bible or in other accepted authority. Education was essentially a

> preparation for adult life, and it was totally divorced from the child's present life. . . .
> this kind of education twisted, corroded, and warped the lives of children, creating
> truants and delinquents and personal maladjustments; and it made of childhood a
> period of despair and torture. For in these [traditional] schools there was no inter-
> est in the wholesome development of the whole child, in its growth, in his ethical,
> communal, or familiar adjustments. It was concerned primarily and almost solely
> with the child's mastery of subject matter.[49]

Replacing outdated and even harmful forms of instruction with one based
upon the latest scientific insights into child and adolescent development
seemed a pressing necessity.

Discussions of educational policy under Dewey's influence were liberally
spiced with phrases like "'recognizing individual differences,' 'personality
development,' 'the whole child,' 'social and emotional growth,' 'creative self-
expression,' 'the needs of learners,' 'intrinsic motivation,' 'persistent life situ-
ations,' 'bridging the gap between home and school,' 'teaching children, not
subjects,' 'adjusting the school to the child,' 'real life experiences,' 'teacher-pupil
relationships,' and 'staff planning.'"[50] Ravitch characterizes this as "a rhetorical tradition of inflated pedagogical language characterized by invocations of
democracy and other lofty ends for whatever was proposed. . . . it had become
the fashion in the education world to claim that every new idea was more progressive, more modern, and more democratic than whatever it superseded"
(Ravitch 2000, 124–25).

In *Anti-intellectualism in American Life*, Hofstadter contended that "the
notion that education is growth" had become "one of the most mischievous
metaphors in the history of modern education. Growth is a natural, animal
process, and education is a social process." While the "arbitrary authority of
the teacher has been lessened," it has been replaced by "a subtle manipulation,
which requires self-deceit on the part of the teacher and often inspires resentment in the child." In order—unsuccessfully—to remove the fear of failure,
"devices introduced to remove it have created frustrations arising from a lack
of standards, of recognition, of a sense of achievement."[51]

Because of the loss of faith in intellectual effort, Dewey critic Arthur
Bestor contended, setting the goals of education had inappropriately been
left in the hands of specialists in pedagogy who were unqualified to deal
with such basic questions. "The idea that there can be a 'curriculum expert'
is as absurd as the idea that there can be an expert on the meaning of life."
There had been a fundamental displacement of the task of setting the goals
for education, based on an understanding of the requirements for human
flourishing, from those entitled to deliberate about such consequential

matters, parents, and society as a whole through a democratic process. After all, pedagogy was an applied science that "answers practical questions, not ultimate and philosophical ones. . . . The question of *what* subjects should be taught . . . cannot be answered on the basis of pedagogical considerations alone, for it involves the ultimate purposes of education." As a result, "we have permitted the content of public school instruction to be determined by a narrow group of specialists in pedagogy, well-intentioned men and women, no doubt, but utterly devoid of the qualifications necessary for the task they have undertaken."[52]

Bestor noted that "Progressive Education" had begun as a strategy of classroom reform "to accomplish more effectively the purposes which citizens, scholars, and scientists had agreed were fundamental," but that over time it had begun "to imply the substitution of new purposes." It would perhaps be more accurate that the enthusiasm of some for the new instructional practices was originally and continued to be based on a concern to make classrooms more child-friendly and engaging, but that for others it had always rested upon a fundamental philosophical commitment to a view of human life which placed an emphasis upon process rather than upon any clear goals.

In what was in some respects an even more fundamental critique of Progressive Education, sociologist David Riesman charged that the lamentable dominance of what he called the "other-directed" personality in American life could be blamed in part on schools that placed an excessive emphasis on adjustment to the group rather than on individual competence. His book *The Lonely Crowd* (1950) was widely read—indeed, at well over a million copies, it may be the best-seller of all time in sociology—and provoked self-examination by many Americans. In effect, what Riesman (and his coauthors) did was to revive Rousseau's warning, in *Emile*, about the inauthenticity of a life concerned primarily to impress and please others.

Criticism of the effects of Progressive Education was voiced, in Canada, by Helen Neatby in *So Little for the Mind: An Indictment of Canadian Education* (1953). Neatby blamed the influence of Dewey that Canadian educators

neglected formal grammar and written composition, de-emphasized history and the great works of literature, put too much faith in guidance and extra-curricular activities, and were far too casual about promotion and graduation standards. The schools must abandon their "life adjustment" goals and "concentrate on the intellectual aspects of education, on providing children with intellectual preparation for citizenship." This approach called for teachers with stronger liberal arts backgrounds and a curriculum based on the essential values of western civilization.[53]

According to Neatby, "progressive education is . . . anti-intellectual because progressive educators make no attempt to discipline and train minds; anti-cultural because children are no longer required to appreciate and understand their inheritance; anti-moral because educators no longer are willing to discuss right and wrong actions."[54]

In what many consider the most important book about American schools in several decades, E. D. Hirsch, Jr describes the "American Educational Thoughtworld" as "a juggernaut that crushes independence of mind."[55] Unlike Bestor, Neatby, and the other critics from the 1950s, Hirsch builds his case on the disproportionately negative effect of a curriculum light on systematically presented content upon children from homes where they are not acquiring elements of this content, and the intellectual habits associated with it, outside of school. "A systemic failure to teach all children the knowledge they need in order to understand what the next grade has to offer," Hirsch charges, "is the major source of avoidable injustice in our schools."[56]

This relegation of many children to an instructional program which does not provide the "cultural literacy" required to enable them to make a success of their further education grows directly out of what, among advocates of Progressive pedagogy, had seemed a necessary reform.

> By the 1950s, educators were ready to accept as a fact that many children simply could not benefit from the traditional aspects of the curriculum. Increasingly, the doctrine of the "whole child" was used to disparage academic concerns. . . . By the 1950s, a principal could argue in a national professional journal that the junior high school curriculum should be "improved" by devoting less attention to reading, writing, and mathematics because "not every child has to read, figure, write and spell" and "many of them either cannot or will not master these chores." The antidemocratic nature of this self-fulfilling prophecy directly contradicted Dewey's emphasis on education as a vehicle for attaining a more egalitarian society.[57]

This emphasis has been restated by Hirsch from a very different philosophical basis. Noting that many of the proposals for school reform—especially from those on the Left who oppose the standards movement (of which the latest manifestation is No Child Left Behind)—call for greater efforts to make the curriculum "relevant," Hirsch points out that these

> reform proposals continue to be based on a sincere but quite inaccurate belief that a fact-oriented classroom prevails in American public schools today, whereas, in reality, the most striking feature of our elementary schools is that the anti-rote-learning reforms being advocated are already firmly in place.

This is especially damaging because it denies children who do not enter school with the necessary background knowledge and habits the chance to begin to catch up through systematic instruction. "It is not too much to say that an antiknowledge attitude is the defining element in the worldview of many early-childhood educators and reformers."[58]

The characteristic strategies advocated by educational theorists, according to Hirsch, merely compound the problems. For example, to stress critical thinking while de-emphasizing knowledge *reduces* a student's capacity to think critically. Giving a child constant praise to bolster self-esteem regardless of academic achievement breeds complacency, or skepticism, or both, and, ultimately, a *decline* in self-esteem. For a teacher to pay significant attention to each individual child in a class of twenty to forty students means individual *neglect* for most children most of the time.[59]

A rather different analysis of the weakness of the Progressive approach to education was advanced by two Canadian critics:

> the animus driving the reforms is an extravagant expectation of how much education and technical prowess can do to remake human life. . . . Underlying this hope is the Rousseauan view that human relations should resonate with an authenticity richer than our observable and customary interactions as members of society—as husbands and wives, as mechanics and politicians, as soldiers and poets, as teachers and pupils, as skilled craftsmen and apprentices. These roles and functions are "inauthentic," it is said, and the source of invidious distinctions. . . . The world evoked by the revolutionary is a dream because it eclipses the reality where the burdens of existence have to be nobly and justly shouldered—disease, labour, early death, injustice at the hands of the stronger, pragmatic compromise with others, tragic judgments, painful choices. In our view, the dream-world of the reformers gives rise to an education which does not exercise its responsibility in forming those characteristic virtues—charity, forgiveness, honour, righteous anger, compassion, dignity—through which we express our humanity.[60]

From Hirsch, then, the charge that "Progressive" pedagogy reinforces social and economic inequality by failing to provide poor children with the intellectual tools needed to make a success of their education; from Emberley and Newell the charge that it provides all children with an unrealistic dreamworld which ill-prepares them for the realities of the human condition.

And what about the child's first educators, his or her parents? The Canadian critics note that "the reformers see parents and teachers largely as impediments to the success of their agenda."[61]

If true, that would be nothing new. Rousseau, imagining Émile's education, specified that "He ought to honor his parents, but he ought to obey only me. That is my first or, rather, my sole condition."[62] In the utopian socialist Fourier's *Natural Education*, "Children are to be taken away from their parents and entrusted to public nurses, more faithful to nature than they."[63] One looks in vain, in the voluminous writing of Horace Mann and John Dewey, for an appreciation of the role of parents in guiding the education of their children. Nor is this attitude confined to an elite of educational theorists; in a recent survey, "When asked 'who should have the greatest influence in deciding what is taught in the public schools of your community?' only 2 percent of teachers answered that it should be parents."[64] As, generation after generation, the education level of parents themselves rises, it is not surprising that a gap has opened between parents and public schools, and that more than a million children, in North America, are now schooled at home. "What the future promises, parents fear, is a situation in which their children have neither been prepared for life's practical necessities nor supplied with the moral substance associated with a meaningful existence."[65]

Arguably, the greatest challenge today for educational policy is to find a way to rebuild the confidence that should exist between parents and the schools to which they entrust their children.

Chapter Ten

Concluding Reflections

While I was making final revisions to this book—literally in the last three weeks—I was asked to be expert witness for the school district defendants in *La Rue v. Douglas County*, a case challenging the decision of the district to offer scholarships for 500 of its students to attend approved private schools. The Colorado Constitution adopted in 1876 forbids public funding of "sectarian" schools, and the purpose of my testimony was to show that such language in the constitutions of most states had been adopted in a politically orchestrated national movement in the late nineteenth century to frighten voters about the alleged intentions of the Catholic Church to undermine public schools and other cornerstones of American life.

Although this book is by no means focused on the debates over educational vouchers, I was struck with how much of my account of the development of the relationship of government and schools in the United States was relevant to those debates. Not only does Chapter Seven discuss the conflicts that led to the contested provision in the Colorado Constitution, but in a sense the whole narrative helps to explain why the American political system has found it so difficult to accommodate the desire of many families for schools that reflect their religious convictions or their desire for a distinctive pedagogy. I've published detailed accounts of more than a score of other western democracies that have made that accommodation;[1] why does America fail to live up to the commitment of the International Covenant on Economic, Social and Cultural Rights (1966), "to have respect for the liberty of parents . . . to choose for their children schools, other than those established by public authorities, which conform to such minimum educational standards as may be laid down or approved by the State and to ensure the religious and moral education of their children in conformity with their own convictions" (Article 13, 3)?[2]

What I have tried to show is how a set of ideas about the unique function of the public school and of public school teachers in American life, especially in relation to the heavy immigration over much of the nineteenth century, made it difficult to imagine a system that would be pluralistic, like those that developed in Canada and Australia, in England and Germany, in Belgium, and The Netherlands. The intensely local nature of almost all decisions about what would occur in each public school in most American communities made it possible in most cases to accommodate the religious and other preferences of parents without this becoming a matter of political debate and compromise as it did in other countries. When conflict arose in New York City in the 1830s, the solution was to abandon the attempt to provide "neutral" schooling across the city and instead entrust education to the ward system, where the sorts of accommodations could be made that were occurring and would continue in smaller communities.

The great exception, discussed in Chapter Seven, was the conflict over Catholic schooling in the 1870s; on this, the Protestant majority was persuaded to admit no possibility of compromise and to seek to enshrine provisions forbidding public funds for Catholic schools in the federal and state constitutions. It is clear from the rhetoric that accompanied this process that participants believed that nonnegotiable principles were at stake, principles that could not be entrusted to the ordinary process of democratic deliberation in local communities.

Perhaps the time has come, however, that Vicar Apostolic Machebeuf rather wistfully predicted in his plea to the Colorado Constitutional Convention, to leave this question up to the ordinary political process: "we look forward hopefully to the future. A day shall at last dawn—surely it shall—when the passions of this hour will have subsided; when the exigencies of partisan politics will no longer stand in the way of right and justice, and political and religious equality shall again seem the heritage of the American citizen."[3]

A number of factors seem to be at work to this end. One is that the Catholic Church itself has changed radically in its stance toward modernity and democracy, and has become, in popular perception, thoroughly mainstream; it is remarkable that, at present, there is not a single Protestant on the United States Supreme Court. Another is that "private school" is no longer essentially equivalent to Catholic school. The latest figures from the federal government suggest that, of 5 million pupils in private elementary and secondary schools, only about 38 percent are in Catholic, 20 percent in evangelical Protestant, 2 percent in Jewish, and 0.2 percent in Muslim schools, with the balance in a scattering of schools of very varied identity and mission.[4]

A third factor is that Americans have come to have a different attitude toward cultural diversity, which for most is no longer seen as threatening national identity. This necessarily implies a greater acceptance for structural pluralism, even in publicly supported education:

> the issue is one of human respect. In a multicultural society respect must necessarily be accorded to all groups. And if it is to mean anything, it must be evidenced not just by pleasant verbal affirmations such as "celebrate diversity." It must be instantiated in a society's institutions and policies—and these must include government assistance to parochial schools.[5]

Yet another factor may be a widespread loss of faith in public schools, fueled both by disappointing results on cross-national comparisons of academic outcomes, and also by severing of the rootedness of schools in local communities. While formally the situation continues much as before, the actual links have become much weaker as a result of a combination of consolidation of school districts, professionalization of educational administration, the unresponsiveness of teacher unions to the concerns of parents, and the continually growing role of state regulation and federal program requirements. "In recent years, the public schools have undergone intense and not undeserved criticism for failing to prepare students adequately for higher education or the workforce. At the same time, the hope of using schools to achieve the social goal of desegregating American society has faded, as has the belief in the public-school mission to inculcate democratic virtues. In this more critical and less optimistic atmosphere, the idea of seeking alternatives to public schools has become more attractive."[6]

While there is a residual loyalty to the idea of public schools, more and more parents are seeking alternatives, not only in private schools, but also in charter schools (legally "public" but functionally private), home schooling, and "cyberschooling." After all, many feel, there is no reason not to extend to the schooling of their children the consumerist habits which prevail in other domains of life.[7]

As a result of these factors, and no doubt others, the old dichotomy public/private no longer defines the terms of debate over educational policy or the approaches under consideration in state capitals and at the national level—and even locally, as in the case of Douglas County, Colorado. In addition, At the same time, the extreme financial pressure that is causing hundreds of Catholic and evangelical Protestant schools that have been providing good service to families with modest resources to close or threaten to do so has made it urgent to find mechanisms to keep them afloat. Nor does the religious character of such schools pose such a barrier as it once did. The anti-aid provisions language of most state constitutions

> no longer divides, for purposes of public funding, the Protestant public schools from the Catholic private schools. Instead, they divide the thoroughly secularized public schools and other public institutions from a growing array of private religious schools and other private religious entities. They divide persons with religious affiliations or religious purposes from persons with non-religious affiliation and purposes. This operation is fully consonant with the changing dynamic of religious conflicts in modern American society. As Ira Lupu and Robert Tuttle have observed, "the religious wars in the United States in the early twenty-first century are not Protestant vs. Catholic, or Christian vs. Jew, or even the more plausible Islam vs. all others. They are instead the wars of the deeply religious against the forces of a relentlessly secular commercial culture."[8]

In this changed climate, it seems likely that most of those Americans who do not want religious elements in the schools that their children attend do not see any problem with other children attending schools whose religious character is preferred by their parents. Nor does this mean that we are likely to see a restoration, in government-operated schools, of the religious elements prevalent in the nineteenth and often in the twentieth century as well. I find persuasive the conclusion, by Jeffries and Ryan: it is

> likely that the emerging political combination in favor of government aid to religious education will prove, sooner or later, to be irresistible. We do not, however, foresee an end to secularism in public education. In contrast to the political revolution on school aid, no new coalition has formed to overturn the Court's decisions outlawing school prayer and Bible reading. . . . While the growing religious diversity of private schools makes government funding seem more "neutral" and hence more acceptable, the growing religious diversity of public school students makes it more and more difficult to envision any religious exercise that would not favor some faiths and offend others. We therefore predict that the constitutional prohibition against religious exercises in the public schools will remain intact.[9]

On the basis of structural pluralism, there is reason to hope that we can stop fighting over religion and schools and agree to disagree as is appropriate in a free society.

In the light of this new openness to change in the prevailing model of public education, let us revisit the three aspects of American schooling with which this study began and see what policy conclusions follow.

PUBLIC EDUCATION AS AN OBJECT OF FAITH

The strong belief in the importance of education for society as well as for individuals that characterized so many American leaders as well as ordinary citizens throughout the nineteenth century has made public debate over how to reform our educational system difficult. The excessive rhetoric associated with the Common School movement, rhetoric that became even more heated as Catholic immigration swelled, and in particular the hostility expressed toward privately sponsored religious schools, set a pattern that has continued to frustrate the adoption of educational policies appropriate to a diverse nation that proclaims the free exercise of religion as a basic principle. Much of the energy of the education reformers of the "common school revival" had less to do with the unavailability of elementary schooling than it did with opposition to such schooling under private auspices.

Critics of the present system, like their predecessors, are falsely accused of being enemies of education, or of wanting to destroy the public school. Unhealthy obsession with defending the status quo obscures the dysfunctional character of the present arrangements, particularly in urban districts where decisions that affect millions of students—and their teachers—are made through bureaucratic processes that have little to do with education and, all too often, are indeed anti-educational. Student effort and teacher morale suffer from the sense of being cogs in a vast machine.

The inefficiencies of a heavily bureaucratized system are grudgingly accepted by most Americans as a cost associated with the mission of the public school, but a more fundamental objection is that of families with strong views about the education that they want their children to receive. For them the monopolistic public education system is experienced as oppressive but, often, inescapable. The United States should not continue to lag behind other western democracies in showing respect for the right of parents to make decisions about the education of their own children.

American public education should be "disestablished," just as state churches were in the decades after the Revolution.[10] The resulting emulation and competition among religious groups has played a major role in the continuing dynamism of Christianity in the United States compared with countries retaining church establishments,[11] and there is every reason to believe that education in the United States would similarly flourish if the present "establishment" were dismantled under arrangements that protected the interests of the most vulnerable children. Public education should be no more synonymous with government-operated schools than public health is with government-operated hospitals, though government should play a significant role in both cases, setting standards and ensuring universal coverage.

The public school should be "demythologized," without lessening in the slightest our high expectations; it should be liberated to provide a true education and not simply instruction, to be as concerned about the character of its students as it is about their academic accomplishments. That is only possible if we give up the fruitless effort to make public education "neutral," as though anything so intimately associated with the shaping of human beings could ever avoid choices among alternative views of human flourishing. The sort of lowest-common-denominator schooling into which public schools have been forced, the "defensive teaching" in which their teachers engage to avoid controversy, can never provide a rich educational environment.

It is also high time that the American legal system remove the relics of the anti-Catholic bias that placed such a strong mark on its provisions for education during just the same decades when racial bias was being formalized in the laws of many states and tolerated by the courts. "These [anti-aid] provisions no doubt reflected many ideas and agendas, but prominent among them were religious rivalry and anti-Catholic prejudice. In *Everson* and its progeny, the Supreme Court applied this legacy to the nation. At least in its historical antecedents, the constitutional ban against aid to sectarian schools was indeed a doctrine 'born of bigotry.'"[12] The racial provisions have rightly been purged through a series of judicial and legislative reforms, and discrimination on the basis of religion should be eliminated as well.

The point is not to favor or promote schooling on a religious basis, but to ensure that those who act out of religious motivations are not thereby disadvantaged in comparison with others engaging in the same lawful activities from secular motivations. The issue is equal protection under the law, and ensuring that government does not engage in what the Supreme Court has called "viewpoint discrimination."[13]

Funding is by no means the only issue; those who seek an alternative to the lowest-common-denominator schooling provided under government auspices have every reason to be concerned about the strings that may come with public funding . . . and, indeed, without it. It is always tempting for government, whether in a totalitarian system[14] or in a democracy,[15] to impose what the French call a *pédagogie d'Etat*, seeking to impose uniformity of vision and attitudes. This was illustrated by recent controversy in Spain over the government's imposition of a curriculum of *Educación para la Ciudadanía y los Derechos Humanos* on Catholic schools, although some of its elements were in conflict with Catholic teaching. This is thorny ground: balancing society's need that children develop the habits and attitudes that permit adults to live together, while showing respect for differing perspectives on matters of conscience. For government to seek to shape the beliefs of young people threatens the free exercise of religion which is fundamental to the American system and its jurisprudence.

LOCAL AND PARENTAL CONTROL

As we have seen, American society and its educational institutions at all levels have remained stubbornly resistant to central direction. Despite the grand schemes proposed in the early years of the republic, the fate of national plans for education suggest what Madison more than once proposed: that our strengths will be found not in uniform schemes imposed from a centralized government above, but in local initiative, diversity, and competition, including both the freedom of students to choose schools and the freedom of schools to experiment. Moreover, we find in both Franklin and Jefferson support for the idea that local initiative should mean above all parental involvement, not only because the schools and students' development require it, but equally because parents need the civic education that comes through collectively formulating and pursuing serious goals.[16]

What has developed in recent decades, however, is a substantial emptying-out of the content of democratic localism in education, without a corresponding increase in real control from society as a whole. Professional educational administrators and the teacher unions have, between them, come to shape educational practice in countless ways that are beyond the reach of the democratic process, whether at the local, state, or national level. Seldom are real issues of how, much less why, to educate put before parents and other citizens. Most parents have little appetite to debate these questions, but they are eager to choose among schools with distinctive missions when the alternatives are explained clearly. We demonstrated that in Massachusetts in the 1980s when I was responsible for educational equity and worked with a dozen cities to create choice-based desegregation plans based on clear differentiation of schools.[17] Parents were much more interested in choice than in "voice." This in turn made it possible for the teachers in each school to work together to fashion a distinctive approach or mission that would be attractive to parents. Too often,

> [i]n our efforts to help public schools respond to the needs of an increasingly diverse population, we have made public education more rule-bound, rights-driven, and divided into specialties; we have removed decision-making from the school level and centralized it in district offices, courts, and state departments of education. . . . We had reasons to do these things but the results have not been good.[18]

Through a process combining bureaucratic elaboration and "professional" norms, the fifteen thousand school districts and the hundred thousand public schools in the United States have become, in many respects, as alike as peas in a pod, except in the one respect in which they *ought* to be similar: high expectations for all pupils to master the common skills and knowledge essential for successful participation in the society, its political system, and its economy.

American education is, fortunately, now undergoing a reinvention of localism, in the form of charter schools and other innovations that place significant decisions back in the hands of those engaged with shaping and maintaining an individual school: teachers and other school staff (and students as appropriate) in dialogue with parents and community institutions and supporters, as in the nineteenth century. Since the barriers of distance have been greatly reduced, such school communities can be formed on the basis of choice rather than of geography. Some forward-looking school districts are promoting what, in Massachusetts, are called "innovation schools," described as "unique schools [that] operate with increased autonomy and flexibility in six key areas: curriculum; budget; school schedule and calendar; staffing (including waivers from or exemptions to collective bargaining agreements); professional development; and school district policies."[19] A bolder proposal calls for local school districts to stop operating schools altogether, and become contracting bodies:

> [c]ontracting would ... redefine a public school board as a local community agent responsible for providing a portfolio of school alternatives that meet the needs of the community's children. School boards would no longer have authority to run schools directly or to create systems of regulation that exhaustively constrain what all schools may do. They would no longer have responsibility for directly hiring, evaluating, paying, or dismissing teachers, administrators, or other employees for individual schools. Their only responsibility would be finding, hiring, paying, and/monitoring the performance of the independent contractors that would run schools. ... The local board ... would monitor schools to determine that all admit students without respect to race or income, that no child is obliged to attend a bad school, and that students attending failing schools are provided with viable alternatives. ... Schools could therefore run consistent and coherent programs, free of the need to be all things to all people.[20]

It is impossible to keep track of all of the new arrangements taking shape across the country. Paradoxical as it may seem, this is made possible by the enhanced role of government in setting expectations for academic outcomes in order to protect the interests of students and of society. Such clarity (missing for far too long) about accountability for results allows the educators working in individual schools to find their own solutions to the challenges they face without putting children at risk. Ludger Woessmann and others have shown, based on international comparative data, that it is those educational systems combining strong external accountability with school-level autonomy and choice that produce the most impressive academic results.[21]

PSEUDO-PROFESSION OR SECULAR CLERGY?

To create a true profession, teachers need to work under professional conditions in which they collaborate with colleagues to make the day-to-day and longer-term decisions about their work, free to use their best judgment based on a sound grasp of the available research and their own experience. As with the established professions, they should do so under the discipline of commonly understood norms of ethical and effective practice, and with a responsibility to the client. In the case of teachers, this client is not simply the student (as suggested by Dewey and others who saw themselves as knowing better than parents what was in the best interest of the child) but also the family; it is essential to rebuild the relationship of confidence between schools and families that, as we have seen, were disrupted by the ideology that developed to sustain an exalted view of the teacher's mission.

The relationship of trust that existed between nineteenth-century teachers and the parents of the children in their classes can be rebuilt, but on a higher level, with more ambitious expectations on both sides reflecting the fact that both parents and teachers are themselves far better educated. This appears to be occurring at many public schools that enroll their students on the basis of parental choice, whether magnet or charter schools or some variation. In such cases, teachers see themselves as accountable to parents, not hiding behind a "sacred mission" that gives them a superior insight into the goals of human development. By spelling out clearly what they will seek to accomplish for the children entrusted to them, not in the windy generalities of "we believe that every child can learn" and "we foster creativity" but in specifics of what students will come to know and be able to do, schools that are freely chosen by parents are in turn free to pursue those goals without apology and with the full support of families.

Only under such conditions will schoolteaching become a true profession.

Notes

Preface

1 Mattingly (1975), xi.
2 Labaree (1997), 134–35.

Introduction: Weaknesses and Strengths of the American Model of Schooling

1 Tyack and Hansot (1982), 4.
2 Tyack and James (1986), 39.
3 Mattingly (1975), 68.
4 Kuhn (1962).
5 Cavanaugh (2009), 6.
6 Moe (2000), 87–88.
7 Gutmann (1987), 65, 70.
8 Tyack and Hansot (1982), 10.
9 Peterson (2010).
10 Tyack and Hansot (1982), 18.
11 In Schleifer (2000), 163, 169.
12 Tocqueville (1988), 12.
13 Tocqueville (1988), 68.
14 Described in Glenn (1988), chapter 1.
15 Tocqueville (1988), 63, 90.
16 Tocqueville (1988), 95, 96.
17 Tocqueville (1988), 673, 680–81.
18 Tocqueville (1988), 691–93.
19 Thabault (1982), 80–81.
20 Madison (1999), 410.
21 *West Virginia State Board of Education v. Barnette*, 319 US 624 (1943).
22 Moe (2011), 114.
23 Labaree (1997), 261.
24 See, for example, American Federation of Teachers (2008).
25 See Glenn and De Groof (2004) for descriptions of the balance struck in 40 countries.

26 Steinberg (1997), 13, 67.
27 Glenn (1988), 35–37.
28 Tyack (1974); Tyack and Hansot (1982).
29 Callahan (1962).
30 Wesley (1957), 82.
31 Tyack and Hansot (1990), 47.

Chapter One: Colonial Background

1 May (1976), 32.
2 Lockridge (1974), 68–69.
3 Monroe (1971), 108.
4 Pangle and Pangle (1993), 20.
5 In Axtell (1976), 4.
6 In Cohen (1974a), I, 383.
7 Lockridge (1974), 13.
8 In Cohen (1974a), I, 393.
9 Monroe (1971), 106.
10 In Cohen (1974a), I, 395.
11 Cole (1957), 70.
12 Lockridge (1974), 69, 63.
13 Lockridge (1974), 99.
14 In Cohen (1974a), I, 394.
15 In Cohen (1974a), I, 394.
16 In Cohen (1974a), I, 398.
17 Monroe (1971), 109–10.
18 In Cohen (1974a), I, 402–03.
19 Axtell (1976), 170.
20 Monroe (1971), 113.
21 Axtell (1976), 183.
22 Monroe (1971), 154.
23 Hendrick (1966).
24 Cremin (1970), 557.
25 Mattingly (1975), 45.
26 Cohen (1974b), 82.
27 Axtell (1976), 173.
28 Axtell (1976), 176–77.
29 Teaford (1970), 290, 295, 300.
30 Welter (1962), 13.
31 In Cohen (1974a), I, 439.
32 Monroe (1971), 128.
33 Lockridge (1974), 5.
34 In Cohen (1974a), I, 345.
35 Monroe (1971), 53.

36 In Calhoun (1969), 7–8.
37 Cohen (1974a), I, 458.
38 Monroe (1971), 59.
39 Kaestle (1973a), 5–6.
40 Monroe (1971), 69.
41 Monroe (1971), 71.
42 Kilpatrick (1912), 40, 81, 141.
43 Cohen (1974a), I, 353.
44 Kilpatrick (1912), 100.
45 Monroe (1971), 81.
46 Cremin (1977), 23–24.
47 Reisner (1930), 104–105.
48 Monroe (1971), 82–7; see Glenn (2011c), 24; Glenn (2011b), 27.
49 Kaestle (1973a), 2.
50 Monroe (1971), 91.
51 In Cohen (1974a), I, 359.
52 See Glenn (2011a), 8–9.
53 Franklin (1984), 472–74.
54 Welter (1962), 19.
55 Franklin (1979), 29; see also Glenn (2011b), 24, 39.
56 Lockridge (1974), 73.
57 Kaestle (1973a), 1, 5.
58 Kaestle (1973a), 19–20.
59 Franklin (1984), 1313–14.
60 Bailyn (1960), 17–18.
61 In Bailyn (1960), 18.
62 In Cremin (1970), 502.

Chapter Two: The Idea of Forming Citizens

1 In Smith (1990), 54.
2 In Rudolf (1965), 45.
3 Brown (1996), 66.
4 *Constitution* (1981), 29–30.
5 Tyack, James, and Benavol (1987), 30.
6 In Cohen (1974a), II, 729.
7 In Pangle and Pangle (1993), 96.
8 In Pangle and Pangle (1993), 29; italics in original.
9 In Pangle and Pangle (1993), 29.
10 Aristotle (1944), VIII, 1, 1337a, 635.
11 Montesquieu (1989), 72.
12 Washington (1997), 750.
13 Washington (1997), 971.

14   Washington (1997), 1026.
15   Monroe (1971), 199–200.
16   In Cohen (1974a), II, 954.
17   Jefferson (1984), 365.
18   Jefferson (1984), 367, 372–73.
19   Jefferson (1984), 859.
20   See Glenn (1988), 18–30.
21   In Welter (1962), 28.
22   Jefferson (1984), 272.
23   Jefferson (1984), 1305–09.
24   Addis (2003), 16.
25   Honeywell (1931), 37; Jefferson (1984), 1387–88.
26   Jefferson (1984), 1379.
27   In Pangle and Pangle (1993), 115.
28   Jefferson (1984), 211.
29   Addis (2003), 36; Cremin (1980), 157–58.
30   Addis (2003), 143.
31   Miller (1961), 127.
32   Elkins and McKitrick (1995), 310.
33   In Malone (1962), 47.
34   In Hazen (1964), 266.
35   Smith (1990), 115, 134.
36   May (1976), 225.
37   Unger (1998), 85.
38   Hazen (1964), 267.
39   In Rudolf (1965), 113, 127; italics in original.
40   In Rudolf (1965), 138, 141.
41   May (1976), 235.
42   In Rudolf (1965), 210.
43   In Rudolf (1965), 170, 211.
44   In Rudolf (1965), 309–11.
45   Rush (1965), 10.
46   Rush (1965), 17.
47   Rush (1965), 5–6.
48   Rush (1965), 22.
49   Rush (1965), 10.
50   Rush (1965), 12, 7.
51   Rush (1965), 10.
52   Rush (1965), 11.
53   In Noll (2002), 374.
54   Hawke (1971), 317.
55   May (1976), 235.
56   In Dunn (1999), 38.

57   Dunn (1999), 40.
58   Dunn (1999), 41.
59   Messerli (1972), 11.
60   May (1976), 223.
61   In Johnson (2002), 81.
62   In Butts (1978), 79.
63   Kaestle (1973a), 35–36.
64   See Glenn (2011a), 22–31.
65   Bestor (1950), 7.
66   In Bestor (1948), 351.
67   Watkinson (1990), 363.
68   Farrell (1938), 357.
69   In Silver (1969), 55, 65.
70   In Silver (1969), 130, 144, 73.
71   In Harrison (1967), 77.
72   Bestor (1950), 227.
73   Power (1996), 70.
74   Burgess (1963), 67, 70.
75   Eckhardt (1984), 216, 203.
76   In Cohen (1974a), II, 1053–56.
77   Pessen (1985), 273; Nasaw (1979), 49.
78   Welter (1962), 46.
79   Mirel (1999), 49.
80   Kaestle (1983), 145.
81   Brown (1996), 161.
82   In Eckhardt (1984), 218; Beecher (1852), 92.
83   Kaestle (1982), 134.
84   Cremin (1980), 287.
85   In Wesley (1957), 169.
86   Martineau (1837), II, 278.
87   Thomas (1965), 677.
88   Harrison (1967), 88.
89   May (1976), 229.

Chapter Three: Religion as Source of Cooperation

1   See Glenn (1988), 179–95.
2   Fraser (1985), 28.
3   See Casanova (1994), 29.
4   Esbeck (2004), 1458, 1553.
5   Curran (1975), 20; Smith (1926), 108; Kaestle and Vinovskis (1980), 171.
6   Smith (1965), 36.
7   Jorgenson (1952), 14.

8 Bushnell (1847).
9 McLoughlin (1968), 70.
10 Sklar (1973), 78.
11 Beecher (1864), 44–45; italics in the original.
12 In Nasaw (1979), 60.
13 In Jorgenson (1952), 15.
14 In Kaestle (1982), 133.
15 Wesley (1957), 43, 50.
16 McLoughlin (1968), 4.
17 Cremin (1980), 33.
18 Everett (1859), 236.
19 In Kaestle (1983), 98.
20 Brooks (1837), 11.
21 Brooks (1867), 8.
22 Mann (1848), 40–41.
23 Mann (1846), 64–65.
24 Mann (1845), 16–17.
25 See Glenn (1988), chapters 6 and 7.
26 In McLoughlin (1968), 70–85.
27 Boyer (1978), 12.
28 Noll (2002), 198.
29 Butler (1990), 268.
30 In Tyack and Hansot (1981), 5.
31 Noll (2002), 182, 193.
32 Kaestle (1973a), 121.
33 Smith (1965), 40–41.
34 In Fraser (1985), 183.
35 Cremin (1980), 66.
36 Berger and Neuhaus (1996).
37 Smith (1967), 690.
38 In Fraser (1985), 194.
39 Boyer (1978), 35.
40 In Cohen (1974a), II, 976.
41 In Cohen (1974a), II, 979.
42 Kaestle (1983), 45.
43 Fraser (1985), 32, 41.
44 Vinovskis (1985), 81–82.
45 Johnson (1978), 13, 118.
46 Starr (1971), 87, 107.
47 See Glenn (1988) for a discussion of this process.
48 Cremin (1980), 67.
49 McCluskey (1958), 17n.
50 Channing (1903), 386–87.

51 Mann (1845), 15.
52 Anonymous (1848).
53 Humphrey (1844), 52–53.
54 See "The Common School as a Religious Institution" 146–78 and "The Gathering Protestant Consensus on Religious Schooling" 230–34 in Glenn (1988).
55 Gordon (1978), 557–58.
56 Mann (1847), 233.
57 Mann (1848), 9.
58 Mann (1849), 98–99.
59 Mann (1849), 103, 113.
60 Sears (1852), 26–27.
61 See Glenn (2011b), x–y.
62 Hamburger (2004), 227–28.
63 Green (1992), 43.
64 Justice (2005), 190–91, 208.
65 McAfee (1998), 38.
66 Justice (2005), 113.
67 Justice (2005), 109, 61, 112.
68 Justice (2005), 221.
69 McAfee (1998), 39.
70 Justice (2005), 143.
71 Justice (2005), 74.
72 See Glenn (1988), 216–17.
73 Justice (2005), 195–96.
74 Justice (2005), 197–98, 209.

Chapter Four: Schooling and Local Democracy

1 Bailyn (1960), 48.
2 Tyack and Hansot (1982), 5.
3 Johnson-Weiner (2006).
4 Wickersham (1886), 184–85.
5 Kaestle (1973a), 55.
6 Welter (1962), 23; Monroe (1971), 204, 317.
7 Bailyn (1960), 27.
8 Monroe (1971), 205–07.
9 MacMullen (1991), 109–10.
10 In Brown (1996), 51.
11 Vinovskis (1985), 76.
12 In Cremin (1970), 521.
13 Bailyn (1960), 18.
14 Messerli (1972), 12.
15 Messerli (1972), 12.

16 Gordon (1978), 560.

17 Monroe (1971), 277.

18 Reisner (1922), 353f.

19 Mann (1841), 21–22; Mann (1845), 77.

20 Messerli (1972), 396.

21 Martineau (1837), I, 196.

22 Monroe (1971), 280.

23 Tyack and Hansot (1990), 49.

24 Kaestle (1983), 8.

25 In Rudolf (1965), 136.

26 Unger (1998), 8–9.

27 Sklar (1973), 170–71.

28 In Johnson (2002), 75.

29 Pangle and Pangle (1993), 133.

30 MacMullen (1991), 7.

31 In Unger (1998), 36.

32 Tyack and Hansot (1990), 18.

33 Kaestle (1983), 24.

34 See Glenn (1988), x–y.

35 Reisner (1930), 311.

36 Kaestle (1983), 10.

37 Katz (1975), 155.

38 In Calhoun (1969), 110–11.

39 In Kaplan (1948), 374.

40 Schultz (1973), 32.

41 In Calhoun (1969), 131.

42 Text in Cohen (1974a), II, 732–38.

43 Katz (1975), 49.

44 Galenson (1997), 271, 274–75.

45 Reisner (1930), 282–83.

46 Monroe (1971), 282, 329, 285.

47 Lottich (1962), 52–53, 56; Kaestle (1983), 186–87.

48 Cremin (1977), 69.

49 Pulliam (1967), 193–94.

50 Baumgarten (1994), 172–73.

51 Baumgarten (1994), 175.

52 Troen (1975), 6.

53 Troen (1975), 11, 33.

54 Starr (1971), 94.

55 Jorgenson (1987), 104, 6.

56 Jorgenson (1987), 4.

57 Nasaw (1979), 55–56.

58 Kaestle (1983), 50–51.

59   Dunn (1958), 228.
60   Monroe (1971), 286.
61   Dunn (1958), 232.
62   Reisner (1922), 393.
63   Reinders (1964), 182.
64   Cremin (1977), 63–65.
65   Brown (1996), 144.
66   Cohen (1974a), II, viii–ix.
67   Jorgenson (1952), 11.
68   Eaton (1961), 40, 252, 258.
69   Reinders (1964), 183–86.
70   Tocqueville (2000), 289.
71   In Cohen (1974a), II, 1069.
72   Tocqueville (2000), 651–53.
73   Brown (1996), 74.
74   In Sizer (1964), 86–87.
75   Kaestle (1983), 13.
76   Nasaw (1979), 34.
77   Cremin (1970), 545.
78   Kaestle (1983), 164.
79   Tyack and James (1986), 66.
80   Kaestle (1983), 13, 166–67; Walsh (1901), 7–14; Justice (2005), 197–98; for
     the context of public funding of parochial schools in Lowell, see Cremin
     (1980), 417–18.
81   In Cohen (1974a), II, 1026.
82   In Herbst (1989), 16.
83   MacMullen (1991), 145.
84   In Katz (1975), 27.
85   Cremin (1980), 165.
86   Edwards and Richey (1968), 223.
87   Kaestle and Vinovskis (1980), 34.

Chapter Five: Schooling as Protection for Society

1   Kaestle (1983), 30.
2   Reisner (1922), 356f.
3   Monroe (1971), 209.
4   Katz (1971), 299.
5   See Anonymous (1809); Kaestle (1973b).
6   Ravitch (1974), 9–11.
7   In Cohen (1974a), II, 983.
8   Kaestle (1973a), 71.
9   Sheller (1982), 25.
10   Cohen (1974a), II, ii.

11 Sheller (1982), 30.
12 Sheller (1982), 25–26.
13 Sheller (1982), 34.
14 Pessen (1985), 63.
15 In Katz (1971), 315.
16 Butts (1978), 12; Wickersham (1886), 256–59.
17 Franklin (1979), 32.
18 In Monroe (1971), 208.
19 Kaestle (1983), 31.
20 In Wickersham (1886), 266; McCadden (1937), 19.
21 Monroe (1971), 296–98.
22 In Cohen (1974a), II, 981.
23 In Butts (1978), 59.
24 Katz (1971), 319.
25 Reisner (1922), 366.
26 Kaestle (1983), 117.
27 Galenson (1997), 279.
28 See Glenn (2011b), x–y.
29 Gardner (1855), 978–86.
30 Shapiro (1960), 213.
31 Monroe (1971), 189.
32 See Bureau of the Census (1976), 106–08.
33 Handlin (1968), 51–52.
34 Abbott (1926), 338.
35 Tyack (1974), 30–31.
36 Gardner (1855).
37 Billington (1937), 7.
38 Hamburger (2004), 231–32.
39 Elson (1964), 53–54.
40 Billington (1938), 44.
41 In Fraser (1985), 44.
42 *Biblical Repertory* (1830), 225.
43 In Esbeck (2004), 1545n; in Sklar (1973), 116.
44 Sklar (1973), 113–14.
45 In Cohen (1974a), II, 991.
46 In Cohen (1974a), II, 995.
47 In Cohen (1974a), II, 995–97.
48 Galenson (1998), 26–31.
49 Galenson (1995), 400.
50 Text in Tyack (1967), 148–50.
51 In Howe (1997), 163.
52 Anonymous (1848), 168–69.
53 Bushnell (1880), 299–303.
54 Mulkern (1990), 61, 82.

55 Mulkern (1990), 76, 138–39.
56 Mulkern (1990), 123.
57 Ravitch (1974), 7.
58 Kaestle (1973a), 41.
59 Justice (2005), 31.
60 Kaestle (1973a), 82.
61 Justice (2005), 31.
62 In Cohen (1974a), II, 1120–21.
63 Katz (1987), 28–29.
64 Kaestle (1983), 166
65 Smith (1966), 687.
66 In Katz (1971), 299.
67 In Cohen (1974a), II, 1123–25.
68 In Welter (1971), 112.
69 Kaestle (1973a), 86.
70 Ravitch (1974), 20–21; Kaestle (1973a), 57.
71 In Katz (1975), 8–9.
72 Kaestle (1973a), 168–69.
73 Ravitch (1974), 19, 12.
74 In Cohen (1974a), II, 1126–27.
75 Ravitch (1974), 32, 53, 45.
76 In Calhoun (1969), 162.
77 In Welter (1971), 100–01; emphasis in original.
78 In Welter (1971), 103.
79 Katz (1975), 13.
80 In Kaestle (1973a), 117.
81 Katz (1971), 302.
82 In Welter (1962), 85.
83 Messerli (1972), 343.
84 Curran (1975), 100.
85 In Calhoun (1969), 165–67.
86 Justice (2005).
87 Ravitch (1974), 61–63.
88 Ravitch (1974), 64.
89 Calhoun (1969), 143.
90 Kaestle (1973a), 170–78.
91 Kaestle (1973a), 189.
92 Katz (1975), 12.
93 In Carey (2004), 87.
94 In Power (1996), 105.
95 Sears (1855), 47.
96 Sears (1856), 42.
97 Kaestle (1973a), 99, 118, 186.

Chapter Six: Toward the Educator-State

1   See Glenn and De Groof (2004).
2   Spear (1876), 60–61.
3   Tanner and Tanner (1990), 109.
4   Handy (1991), 62.
5   Tyack and Hansot (1982), 103.
6   In Cohen (1974a), II, 794–95.
7   In Cohen (1974a), II, 794, 797.
8   See Glenn (2011b), x–y.
9   Reisner (1922), 343
10 Reisner (1930), 291.
11 Glenn (2011b), 29–37.
12 Tyack and James (1986), 54.
13 Reisner (1930), 327.
14 In Darling (1925), 250.
15 Reisner (1922), 347, 391.
16 Tocqueville (2000), 87.
17 Brown (1996), 139.
18 In Welter (1962), 30–31.
19 Messerli (1972), 108–09.
20 Carter (1826), 48, 16.
21 Dunn (1999), 114.
22 Messerli (1972), 319.
23 In Calhoun (1969), 158.
24 Gordon (1978), 564.
25 For a more extensive discussion of the role of Mann in developing a model of state leadership in education, see Glenn (1988), "The State Assumes Educational Leadership," 115–45.
26 In Cohen (1974a), II, 1096–97.
27 In Messerli (1972), 226.
28 In Howe (1997), 161.
29 Messerli (1972), 284.
30 Kaestle (1983), 25.
31 Compayré (1904), 29.
32 Mann (1849), 78.
33 Soldani & Turi (1993), 17.
34 Messerli (1972), 122.
35 Messerli (1972), 135.
36 Howe (1997), 161.
37 Howe (1979), 36.
38 Reisner (1922), 380–87.
39 In Cohen (1974a), II, 1070–71.

40 Cremin (1957), 6.
41 Mann (1855), 50.
42 In Messerli (1972), 249.
43 In Glenn (1988), 80.
44 Messerli (1972), 263–64.
45 Mann (1840), 96.
46 In Cohen (1974a), II, 1107.
47 In Lannie (1974), 87.
48 Mann (1838), 48, 54–56; Mann (1841), 42.
49 Mann (1839), 154.
50 Mann (1838), 56.
51 Mann (1842), 66–68.
52 Mann (1840), 14.
53 See "The State Assumes Educational Leadership," in Glenn (1988), 115–45.
54 Messerli (1972), 293.
55 Messerli (1972), 307.
56 MacMullen (1991), 33.
57 MacMullen (1991), 52–53, 56.
58 MacMullen (1991), 57, 76.
59 MacMullen (1991), 93, 117, 119.
60 MacMullen (1991), 275.
61 MacMullen (1991), 277.
62 Wickersham (1886), 273.
63 Tocqueville (2000), 62.
64 Kliebard (1982), 95.
65 Katz (1971), 304.
66 In Wickersham (1886), 338.
67 Wickersham (1886), 314.
68 Wickersham (1886), 342–43, 508.
69 Wickersham (1886), 374.
70 In Labaree (1988), 11.
71 Labaree (1988), 67–68.
72 Reisner (1930), 336–37.
73 Wickersham (1870), xvi.
74 Mulhern (1969), 604.
75 Wickersham (1886), 361.
76 Wickersham (1886), 567.
77 Wickersham (1886), 312.
78 See account in Glenn (1988), chapter 5.
79 MacMullen (1991), 341.
80 MacMullen (1991), 119.
81 Cremin (1957), 19.
82 Glenn (1988), 118.

83   Morton (1842), 306–07.
84   Committee on Education (1840), 225. Messerli (1972), 329; text in Welter (1971), 85–96.
85   Committee on Education (1840), 226–27.
86   Committee on Education (1840), 229.
87   Kaestle and Vinovskis (1980), 229.
88   Kaestle and Vinovskis (1980), 215–16.
89   Morton (1845), 120.
90   In Katz (1995), 17.
91   Power (1996), 107, 113–14.
92   Jefferson (1984), 1379; Addis (2003), 17.
93   In Butts (1978), 86–87.
94   Power (1996), 107.
95   In Cohen (1974a), II, 1057.
96   Kaestle (1983), 155.
97   Nasaw (1979), 54.
98   McCadden (1937), 262–63, 268.
99   Cremin (1977), 20–21.
100 Reisner (1922), 387.
101 Kaestle (1983), 95.
102 Messerli (1972), 337.
103 Messerli (1972), 342.
104 Messerli (1972), 343.
105 See Glenn (1988), chapter 3.
106 Kaestle (1983), 219.
107 May (1866), 37.
108 Welter (1962), 119.
109 Tyack, James, and Benavot (1987), 42.
110 In Tyack and James (1986), 52–53.
111 Berrol (1982), 34.
112 In Cohen (1974a), II, 1115–16.
113 In Ensign (1969), 176.
114 Wickersham (1870), xiii.
115 *Debates of the Convention* (1873), volume VII, 691.
116 Ensign (1969), 177.
117 Hodge (1846).
118 Packard (1841), 146–47.
119 See Glenn (2011a).
120 Whitescarver (1993), 457–58, 475, 478.
121 Tyack and James (1986), 49.
122 Brown (1996), 98.
123 Kaestle (1983), 158.
124 Duncan (2003), 513.

Chapter Seven: Religion as Source of Conflict

1   Glenn (2011a), 73–93; Glenn (1988), 50–62, 238–49.
2   See Glenn (2011a), 103–09.
3   In McAfee (1998), 179.
4   Partin (1969), 39.
5   Pécout (1999), 188.
6   Pius IX (1864).
7   4 *Congressional Record* 5577–78 (1876).
8   Spear (1876), 28.
9   Bushnell (1880), 299–303.
10   Hamburger (2004), 194.
11   Ross (1994), 24, 68.
12   Dwyer (1998), 15, 23, 164–65.
13   Strong (1963), 65; emphasis in original.
14   Anonymous (1848), 147, 149, 151, 168–69.
15   Cavanaugh (2009).
16   *Zelman v. Simmons–Harris*, 536 U.S. 639 (2002), Stevens, J., dissenting.
17   Glenn (2011a), 123–53.
18   Spear (1876), 65.
19   Justice (2005), 2.
20   Justice (2005), 3–4.
21   McAfee (1998), 23–24.
22   Stowe (1844), 37.
23   Cheever (1854), iii–iv.
24   McAfee (1998), 41.
25   McAfee (1998), 27–29.
26   Green (1992), 51–52.
27   In Green (1992), 52n.
28   Handy (1984), 87.
29   *Rocky Mountain News*, December 30–31, 1875.
30   Baer (1990), 449.
31   Allyn (1853), 25; Cheever (1854), xi.
32   Dunn (1958), 181–82.
33   4 *Congressional Record* 5590 (1876).
34   Dunn (1958), 207, 211.
35   Peterson (1985), 43.
36   Chapman (2009), 5–6.
37   Chapman (2009), 7, 11.
38   See Glenn (2011c), 74–80.
39   Green (1992), 49, quoting William Hesseltine.
40   Hamburger (2004), 322.
41   Green (1992), 44.

42   McAfee (1998), 192.
43   Green (1992), 47–48.
44   4 *Congressional Record* 5589 (1876).
45   Mitchell and Skelton (1966), 42.
46   See Glenn (2011b), 68–75.
47   Prucha (1976), 307.
48   Green (1992), 52.
49   In Green (1992), 50.
50   Noel (1989), 35–36.
51   In Green (1992), 58n, from 19 *Congressional Record* 1218 (1888).
52   4 *Congressional Record* 5585 (1876).
53   4 *Congressional Record* 5586–88 (1876).
54   *Rocky Mountain News*, December 19, 1875.
55   In Hensel (1961), 352.
56   Parker (1992), 46, 112.
57   Hensel (1961), 354.
58   Wesley (1957), *passim.*
59   *Rocky Mountain News*, December 30, 1875.
60   *Rocky Mountain News*, January 11, 1876.
61   *Rocky Mountain News*, January 13, 29, February 2, 1876.
62   Hensel (1961), 354.
63   *Rocky Mountain News*, January 24, 1876.
64   *Proceedings* (1907), 330–31.
65   *Rocky Mountain News*, March 17, 1876.
66   Peterson (1985), 44.

Chapter Eight: Redefining the Teacher

1   Lucas (1997), 5.
2   In Rudolf (1965), 136.
3   In Kaestle (1983), 21.
4   Wesley (1957), 342.
5   Lucas (1997), 50.
6   Zilversmit (1993), 22.
7   Eaton (1961), 140.
8   Reisner (1930), 313.
9   Jorgenson (1952), 17.
10   Messerli (1972), 254.
11   In Barnes (1991), 4.
12   Herbst (1989), 23.
13   Herbst (1989), 23.
14   In Sklar (1973), 52.
15   Martineau (1837), 257–58.

16　In Sklar (1973), 76, 98.

17　In Sklar (1973), 114.

18　Cremin (1980), 145.

19　In Preston (1993), 536.

20　In Cohen (1974a), III, 1318.

21　Baumgarten (1994), 189.

22　In Sklar (1973), 173.

23　In Sklar (1973), 114.

24　Baumgarten (1994), 190.

25　Burstyn (1974), 396.

26　Preston (1993), 531; Vinovskis and Bernard (1978), 868; Bernard and Vinovskis (1997), 333.

27　Bledstein (1976), 120.

28　Bernard and Vinovskis (1997), 333; Vinovskis and Bernard (1978), 868.

29　In Johnson (2002), 99; Sklar (1973), 97.

30　Sklar (1973), 97, 136.

31　In Cohen (1974a), III, 1318.

32　Sklar (1973), 97–98, 180.

33　Ogren (2005), 192.

34　Lucas (1997), 14.

35　Preston (1993), 536–37.

36　In Cohen (1974a), III, 1328–34.

37　See Glenn (2011c), 97–98.

38　Preston (1993), 538–39.

39　Capen and Labaree (1947), 347–48.

40　Pangle and Pangle (1993), 104.

41　Beadie (1993), 553–56.

42　Messerli (1972), 299; Herbst (1989), 57.

43　MacMullen (1991), 157–60.

44　Mattingly (1975), 61, 67.

45　Ogren (2005), 21.

46　See Wesley (1957).

47　Carter (1826), 43, 49–50.

48　Rushdoony (1979), 39.

49　Glenn (2011a), 55–56, 91.

50　Cousin (1835), 62.

51　Stowe (1836); Travers (1969), 84.

52　In Blumenfeld (1981), 178–79.

53　In Brooks (1856), 338–39.

54　Mann (1838).

55　In Cohen (1974a), II, 1077.

56　and Barnard (1959), 394.

57 Everett (1859), 335–36.
58 In Katz (1971), 307.
59 Katz (1971), 307.
60 Lucas (1997), 24.
61 Messerli (1972), 323, 368.
62 Herbst (1989), 69.
63 Cohen (1974a), II, xix.
64 Lucas (1997), 54.
65 Ogren (2005), 77.
66 Wright (1930), 364.
67 Ogren (2005), 25.
68 Messerli (1972), 340.
69 In Kaestle (1983), 156.
70 Lucas (1997), 23.
71 Ogren (2005), 22, 56; see Glenn (2011b), x–y.
72 Herbst (1989), 94.
73 Kaestle (1983), 131.
74 Lucas (1997), 53; Ogren (2005), 57.
75 Beadie (1993), 562.
76 Ogren (2005), 17–18.
77 Lucas (1997), 39.
78 In Ogren (2005), 38.
79 Ogren (2005), 39.
80 Wesley (1957), 344.
81 Ogren (2005), 30, 44.
82 Ozouf and Ozouf (1992), 264.
83 Durkheim (1973), 75, 155.
84 Wesley (1957), 27.
85 Wesley (1957), 30.
86 Wesley (1957), 119.
87 Dewey (1986), 58.
88 See Charlton (1963).
89 Crunden (1984), 40.
90 Crunden (1984), 57.
91 Dewey (1974), 439.
92 Dewey (1987), 168.
93 Rockefeller (1991), 19.
94 Bankston and Caldas (2009), 31–32.
95 Wesley (1957), 110.
96 Wesley (1957), 50.
97 Wesley (1957), 343.
98 Ogren (2005), 44.

99   Ogren (2005), 38.
100   Zilversmit (1993), 170–71.
101   Ogren (2005), 132; Lucas (1997), 66.
102   Wesley (1957), 114–15.
103   Wesley (1957), 122.
104   Wesley (1957), 145.
105   Murphy (1990), 249.
106   Murphy (1990), 23.
107   Dewey (1988c), 326.
108   Rockefeller (1991), 286.
109   Kilpatrick (1925), 523.
110   Farkas and Johnson (1997), 12.
111   Murphy (1990), 36, 45, 231.
112   Lortie (1969), 14, 36.
113   Lortie (1969), 37.

Chapter Nine: *The Educators Find Their Prophet*

1   Cremin (1961), 120.
2   Neatby (1953), 23.
3   Ryan (1995), 148–49.
4   Dewey (1966), 137.
5   Hofstadter (1970), 379.
6   Fott (1998), 35.
7   Dewey (1966), 69; Dewey (1984), 131; Dewey (1966), 137.
8   Lynd (1953), 247, 278.
9   Rockefeller (1991), 426.
10   Dewey (1966), 76, 215–16.
11   Egan (2002), 131.
12   Ryan (1995), 338.
13   Ryan (1995), 349.
14   Hofstadter (1970), 375.
15   Dewey (1966), 79, 87.
16   Kilpatrick (1926), 96.
17   Dewey (1966), 100.
18   Kilpatrick (1926), 58.
19   Dewey (1971), 103.
20   Dewey (1988a), 89.
21   Dewey (1988d), 228–31.
22   Dewey (1988a), 174, 179.
23   Dewey (1988b), 167.
24   Dewey (1966), 107.

25 Whitehead (1929), 57.
26 Dewey (1966), 107–09.
27 Dewey (1956), 17.
28 Zilversmit (1993), 176.
29 Sugg (1978), 192, 205.
30 Dewey (1966), 120.
31 Tanner and Tanner (1990), 90.
32 Dewey (1966), 127, 130.
33 Dewey (1966), 132.
34 Hofstadter (1970), 385.
35 Dewey (1988d), 216, 221.
36 Zilversmit (1993), 176; May (1976), 153.
37 In Cremin (1961), 126.
38 In Rockefeller (1991), 331.
39 Cremin (1961), 225.
40 Dewey (1966), 22.
41 Dewey (1966), 79.
42 Tyack (1974), 23.
43 Dewey (1987), 61.
44 Dewey and Childs (1989), 101.
45 Dewey (1966), 273.
46 Sugg (1978), 186.
47 Rousseau (1979), 120.
48 Smith (1949), 93.
49 Tenenbaum (1951), 114.
50 Cremin (1961), 328.
51 Hofstadter (1970), 373, 390.
52 Bestor (1985), 40–43.
53 Stamp (1982), 192.
54 Kach and Mazurek (1992), 192, 195.
55 Hirsch (1996), 2.
56 Hirsch (1996), 33.
57 Zilversmit (1993), 174.
58 Hirsch (1996), 49, 54.
59 Hirsch (1996), 66.
60 Emberley and Newell (1994), 6.
61 Emberley and Newell (1994), 7.
62 Rousseau (1979), 53.
63 Boyd (1966), 364.
64 Coulson (1999), 152.
65 Emberley and Newell (1994), 5.

Chapter Ten: Concluding Reflections

1   Glenn and De Groof (2004).
2   http://treaties.un.org/doc/Treaties/1976/01/19760103%2009-57%20PM/
     Ch_IV_03.pdf.
3   *Proceedings* (1907), 330–31.
4   http://nces.ed.gov/surveys/pss/tables/table_2008_14.asp.
5   Fowler (1997), 169.
6   Jeffries and Ryan (2001), 366.
7   Ballion (1982).
8   Duncan (2003), 523.
9   Jeffries and Ryan (2001), 283–84.
10   McCarthy, Skillen, and Harper (1982).
11   Casanova (1994).
12   Jeffries and Ryan (2001), 305.
13   Duncan (2003), 550, 567.
14   See Glenn (1995) for the use of schooling by communist regimes.
15   See Glenn (2000) for discussion of government regulation of faith-based
     schools and social agencies in the United States and other democracies.
16   Pangle and Pangle (1993), 286–87.
17   See Glenn (2009).
18   Hill, Pierce, and Guthrie (1997), 11.
19   http://www.mass.gov/?pageID=eduterminal&L=7&L0=Home&L1=Govern
     ment&L2=Special+Initiatives&L3=Education+for+the+21st+Century&L4
     =Commonwealth+Readiness+Project&L5= Readiness+Goal+4+-+I
     nnovation&L6=Innovation+Schools&sid=Eoedu&b=terminalcontent&f=i
     nnovation_schools&csid=Eoedu.
20   Hill, Pierce, and Guthrie (1997), ix–x.
21   Woessmann, Luedemann, Schuetz, and West (2009).

Bibliography

Abbott, Edith, editor. 1926. *Historical Aspects of the Immigration Problem: Selected Documents.* Chicago: University of Chicago Press.

Addis, Cameron. 2003. *Jefferson's Vision for Education, 1760–1845.* New York-Bern-Frankfurt am Main: Peter Lang.

Allyn, Robert. 1853. *An Appeal to Christians.* East Greenwich, RI: John B. Lincoln.

Angus, David L. and Jeffrey E. Mirel. 1999. *The Failed Promise of the American High School, 1890–1995.* New York: Teachers College Press.

Aristotle. 1944. *Politics,* translated by H. Rackham. Cambridge, MA: Harvard University Press.

Axtell, James. 1976. *The School Upon a Hill: Education and Society in Colonial New England.* New York: W. W. Norton.

Baer, Richard. 1990. "The Supreme Court's Discriminatory Use of the Term 'Sectarian.'" *Journal of Law and Politics* IV, 3 (Spring), 449–68.

Bailyn, Bernard. 1960. *Education in the Forming of American Society.* New York: Random House.

Ballion, Robert. 1982. *Les consommateurs d'école.* Paris: Stock.

Bankston, Carl L., III and Stephen J. Candas. 2009. *Public Education--America's Civil Religion: A Social History.* New York: Teachers College Press.

Barman, Jean and Neil Sutherland. 1995. "Royal Commission Retrospective." In *Children, Teachers and Schools in the History of British Columbia,* edited by Barman, Sutherland, and Donald Wilson. Calgary: Detselig Enterprises. pp. 411–26.

Barnard, Henry. 1859. *American Educational Biography.* New York.

Barnes, Howard A. 1991. *Horace Bushnell and the Virtuous Republic.* Metuchen, NJ: Scarecrow Press.

Baumgarten, Nikola. 1994. "Education and Democracy in Frontier St. Louis: The Society of the Sacred Heart." *History of Education Quarterly* 34, 2 (Summer), 171–92.

Beadie, Nancy. 1993. "Emma Willard's Idea Put to the Test: The Consequences of State Support of Female Education in New York, 1819–67." *History of Education Quarterly* 33, 4 (Special Issue on the History of Women and Education, Winter), 543–62.

Beecher, Catharine E. 1864. *Religious Training of Children in the School, the Family, and the Church.* New York: Harper and Brothers.

Beecher, Lyman. 1935. *A Plea for the West*, Second Edition. Cincinnati: Truman and Smith.

—. 1852. *Lectures on Political Atheism and Kindred Subjects; Together with Six Lectures on Intemperance. Dedicated to the Working Men of the United States.* Boston: John F. Jewett & Company.

Berger, Peter L. and Richard John Neuhaus. 1996. "To Empower People" (1977), republished in *To Empower People: From State to Civil Society,* edited by Michael Novak. Washington, DC: American Enterprise Institute.

Bernard, Richard M. and Maris A. Vinovskis. 1997. "The Female School Teacher in AnteBellum Massachusetts." *Journal of Social History* 10, 3, 332–45.

Berrol, Selma. 1982. "Public Schools and Immigrants: The New York City Experience." In *American Education and the European Immigrant, 1840–1940,* edited by Bernard J. Weiss. Urbana (IL): University of Illinois Press. pp. 31–43.

Bestor, Arthur, editor. 1948. *Education and Reform at New Harmony: Correspondence of William Maclure and Marie Duclos Fretageot 1820–1833.* Indianapolis: Indiana Historical Society.

—. 1950. *Backwoods Utopias: The Sectarian and Owenite Phases of Communitarian Socialism in America: 1663–1829.* Philadelphia: University of Pennsylvania Press.

—. 1985. *Educational Wastelands: The Retreat from Learning in Our Public Schools,* Second Edition. Urbana: University of Illinois Press.

Billington, Ray Allen. 1937. "The Burning of the Charlestown Convent." *The New England Quarterly* 10, 1 (March), 4–24.

—. 1938. *The Protestant Crusade, 1800–1860: A Study of the Origins of American Nativism.* New York: Macmillan.

Bledstein, Burton J. 1976. *The Culture of Professionalism.* New York: W. W. Norton.

Blumenfeld, Samuel L. 1981. *Is Public Education Necessary?* Old Greenwich, CT: DevinAdair.

Boyd, William. 1966. *The History of Western Education*, Eighth Edition. New York: Barnes & Noble.

Boyer, Paul. 1978. *Urban Masses and Moral Order in America, 1820–1920.* Cambridge: Harvard University Press.

Bradley, Gerard V. 1987. *Church-State Relationships in America.* New York: Greenwood Press.

Brooks, Charles. 1837. *Elementary Instruction: An Address Delivered before the Schools and the Citizens of the Town of Quincy, July 4, 1837,* Quincy, MA: John A. Green.

—. 1856. "Moral Education: The Best Methods of Teaching Morality in the Common Schools." *American Journal of Education,* March.

—. 1867. *An Appeal to the Legislatures of the United States in Relation to Public Schools.* Cambridge, MA: John Wilson.

Brown, Richard D. 1996. *The Strength of a People: The Idea of an Informed Citizenry in America, 1650–1870.* Chapel Hill: University of North Carolina Press.

Bureau of the Census. 1976. *Historical Statistics of the United States: Colonial Times to 1970*. Volume I. Washington, DC: US Department of Commerce.

Burgess, Charles. 1963. "William Maclure and Education for a Good Society." *History of Education Quarterly*, Vol. 3, No. 2. pp. 58–76.

Burstyn, Joan N. 1974. "Catharine Beecher and the Education of American Women." *The New England Quarterly* 47, 3, 386–403.

Bushnell, Horace. 1847. *Discourses on Christian Nurture*. Boston: Sabbath School Society.

—. 1880. *Life and Letters*. New York: Harper and Brothers.

Butler, Jon. 1990. *Awash in a Sea of Faith: Christianizing the American People*. Cambridge: Harvard University Press.

Butts, R. Freeman. 1978. *Public Education in the United States: From Revolution to Reform*. New York: Holt, Rinehart and Winston.

Calhoun, Daniel. 1969. *The Educating of Americans: A Documentary History*. Boston: Houghton Mifflin.

Callahan, Raymond E. 1962. *Education and the Cult of Efficiency: A Study of the Social Forces That Have Shaped the Administration of the Public Schools*. Chicago: University of Chicago Press.

Capen, Eliza Paul and Leonard W. Labaree. 1947. "Zilpah Grant and the Art of Teaching: 1829." *The New England Quarterly* 20, 3, 347–64.

Carey, Patrick W. 2004. *Orestes A. Brownson: American Religious Weathervane*. Grand Rapids: Eerdmans.

Carlton, F. T. 1907. "The Workingmen's Party of New York City: 1829–1831." *Political Science Quarterly* 22, 3, 401–15.

Carter, James G. 1826. *Essays upon Popular Education, Containing a Particular Examination of the Schools of Massachusetts, and an Outline of an Institution for the Instruction of Teachers*. Boston: Bowles and Dearborn.

Casanova, José. 1994. *Public Religions in the Modern World*. Chicago: University of Chicago Press.

Cavanaugh, William L. 2009. *The Myth of Religious Violence: Secular Ideology and the Roots of Modern Conflict*. Oxford: Oxford University Press.

Channing, William Ellery. 1903. "Remarks on Education" (1833). In *Works*, Volume I. Boston: American Unitarian Association.

Chapman, Cornelius. 2009. *The Know-Nothing Amendments: Barriers to School Choice in Massachusetts*. Boston: Pioneer Institute White Paper 46, April.

Charlton, D. G. 1963. *Secular Religions in France, 1815–1870*. London: Oxford University Press.

Cheever, George B. 1854. *Right of the Bible in Our Public Schools*. New York: Robert Carter and Brothers.

Cohen, Sheldon S. 1974. *A History of Colonial Education: 1607–1776*. New York: John Wiley & Sons.

Cohen, Sol. 1974. *Education in the United States: A Documentary History*, I–V. New York: Random House.

Cole, Norwood M. 1957. "The Licensing of Schoolmasters in Colonial Massachusetts." *History of Education Journal* 8, 2 (Winter), 68–74.

Committee on Education, Massachusetts House of Representatives. 1840. "Report." *The Common School Journal* II, 15 (August 1), 224–29.

Compayré, Gabriel. 1904. *The History of Pedagogy*, translated by W. H. Payne. Boston: D. C. Heath.

Constitution of the Commonwealth of Massachusetts. 1981. Part the Second, Chapter V, Section II, "The Encouragement of Literature, etc." Boston: Office of the Massachusetts Secretary of State.

Cord, Robert L. 1982. *Separation of Church and State.* New York: Lambeth Press.

Coulson, Andrew J. 1999. *Market Education: The Unknown History.* New Brunswick: Transaction.

Cousin, Victor. 1835. *Report on the State of Public Instruction in Prussia*, translated by Sarah Austin. New York: Wiley and Long.

Cremin, Lawrence. 1957. "Introduction." In *The Republic and the School: Horace Mann on the Education of Free Men.* New York: Teachers College Press. pp.3–28

—. 1961. *The Transformation of the School: Progressivism in American Education, 1876–1957.* New York: Random House.

—. 1970. *American Education: The Colonial Experience 1607–1783.* New York: Harper & Row.

—. 1977. *Traditions of American Education.* New York: Basic Books.

—. 1980. *American Education: The National Experience 1783–1876.* New York: Harper & Row.

Crunden, Robert M. 1984. *Ministers of Reform: The Progressives' Achievement in American Civilization, 1889–1920.* Urbana: University of Illinois Press.

Cuban, Larry. 1993. *How Teachers Taught: Constancy and Change in American Classrooms, 1890–1990*, Second Edition. New York: Teachers College Press.

Curran, Thomas J. 1975. *Xenophobia and Immigration, 1820–1930.* Boston: Twayne.

Darling, Arthur Burr. 1925. *Political Changes in Massachusetts, 1824–1848: A Study of Liberal Movements in Politics.* New Haven: Yale University Press.

Debates of the Convention to Amend the Constitution of Pennsylvania: Convened at Harrisburg, November 12, 1872, Adjourned, November 27, to Meet at Philadelphia, January 7, 1873. 1873. Philadelphia: B. Singerly.

Dewey, John. 1956. *The Child and the Curriculum and The School and Society.* Chicago: University of Chicago Press.

—. 1966. *Democracy and Education* (1916). New York: The Free Press.

—. 1971. *The Early Works, 1882–1898, 4: 1893–1894.* Carbondale: Southern Illinois University Press.

—. 1972. *The Early Works, 1882–1894, 5: 1895–1898.* Carbondale: Southern Illinois University Press.

—. 1974. "My Pedagogic Creed" (1897). In *John Dewey on Education*, edited by Reginald D. Archambault. Chicago: University of Chicago Press Phoenix Edition. pp.427–39.

—. 1980. *The Middle Works, Volume 10: 1916–1917*, Essays on Philosophy and Education. Carbondale: Southern Illinois University Press.

—. 1984. *Later Works, Volume 5: 1929–1930*, edited by Jo Ann Boydston. Carbondale: University of Southern Illinois Press.

—. 1985. *Later Works, Volume 6: 1931–1932*, edited by Jo Ann Boydston. Carbondale, IL: Southern Illinois University Press.

—. 1986. *Later Works, Volume 9: 1933–1934*, edited by Jo Ann Boydston. Carbondale, IL: Southern Illinois University Press.

—. 1987. "Liberalism and Social Action" (1935). In *Later Works, 11: Essays and "Liberalism and Social Action," 1935–1937*, edited by Jo Ann Boydston. Carbondale, IL: Southern Illinois University Press.

—. 1988a. "Reconstruction in Philosophy and Essays" (1920). In *Middle Works, Volume 13*, edited by Jo Ann Boydston. Carbondale: Southern Illinois University Press.

—. 1988b. "Human Nature and Conduct" (1922). In *Middle Works, Volume 14*, edited by Jo Ann Boydston. Carbondale: Southern Illinois University Press.

—. 1988c. The People and Its Problems. In *Later Works, Volume 2: 1925–1927*, edited by Jo Ann Boydston. Carbondale: Southern Illinois University Press.

—. 1988d. *Later Works, Volume 3: 1927–1928, Essays, Reviews, Miscellany, and "Impressions of Soviet Russia,"* edited by Jo Ann Boydston. Carbondale: University of Southern Illinois Press.

Dewey, John with John L. Childs. 1989. "The Social-Economic Situation and Education" (from *The Educational Frontier*, edited by William H. Kilpatrick, 1933). In *Later Works, Volume 8: 1933*, edited by Jo Ann Boydston. Carbondale, IL: Southern Illinois University Press.

Duncan, Kyle. 2003. "Secularism's Laws: State Blaine Amendments and Religious Persecution." *Fordham Law Review* 72, 493–593.

Dunn, Susan. 1999. *Sister Revolutions: French Lightning, American Light*. New York: Faber and Faber.

Dunn, William Kailer. 1958. *What Happened to Religious Education? The Decline of Religious Teaching in the Public Elementary School, 1776–1861*. Baltimore: Johns Hopkins University Press.

Durkheim, Emile. 1973. *Moral Education: A Study in the Theory and Application of the Sociology of Education* (1925), translated by Everett K. Wilson and Herman Schnurer. New York: Free Press.

Dwyer, James G. 1998. *Religious Schools v. Children's Rights*. Ithaca, NY: Cornell University Press.

Eaton, Clement. 1961. *The Growth of Southern Civilization, 1790–1860*. New York: Harper Torchbooks.

Eckhardt, Celia Morris. 1984. *Fanny Wright: Rebel in America*. Cambridge: Harvard University Press.

Edwards, Newton and Herman Richey. 1968. *The School in the American Social Order*, Second Edition. Boston: Houghton Mifflin.

Egan, Kieran. 2002. *Getting It Wrong From the Beginning*, New Haven: Yale University Press.

Elkins, Stanley and Eric McKitrick. 1995. *The Age of Federalism: The Early American Republic, 1788–1800*. Oxford: Oxford University Press.

Elson, Ruth Miller. 1964. *Guardians of Tradition: American Schoolbooks of the Nineteenth Century*. Lincoln: University of Nebraska Press.

Emberley, Peter C. and Waller R. Newell. 1994. *Bankrupt Education: The Decline of Liberal Education in Canada*. Toronto: University of Toronto Press.

Ensign, Forest Chester. 1969. *Compulsory School Attendance and Child Labor* (Iowa City, Iowa 1921). Reprinted New York: Arno Press and The New York Times.

Esbeck, Carl H. 2004. "Dissent and Disestablishment: The Church-State Settlement in the Early American Republic." *Brigham Young University Law Review* 4, 1385–1592.

Everett, Edward. 1859. *Orations and Speeches on Various Occasions*, Volume II, Fifth Edition. Boston: Little, Brown.

Farkas, Steve and Jean Johnson. 1997. *Different Drummers: How Teachers of Teachers View Public Education*. New York: Public Agenda.

Farrell, Emma L. 1938. "The New Harmony Experiment, an Origin of Progressive Education." *Peabody Journal of Education* 15, 6 (May), 357–61.

Fott, David. 1998. *John Dewey: America's Philosopher of Democracy*. Lanham (MD): Rowman and Littlefield.

Fowler, Robert Booth. 1997. "A Sceptical Postmodern Defense of Multiestablishment: The Case for Government Aid to Religious Schools in a Multicultural Age." In *Everson Revised: Religion, Education, and Law at the Crossroads*, edited by Jo Renée Formicola and Hubert Morken. Lanham, MD: Rowman & Littlefield.

Franklin, Benjamin. 1984. *Writings*. New York: The Library of America.

Franklin, Vincent P. 1979. *The Education of Black Philadelphia: The Social and Educational History of a Minority Community, 1900–1950*. Philadelphia: University of Pennsylvania Press.

Fraser, James W. 1985. *Pedagogue for God's Kingdom: Lyman Beecher and the Second Great Awakening*. Lanham, MD: University Press of America.

Galenson, David W. 1995. "Determinants of the School Attendance of Boys in Early Chicago." *History of Education Quarterly* 35, 4 (Winter), 371–400.

—. 1997. "Neighborhood Effects on the School Attendance of Irish Immigrants' Sons in Boston and Chicago in 1860." *American Journal of Education* 105, 3 (May), 261–93.

—. 1998. "Ethnic Differences in Neighborhood Effects on the School Attendance of Boys in Early Chicago." *History of Education Quarterly* 38, 1 (Spring), 17–35.

Gardner, Henry J. 1855. "Inaugural Address," in Acts and Resolves passed by the Legislature of Massachusetts in the Year 1855, together with the Rolls and Messages. Boston: William White.

Glenn, Charles L. 1987. "Religion, Textbooks and the Common School." *The Public Interest*, July.

—. 1988. *The Myth of the Common School*. Amherst: University of Massachusetts Press.

—. 1995. *Educational Freedom in Eastern Europe*. Washington, DC: Cato Institution Press.

—. 2000. *The Ambiguous Embrace: Government and Faith-based Schools and Social Agencies*. Princeton, NJ: Princeton University Press.

—. 2009. "Segregated Schools and Virtuous Markets." *International Journal for Education Law and Policy* 5, 1–2, 10–23.

—. 2011a. *Contrasting Models of State and School: A Comparative Historical Study of Parental Choice and State Control*. New York and London: Continuum.

—. 2011b. *Native American/First Nations Schooling: From the Colonial Period to the Present*. New York and London: Palgrave Macmillan.

—. 2011c. *African American/Afro-Canadian Schooling: From the Colonial Period to the Present*. New York and London: Palgrave Macmillan.

Glenn, Charles L. and Jan De Groof. 2004. *Balancing Freedom, Autonomy, and Accountability in Education*, I–III. Nijmegen: Wolf Legal Publishing.

Glenn, Charles L. with Ester J. de Jong. 1996. *Educating Immigrant Children: Schools and Language Minorities in 12 Nations*. New York: Garland Publishing.

Gordon, Mary McDougall. 1978. "Patriots and Christians: A Reassessment of Nineteenth-Century School Reformers." *Journal of Social History* 11, 4 (Summer), 554–73.

Graham, Patricia Albjerg. 2005. *Schooling America*. Oxford: Oxford University Press.

Green, Steven K. 1992. "The Blaine Amendment Reconsidered." *The American Journal of Legal History* 36, 1 (January), 38–69.

Gutmann, Amy. 1987. *Democratic Education*. Princeton, NJ: Princeton University Press.

Hamburger, Philip. 2004. *Separation of Church and State*. Cambridge: Harvard University Press.

Handlin, Oscar. 1968. *Boston's Immigrants: A Study in Acculturation*, Revised Edition. New York: Atheneum.

Handy, Robert T. 1984. *A Christian America: Protestant Hopes and Historical Realities*. Oxford: Oxford University Press.

—. 1991. *Undermined Establishment: Church-State Relations in America, 1880–1920*. Princeton, NJ: Princeton University Press.

Harrison, J. F. C. 1967. "'The Steam Engine of the New Moral World': Owenism and Education, 1817–1829." *The Journal of British Studies* 6, 2 (May), 76–98.

Hawke, David F. 1971. *Benjamin Rush: Revolutionary Gadfly*. New York: Irvington Publishers.

Hazen, Charles D. 1964. *Contemporary American Opinion of the French Revolution*. Gloucester, MA: P. Smith.

Hendrick, Irving G. 1966. "A Reappraisal of Colonial New Hampshire's Effort in Public Education." *History of Education Quarterly* 6, 2 (Summer), 43–60.

Hensel, Donald W. 1961. "Religion and the Writing of the Colorado Constitution." *Church History* 30, 3 (September), 349–60.

Herbst, Jurgen. 1989. *And Sadly Teach: Teacher Education and Professionalization in American Culture*. Madison: University of Wisconsin Press.

Hill, Paul T., Lawrence C. Pierce, and James W. Guthrie. 1997. *Reinventing Public Education*. Chicago: University of Chicago Press.

Hirsch, Jr, E. D. 1996. *The schools we need . . . and why we don't have them*. New York: Doubleday.

Hodge, Charles. 1846. "The General Assembly, Parochial Schools." *Princeton Review* 18.

Hofstadter, Richard. 1970. *Anti-intellectualism in American Life*. New York: Alfred A. Knopf.

Honeywell, Roy J. 1931. *The Educational Work of Thomas Jefferson*. Cambridge: Harvard University Press.

Howe, Daniel Walker. 1979. *The Political Culture of the American Whigs*. University of Chicago Press.

—. 1997. *Making the American Self: Jonathan Edwards to Abraham Lincoln*. Cambridge: Harvard University Press.

Humphrey, Heman. 1844. "Extracts from the Introductory Lecture." *The Common School Journal* VI, 4 (February 15), 50–53.

Issel, William H. 1967. "Teachers and Educational Reform during the Progressive Era: A Case Study of the Pittsburgh Teachers' Association." *History of Education Quarterly* 7, 2 (Summer), 220–33.

Jefferson, Thomas. 1984. *Writings*. New York: The Library of America.

Jeffries, Jr, John C. and James E. Ryan. 2001. "A Political History of the Establishment Clause." *Michigan Law Review* 100, 2 (November), 279–370.

Johnson, Paul E. 1978. *A Shopkeeper's Millennium: Society and Revivals in Rochester, New York, 1815–1837*. New York: Hill and Wang.

Johnson, Tony W., editor. 2002. *Historical Documents in American Education*. Boston: Allyn and Bacon.

Johnson-Weiner, Karen M. 2006. *Train Up a Child: Old Order Amish and Mennonite Schools*. Baltimore: Johns Hopkins University Press.

Jorgenson, Lloyd P. 1952. "The American Faith in Education." *History of Education Journal* 4, 1 (Autumn), 11–17.

—. 1987. *The State and the Non-Public School, 1825–1925*. Columbia, MO: University of Missouri Press.

Justice, Benjamin. 2005. *The War that Wasn't: Religious Conflict and Compromise in the Common Schools of New York State, 1865–1900*. Albany: State University of New York Press.

Kach, Nick. 1992. "The Emergence of Progressive Education in Alberta." In *Exploring Our Educational Past: Schooling in the North-West Territories and Alberta*, edited by Kach and Kas Mazurek. Calgary: Detselig Enterprises. pp. 149–74.

Kaestle, Carl F. 1973a. *The Evolution of an Urban School System: New York City, 1750–1850.* Cambridge: Harvard University Press.

—, editor. 1973b. *Joseph Lancaster and the Monitorial School Movement: A Documentary History.* New York: Teachers College Press.

—. 1982. "Ideology and American Educational History." *History of Education Quarterly* 22, 2 (Summer), 123–37.

—. 1983. *Pillars of the Republic: Common Schools and American Society, 1780–1860.* New York: Hill and Wang.

—. 1987. *Reconstructing American Education.* Cambridge: Harvard University Press.

Kaestle, Carl F. and Maris A. Vinovskis. 1980. *Education and Social Change in Nineteenth-Century Massachusetts.* Cambridge: Cambridge University Press.

Kandel, Isaac Leon. 1943. *The Cult of Uncertainty.* New York: Macmillan.

Kaplan, Sidney. 1948. "The Reduction of Teachers' Salaries in Post-Revolutionary Boston." *The New England Quarterly* 21, 3, 373–79.

Katz, Michael B. 1968. *The Irony of Early School Reform: Educational Innovation in Mid-Nineteenth Century Massachusetts.* Boston: Beacon Press.

—. 1971. "From Voluntarism to Bureaucracy in American Education." *Sociology of Education* 44, 3 (Summer), 297–332.

—. 1975. *Class, Bureaucracy, and Schools.* New York: Praeger.

Kilpatrick, William Heard. 1912. *The Dutch Schools of New Netherland and Colonial New York.* Washington: Government Printing Office.

—. 1925. *Foundations of Method: Informal Talks on Teaching.* New York: Macmillan.

—. 1926. *Education for a Changing Civilization.* New York: Macmillan.

—. 1932. *Education and the Social Crisis: A Proposed Program.* New York: Liveright.

—. 1936. *Remaking the Curriculum*, New York: Newson.

Kliebard, Herbert M. 1982. "Education at the Turn of the Century: A Crucible for Curriculum Change." *Educational Researcher* 11, 1 (January), 16–24.

Kramer, Rita. 1991. *Ed School Follies: The Miseducation of America's Teachers.* New York: Free Press, 1991.

Kuhn, Thomas. 1962. *The Structure of Scientific Revolutions.* Chicago, IL: University of Chicago Press.

Labaree, David F. 1988. *The Making of an American High School: The Credentials Market and the Central High School of Philadelphia, 1838–1939.* New Haven: Yale University Press.

—. 1997. *How to Succeed in School without Really Learning: The Credentials Race in American Education.* New Haven: Yale University Press.

Lannie, Vincent P., editor. 1974. *Henry Barnard: American Educator.* New York: Teachers College Press.

Lockridge, Kenneth A. 1974. *Literacy in Colonial New England.* New York: W. W. Norton.

Lortie, Dan C. 1969. "The Balance of Control and Autonomy in Elementary School Teaching and Their Organization." In *The Semi-Professions and Their Organization*, edited by Amitai Etzioni. New York: The Free Press.

Lottich, Kenneth V. 1962. "Educational Leadership in Early Ohio." *History of Education Quarterly* 2, 1 (March), 52–61.

Lucas, Christopher J. 1997. *Teacher Education in America*. New York: St. Martin's Press.

Lynd, Albert. 1953. *Quackery in the Public Schools*, New York: Grosset & Dunlap.

MacMullen, Edith Nye. 1991. *In the Cause of True Education: Henry Barnard and Nineteenth-Century School Reform*. New Haven: Yale University Press.

Madison, James. 1999. *Writings*. Library of America.

Malone, Dumas. 1962. *Jefferson and the Ordeal of Liberty*. Boston: Little, Brown.

Mann, Horace. 1838. *First Annual Report of the Secretary of the Board*. Boston: Dutton and Wentworth.

—. 1839. "The Advantages of Common Schools, and the Dangers to Which They are Exposed; Addressed to the Professional Men of Massachusetts." *Common School Journal* 1, 9 (May 1).

—. 1840. *Third Annual Report of the Secretary of the Board*. Boston: Dutton and Wentworth.

—. 1841. *Fourth Annual Report of the Secretary of the Board*. Boston: Dutton and Wentworth.

—. 1842. *Fifth Annual Report of the Secretary of the Board*. Boston: Dutton and Wentworth.

—. 1844. *Seventh Annual Report of the Secretary of the Board*. Boston: Dutton and Wentworth.

—. 1845. *Eighth Annual Report of the Secretary of the Board*. Boston: Dutton and Wentworth.

—. 1846. Ninth *Annual Report of the Secretary of the Board*. Boston: Dutton and Wentworth.

—. 1847. *Tenth Annual Report of the Secretary of the Board*. Boston: Dutton and Wentworth.

—. 1848. *Eleventh Annual Report of the Secretary of the Board*. Boston: Dutton and Wentworth.

—. 1849. *Twelfth Annual Report of the Secretary of the Board*. Boston: Dutton and Wentworth.

Martineau, Harriet. 1837. *Society in America*, I & II. New York: Saunders and Otley.

Mattingly, Paul H. 1975. *The Classless Profession*. New York: New York University Press.

May, Henry F. 1976. *The Enlightenment in America*. Oxford: Oxford University Press.

May, Samuel J. 1866. "Address." In *Memorial of the Quarter-Centennial Celebration of the Establishment of Normal Schools in America*. Boston: C.C.P. Moody.

McAfee, Ward M. 1998. *Religion, Race, and Reconstruction: The Public School in the Politics of the 1870s*. Albany: State University of New York Press.

McCadden, Joseph. 1937. *Education in Pennsylvania 1801–1835 and Its Debt to Roberts Vaux*. Philadelphia: University of Pennsylvania Press.

McCarthy, Rockne M., James W. Skillen, and William A. Harper. 1982. *Disestablishment a Second Time: Genuine Pluralism for American Schools*. Grand Rapids, MI: Eerdmans.

McCluskey, Neil G. 1958. *Public Schools and Moral Education: The Influence of Horace Mann, William Torrey Harris, and John Dewey*. New York: Columbia University Press.

McLoughlin, William G., editor. 1968. *The American Evangelicals, 1800–1900: An Anthology*. New York: Harper & Row.

Messerli, Jonathan. 1972. *Horace Mann: A Biography*. New York: Alfred A. Knopf.

Miller, John C. 1961. *The Federalist Era, 1789–1801*. New York: Harper Torchbooks.

Mirel, Jeffrey. 1999. *The Rise and Fall of an Urban School System: Detroit 1907–81*, Second Edition. Ann Arbor: University of Michigan Press.

Mitchell, Frederic and James W. Skelton. 1966. "The Church-State Conflict in Early Indian Education." *History of Education Quarterly* 6, 1 (Spring), 41–51.

Moe, Terry M. 2000. *Schools, Vouchers, and the American Public*. Washington, DC: Brookings Institution.

—. 2011. *Special Interest: Teachers Unions and America's Public Schools*. Washington, DC: Brookings Institution Press.

Monroe, Paul. 1971. *Founding of the American Public School System*. New York: Hafner Publishing.

Montesquieu, Charles-Louis de Secondat. 1989. *The Spirit of the Laws*, translated and edited by Anne M. Cohler, Basia Carolyn Miller, and Harold Samuel Stone. Cambridge University Press.

Morton, Marcus. 1842. "Inaugural Address." In *Acts and Resolves passed by the Legislature of Massachusetts in the Years 1839, 1840, 1841, and 1842, Together with the Rolls and Messages*. Boston: Dutton and Wentworth.

—. 1845. "Inaugural Address." In *Acts and Resolves passed by the Legislature of Massachusetts in the Years 1843, 1844, 1845, Together with the Rolls and Messages*. Boston: Dutton and Wentworth.

Mulhern, James. 1969. *A History of Secondary Education in Pennsylvania* (Philadelphia 1933). Reprinted New York: Arno Press and The New York Times.

Mulkern, John R. 1990. *The Know-Nothing Party in Massachusetts*. Boston: Northeastern University Press.

Murphy, Marjorie. 1990. *Blackboard Unions. The AFT & the NEA, 1900–1980*. Ithaca, NY: Cornell University Press.

Nasaw, David. 1979. *Schooled to Order. A Social History of Public Schooling in the United States*. Oxford University Press.

Neatby, Hilda. 1953. *So Little For the Mind*. Toronto: Clarke, Irwin & Company.

Noel, Thomas J. 1989. *Colorado Catholicism and the Archdiocese of Denver, 1857–1989.* Boulder, CO: University of Colorado Press.

Noll, Mark A. 2002. *America's God. From Jonathan Edwards to Abraham Lincoln.* Oxford University Press.

Null, J. Wesley. 2003. *Disciplined Progressive Educator: The Life and Career of William Chandler Bagley.* New York: Peter Lang.

Nybakken, Elizabeth. 1997. "In the Irish Tradition: Pre-Revolutionary Academies in America." *History of Education Quarterly* 37, 2 (Summer), 163–83.

Ogren, Christine A. 2005. *The American State Normal School.* New York: Palgrave Macmillan.

Ozouf, Jacques and Mona Ozouf. 1992. *La république des instituteurs.* Paris: Gallimard.

Packard, Frederick. 1841. "Religious Instruction in Common Schools." *Princeton Review,* July.

Pangle, Lorraine Smith and Thomas L. Pangle. 1993. *The Learning of Liberty: The Educational Ideas of the American Founders.* Lawrence: University Press of Kansas.

Parker, Anthony Kevin. 1992. *Religious Controversies Surrounding the Colorado Constitutional Convention of 1876.* A Thesis Presented to the Faculty of Denver Seminary.

Partin, Malcolm O. 1969. *Waldeck-Rousseau, Combes, and the Church: The Politics of Anticlericalism, 1899–1905.* Durham, NC: Duke University Press.

Pawa, J. M. 1971. "Workingmen and Free Schools in the Nineteenth Century: A Comment on the Labor-Education Thesis." *History of Education Quarterly* 11, 3, 287–302.

Pécout,Gilles. 1999. *Il lungo Risorgimento: La nascita dell 'Italia contemporanea (1770–1922),* translated by Roberto Balzani. Milan: Bruno Mondadori.

Pessen, Edward. 1985. *Jacksonian America: Society, Personality, and Politics,* Revised Edition. Urbana: University of Illinois Press.

Peterson, Paul E. 1985. *The Politics of School Reform, 1870–1940.* University of Chicago Press.

—. 2010. *Saving Schools: From Horace Mann to Virtual Learning.* Cambridge: Belknap Press of Harvard University Press.

Pius IX. 1864. *Syllabus of Errors.* http://www.papalencyclicals.net/Pius09/p9syll.htm (accessed January 9, 2012).

Power, Edward J. 1996. *Religion and the Public Schools in 19th Century America: The Contribution of Orestes A. Brownson.* New York: Paulist Press.

Preston, J. A. 1993. "Domestic Ideology, School Reformers, and Female Teachers: School Teaching Becomes Women's Work in Nineteenth-Century New England." *The New England Quarterly* 66, 4, 531–51.

Proceedings of the Constitutional Convention Held in Denver, December 20, 1875, to Frame a Constitution for the State of Colorado. 1907. Denver: Smith-Brooks Press.

Prucha, Francis Paul. 1976. *American Indian Policy in Crisis: Christian Reformers and the Indian, 1865–1900.* Norman: University of Oklahoma Press.

Pulliam, John. 1967. "Changing Attitudes toward Free Public Schools in Illinois 1825–1860." *History of Education Quarterly* 7, 2 (Summer), 191–208.

Ravitch, Diane. 1974. *The Great School Wars: New York City, 1805–1973.* New York: Basic Books.

—. 2000. *Left Back: A Century of Failed School Reforms.* New York: Simon & Schuster.

Reinders, Robert C. 1964. "New England Influences on the Formation of Public Schools in New Orleans." *The Journal of Southern History* 30, 2 (May), 181–95.

Reisner, Edward H. 1922. *Nationalism and Education since 1789.* New York: Macmillan.

—. 1930. *The Evolution of the Common School.* New York: Macmillan.

Rockefeller, Steven C. 1991. *John Dewey: Religious Faith and Democratic Humanism.* New York: Columbia University Press.

Ross, William G. 1994. *Forging New Freedoms: Nativism, Education, and the Constitution, 1917–1927.* Lincoln: University of Nebraska Press.

Rousseau, Jean-Jacques. 1979. *Emile, or On Education* (1762), translated by Allan Bloom. New York: Basic Books.

Rudolf, Frederick, editor. 1965. *Essays on Education in the Early Republic.* Cambridge, MA: Harvard University Press.

Rush, Benjamin. 1965. "A Plan for the Establishment of Public Schools and the Diffusion of Knowledge in Pennsylvania." In *Essays on Education in the Early Republic,* edited by Frederick Rudolf. Cambridge, MA: Harvard University Press.

Rushdoony, Rousas John. 1979. *The Messianic Character of American Education.* Nutley, NJ: Craig Press.

Ryan, Alan. 1995. *John Dewey and the High Tide of American Liberalism.* New York: W. W. Norton & Company.

Schleifer, James T. 2000. *The Making of Tocqueville's Democracy in America,* Second Edition. Indianapolis: Liberty Fund.

Schultz, Stanley K. 1973. *The Culture Factory: Boston Public Schools, 1780–1960.* New York: Oxford University Press.

Sears, Barnas. 1852. *Fifteenth Annual Report of the Board of Education, together with the Fifteenth Annual Report of the Secretary of the Board.* Boston: Dutton and Wentworth.

—. 1855. *Eighteenth Annual Report of the Board of Education, together with the Eighteenth Annual Report of the Secretary of the Board.* Boston: Dutton and Wentworth.

—. 1856. *Nineteenth Annual Report of the Board of Education, together with the Nineteenth Annual Report of the Secretary of the Board.* Boston: Dutton and Wentworth.

Shapiro, Samuel. 1960. "The Conservative Dilemma: The Massachusetts Constitutional Convention of 1853." *The New England Quarterly* 33, 2 (June), 207–24.

Sheller, Tina H. 1982. "The Origins of Public Education in Baltimore, 1825–1829." *History of Education Quarterly* 22, 1 (Spring), 23–44.

Siljeström, P. A. 1969. *The Educational Institutions of the United States: Their Character and Organization*, translated by Frederica Rowan (London, 1853). Reprinted New York: Arno Press and The New York Times.

Silver, Harold, editor. 1969. *Robert Owen on Education*. Cambridge University Press.

Sizer, Theodore, editor. 1964. *The Age of the Academies*. New York: Teachers College.

Sklar, Katheryn Kish. 1973. *Catharine Beecher: A Study in American Domesticity*. New Haven: Yale University Press.

Sloan, Douglas, editor. 1973. *The Great Awakening and American Education: A Documentary History*. New York: Teachers College Press.

Smith, Jeffery A. 1990. *Franklin and Bache: Envisioning the Enlightened Republic*. Oxford University Press.

Smith, Mortimer. 1949. *And Madly Teach*. Chicago: Henry Regnery.

—. 1954. *The Diminished Mind: A Study of Planned Mediocrity in Our Public Schools*. Chicago: Henry Regnery.

Smith, Sherman M. 1926. *The Relation of the State to Religious Education in Massachusetts*. Syracuse, NY: Syracuse University Book Store.

Smith, Timothy L. 1965. *Revivalism and Social Reform. American Protestantism on the Eve of the Civil War*. New York: Harper and Row.

—. 1967. "Protestant Schooling and American Nationality, 1800–1850." *The Journal of American History* 53, 4 (March), 679–95.

Soldani, Simonetta and Gabriele Turi. 1993. *Fare gli italiani: Scuola e culture nell 'Italia contemporanea. I. La nascita dello Stato nazionale*. Bologna: Il Mulino.

Spear, Samuel T. 1876. *Religion and the State, or, The Bible and the Public Schools*. New York: Dodd, Mead.

Stamp, Robert M. 1982. *The Schools of Ontario, 1876–1976*. Toronto: University of Toronto Press.

Starr, Kevin. 1971. *Americans and the California Dream, 1850–1915*. New York: Oxford University Press.

Steinberg, Laurence. 1997. *Beyond the Classroom*. New York: Simon and Schuster.

Stowe, Calvin. 1836. *The Prussian System of Public Instruction and Its Applicability to the United States*. Cincinnati: Truman and Smith.

—. 1844. *The Religious Element in Education*. Boston: William D. Ticknor.

Strong, Josiah. 1963. *Our Country* (1891), edited by Jurgen Herbst. Cambridge, MA: Harvard University Press.

Sugg, Jr and Redding S. 1978. *Motherteacher: The Feminization of American Education*. Charlottesville: University of Virginia Press.

Tanner, Daniel and Laurel Tanner. 1990. *History of the School Curriculum.* New York: Macmillan.

Teaford, Jon. 1970. "The Transformation of Massachusetts Education, 1670–1780." *History of Education Quarterly* 10, 3 (Autumn), 287–307.

Tenenbaum, Samuel. 1951. *William Heard Kilpatrick: Trail Blazer in Education.* New York: Harper and Brothers.

Thabault, Roger. 1982. *Mon village: 1848–1914.* Presses de la Fondation nationale des Sciences politiques.

Thomas, John L. 1965. "Romantic Reform in America, 1815–1865." *American Quarterly* 17, 4 (Winter), 656–81.

Tocqueville, Alexis de. 1988. *Democracy in America,* edited by J. P. Mayer, translated by George Lawrence. New York: Harper & Row.

—. 2000. *Democracy in America,* translated by Harvey C. Mansfield and Delba Winthrop. Chicago, IL: University of Chicago Press.

Travers, Paul D. 1969. "Calvin Ellis Stowe and the History of Education." *Peabody Journal of Education* 47, 2 (September), 83–87.

Troen, Selwyn K. 1975. *The Public and the Schools Shaping the St. Louis System, 1838–1920.* Columbia, MO: University of Missouri Press.

Tyack, David. 1966. "The Kingdom of God and the Common School; Protestant Ministers and the Educational Awakening in the West." *Harvard Educational Review XXXVI* (Fall), 447–69.

—, editor. 1967. *Turning Points in American Educational History.* Waltham, MA: Blaisdell Publishing.

—. 1974. *The One Best System: A History of American Urban Education.* Cambridge: Harvard University Press.

Tyack, David and Elisabeth Hansot. 1982. *Managers of Virtue: Public School Leadership in America, 1820–1980.* New York: Basic Books.

—. 1990. *Learning Together: A History of Coeducation in American Schools.* New Haven: Yale University Press.

Tyack, David and Thomas James. 1986. "State Government and American Public Education: Exploring the 'Primeval Forest.'" *History of Education Quarterly* 26, 1 (Spring), 39–69.

Tyack, David, Thomas James and Aaron Benavot. 1987. *Law and the Shaping of Public Education, 1785–1954.* Madison: University of Wisconsin Press.

Tyack, David, Robert Lowe and Elisabeth Hansot. 1984. *Public Schools in Hard Times.* Cambridge, MA: Harvard University Press.

Unger, Harlow Giles. 1998. *Noah Webster: The Life and Times of an American Patriot.* New York: John Wiley.

Vinovskis, Maris A. 1985. *The Origins of Public High Schools.* Madison, WI: University of Wisconsin Press.

Vinovskis, Maris A. and Richard M. Bernard. 1978. "Beyond Catharine Beecher: Female Education in the Antebellum Period." *Signs* 3, 4, 856–69.

Walsh, Louis S. 1901. *The Early Catholic Schools of Lowell, Massachusetts, 1835–1852.* Boston: Whelan.

Wardeberg, Helen L. 1972. "Elementary School Curriculum and Progressive Education." In *A New Look at Progressive Education*, edited by James R. Squire. Washington, DC: Association for Supervision and Curriculum Development. pp. 206–32.

Washington, George. 1997. *Writings.* New York: Library of America.

Watkinson, James D. 1990. "Useful Knowledge? Concepts, Values, and Access in American Education, 1776–1840." *History of Education Quarterly* 30, 3 (Autumn), 351–70.

Welter, Rush. 1962. *Popular Education and Democratic Thought in America.* New York: Columbia University Press.

—, editor. 1971. *American Writings on Popular Education: The Nineteenth Century.* Indianapolis: Bobbs-Merrill.

Wesley, Edgar B. 1957. *NEA: The First Hundred Years.* New York: Harper & Brothers.

Westbrook, Robert B. 1991. *John Dewey and American Democracy.* Ithaca: Cornell University Press.

Whitehead, Alfred North. 1929. *The Aims of Education and Other Essays.* New York: Macmillan.

Whitescarver, Keith. 1993. "Creating Citizens for the Republic: Education in Georgia, 1776–1810." *Journal of the Early Republic* 13, 4 (Winter), 455–79.

Wickersham, J. P. 1870. *Report of the Superintendent of Common Schools of the Commonwealth of Pennsylvania, for the year ending June 6, 1870.* Harrisburg: B. Sincerely, State Printer.

—. 1886. *A History of Education in Pennsylvania.* Lancaster, PA. (Reprinted New York: Arno Press and The New York Times 1969).

Wilson, J. Donald. 1978. "The Pre-Ryerson Years." In *Egerton Ryerson and His Times*, edited by Neil G. McDonald and Alf Chaiton. Toronto: Macmillan of Canada. pp. 19–42.

Woessmann, Ludger, Elke Luedemann, Gabriela Schuetz, and Martin R. West. 2009. *School Accountability, Autonomy and Choice around the World.* Northampton, MA: Edward Elgar.

Wright, Frank W. 1930. "The Evolution of the Normal Schools." *The Elementary School Journal* 30, 5 (January), 363–71.

Zilversmit, Arthur. 1993. *Changing Schools: Progressive Education Theory and Practice, 1930–1960.* Chicago, IL: University of Chicago Press.

Index